THE POINTING LABRADOR

By
Paul and Julie Knutson

Second printing, February 2003

Published by
Clinetop Press
(970) 984-3801 • (970) 704-1313
web: clinetop.com • email: outdoor@clinetop.com

Library of Congress Control Number: 2001088225
ISBN 1-893740-04-8

Dedication

"It is not the critic who counts; not the man who points out how the strong man stumbled or where the doer of deeds could have done them better. The credit belongs to the man who is actually in the arena; whose face is marred by dust and sweat and blood; who strives valiantly; who errs and comes short again and again; who knows the great enthusiasms, the great devotions, and spends himself in a worthy cause; who, at the worst, if he fails, at least fails while daring greatly, so that his place shall never be with those cold and timid souls who knew neither victory nor defeat."

Theodore Roosevelt

This book we dedicate to each other.
It has been a labor of love.
PK & JK

Acknowledgements

Nothing happens without the presence of people who are special, unique, or amazingly knowledgeable. We have had the outstanding opportunity of bumping into a few along the way. There are too many things too many folks have done to list them all, and we would put the reader to sleep. Allow us to mention just a few that made the difference for us. It is important to let them know they are important.

Thanks go to: Jackie Mertens for opening some doors--heck, pointing some doors out. Danny Farmer, for having the doors and making things possible. Judy Aycock, for taking the time to teach, no matter how challenging the student. Jack Bates, for the ridiculously high standards that he never lowers. Delery Guillory and Hershey, for making us believe. Rick and Arlene Trumble, for turning on the light. Kevin Hollern, Charles Scoggin, Larry Morgan, Jim Bonham, Paul Giesenhagen, and all those people who simply thought they had a nice dog.

Thanks, dogs, for making us look good. No one will know how great you are.

Prologue

The book is finished. For the time being, we will spend no more long hours at the desk, trying to find the right words to convey an important thought. Writing a book is an act of arrogance. The assumption is that people will actually pay money to read what you have to say. Why would you spend your money reading the words of two people living in the middle of rural Colorado?

Here's a story that may explain why. One afternoon several years ago, a man knocked on our door. He had just bought a pup and had been told by the breeders to buy our training manual. So he came directly to us and bought the manual and asked a thousand questions. He did not know much of anything about dogs, much less field dogs or hunting. After he left, we never gave him much thought; it was not likely someone that removed from the field would ever do much. A few weeks later, he and his fiancee came out to watch some training and show us their new pup. They told us about all the books they were reading and that the monks said to do this, and so-and-so said to do that. Once again, we gave them little thought since they were going about this in such a helter-skelter approach.

When their dog was six months old they brought it to us for some basic training, force fetch, retrieving and field work. The dog was a nice dog, liked the work. The dog was way ahead of the owner, and when he came to pick his dog up, we did what we could to give him tools so he could continue the work with his dog. He took the dog home to enjoy the hunting season. He would come back out fairly frequently to train with us, again asking countless questions. He certainly seemed determined to make his dog a good hunting dog.

Some time later at a hunt test, someone mentioned hunting in Kansas earlier that season and running into this fellow with this yellow dog. The dog was quite a hunter; so much so, they put their own dog away and hunted with this man's dog. When they mentioned he had a strange name and a yellow pointing Lab, we knew who it was. Another time, at a funeral, of all things, we were talking hunting with someone who had recently returned from a trip further east. They had run into this man with this yellow dog. The dog was a machine, this yellow pointing Lab. So good, in fact, they put their dogs up and hunted with the yellow dog for the afternoon. Now this is getting a little far-fetched, and may seem like literary license is being taken, but it is fact. A client called one day who had had his dog with us the previous year for basic training. The dog was from the other side of the country, but they had been hunting out near the Midwest and had encountered this man with this awesome yellow pointing Lab. They wound up putting their dogs away and hunted with the yellow dog. Now they wanted to bring their own dog back for more training with us since they learned we had been involved with that yellow dog.

This dog we now refer to only as the "Yellow Phantom" has gone on to win the division open to all pointing dogs at the National Finals, held by the National Hunting Dog Association. We could list other hunting challenges this dog has won but that is not the point. There are pictures of him in this book. It would be nice to take credit for having trained that dog and blow our own horn each time someone tells us how the great the dog is. That would not be the truth, however. The dog is what he is because this quiet man was so determined to do the best he could with his dog. He searched for the right way to do things, and then he did them, day after day. He probably does not have the time, either, as he is busy running his own business, but he made the time to work with his dog. He established the most devoted relationship of mutual respect we have ever seen. He would give you his arm before handing over the Yellow Phantom. They ride in the truck together, travel together, and hunt together. They are the definition of success in this business. It is for the "Yellow Phantoms" of every color and type out there that we write this book. May you know what this man and his dog have come to know.

Introduction

The day is a little too warm. The dog is actively searching through the heavy cover. He knows a bird is in there somewhere. You are tired and really ready to call it a morning. You glance back toward the truck where the water and the sandwiches are calling. You turn around and whistle for your dog to follow. Only there is no dog following you. Now you have to turn back around and see what is delaying your buddy. On the other side of the cover strip is your dog, head down and tail out, pointing something. You smile. You walk over to the cover in front of your dog, kicking through the thick grass, and you glance back at your dog. He says the bird is there, now you do your part. You kick a little further, and up in front of you fly two magnificent cock pheasants. You shoot with Old Faithful, watch one bird go down, and then call your dog's name. Your dog beats through the heavy cover one last time, returning proudly with the trophy. One more for the bag, making the drive home all the shorter.

There is often debate about the legitimacy of the retriever that points. There are even more stories from many years past about retrievers that pointed wild game, field champions that pointed on their "right after the National" hunting excursions. In truth, retrievers that point have been around for a very long time, and not just Labradors. There are stories of Chesapeakes, goldens and flatcoat retrievers pointing wild birds. It has not been until the last couple of decades that a concerted, organized effort has existed to develop the Labradors that naturally point.

When you get two long-time bird hunters together, they can argue the phenomenon of the pointing Lab in the same fashion they argue politics or religion. Of course, beginning bird hunters are about the same as old-timers in their fervency regarding the 'real' truth about dogs, and why whatever it is they have is the best of all worlds. Emotion and pride aside, a dog doing what comes naturally to it, with heart and spirit, with confidence, skill, and a teamwork ethic, has to be one of the greatest sights there is. This book will not attempt to convince you that a pointing Labrador is the best dog to hunt. The pointing retriever will not be directly compared to the conventional pointing breeds. This book will tell you about pointing Labradors, and how to make the most of what is within the individual dog. Usually, the dog work itself is the greatest promoter of this type of hunting dog.

What is a Pointing Lab?

A pointing Lab is defined as a dog that will have the natural tendency to freeze upon locating the scent or sight of a live bird. Many breeds of dogs will engage in the predator stance when finding a live animal, and so will many Labs. Pointing is a genetically carried behavior that ultimately does not mask itself as any vestigial behavior. Pointing cannot be taught. Dogs can be taught to stop upon locating a live bird, but as any red-blooded pointer owner can tell you, that is not a point.

There is current investigation regarding genetic markers for pointing. As of this writing, none have been clearly defined. Dog DNA is as yet too complicated to isolate genes for specific behaviors. In time, this may change. For now, pointing appears to be carried genetically, and can be passed on when only one of the parents points. It might also not be passed on when both parents point. There are no definitive data regarding how pointing is carried and passed on. There are no available statistics regarding percentages in a litter, effects of depth of pointing in the background, etc. This is due in part to many dogs probably possessing the pointing characteristic with no one ever knowing it, or many dogs pointing with owners wondering what their "flushing" Lab was doing. Pointing Labs have been around for a long time and it is difficult to define when, where and how this natural pointing came into play, if it ever was a new thing.

Pointing Labs in the early stages might point many things. We have heard tales of grasshoppers, cats, muskrats, mice and pictures of birds being pointed. At first we wrote it off as the fancy of wishful owners. Time has shown it probably was mostly true. Within our own living room, a Grand Master Pointing Retriever asleep on a pheasant-festooned rug awoke with a start, leaped to her feet and pointed a bird image woven into the rug. That was one that had to be seen to be believed. Like any canine that points, Labs might enact their pointing instinct on a variety of strange things. Good upbringing and training will direct that instinct toward live birds in the field.

Why a Pointing Lab?

There are some magnificent pointing breeds out there. To watch a great pointer do its job is a thing of beauty. To watch any talented, skilled animal do its thing is a great pleasure. The key is that the animal has a strong talent, and the ability to develop the skills associated with that talent. That is the beauty of the Labrador retriever. Labs have demonstrated the characteristic of trainability and skill development for a long time. Labs are easily trained to become seeing-eye dogs, handicap assisting dogs, drug-sniffing dogs, family dogs, search and rescue dogs, and hunting dogs. They are generally good-natured and derive a real satisfaction out of serving people and working with them. There are individual exceptions to this, as there are with all things. However, statistics back up the popularity and success of the Lab in many different endeavors.

An intelligent Lab, with the appropriate genetics for hunting and the natural tendency to point, can be an easy dog to train and a great hunting partner. Raised with a certain intent and effort and trained in a fair and appropriate manner, Labs are great and successful partners. They will get out of the vehicle and wait to see what you plan to do. They will hunt with you, not in spite of you. They can view you as an integral part of their activity, and take great satisfaction in sharing their trophies with you. Labs tend to be as much buddy as they are dog, and that is often what compels many folks to buy them. They excel as much with the kids and family at home as they do in the field. They also tend to do just as well at waterfowl hunting or retrieving the pheasant that flew over the icy pond on its last futile flight.

Are There Differences between a Pointing Lab and a Flushing Lab?

There shouldn't be any differences between good Labs, aside from their behavior upon locating a live bird in the field. There are always differences between individuals, but the misconception that the Lab that points should be handled differently or raised differently is just that--a misconception. If misguided breeders of pointing Labs breed for the pointing trait alone, just as breeding for a color trait alone, bad things ultimately result. Greater detail will be given in subsequent chapters on locating a well-bred dog, but a pointing Lab should--in fact, must--be expected to possess all the traits of a good Lab. Those traits include intelligence, strong desire to retrieve, trainability, love of the water, athleticism, and boldness on birds in any form. Pointing Labs are not slower, larger, smaller, or different in any other distinct aspect. They are Labrador retrievers that, given the opportunity, point live game.

This book is written to help people learn about the true nature of the Labrador retriever that points. It is not testimony regarding the pointing Lab in comparison with other breeds of dogs, or pointing Lab people in comparison with other dog owners. There are many interesting ideas regarding this type of dog, some based on reality, some not. Suffice it to say that a good pointing Lab is a great dog to own. They tend to be quite versatile, to borrow a phrase used by other breeds. They love to hunt, they love to work, they enjoy learning and developing their abilities, they love people, and they adore our feathered friends. They relish jumping into the water, and sharing it with you in the form of a big shake. They are enthusiastic, joyful, intent and serious. We have often witnessed good Labs induce lackadaisical hunters to become avid ones, often sacrificing the spouse's good will and much disposable income--just because they were having so much fun with their dogs.

For the individual who plans on having only one hunting dog, the pointing Lab is often an excellent choice. Though the Labrador as a breed is not designed to run non-stop for an entire day, a well built Lab can cover a lot of ground for an extended period of time, and with rest periods, can resume hunting repeatedly. The generally heavier bone structure, muscling and coat do not lend themselves to the marathon characteristics of the big-running bird dogs. This same bone structure, muscling, and coat does lend itself well to any type of waterfowl hunting, in any kind of weather. The Lab is unparalleled in its ability to retrieve ducks and geese, in flowing rivers, icy ponds, through heavy cover and in just about any weather condition. The dogs you will see pictured in this book are used, without exception, for hunting wild pheasant in South Dakota, ducks and geese in Colorado, Nebraska, Kansas, Canada; quail in Arizona, Texas, New Mexico, and Colorado, and even the occasional grouse. They did not begin with all the skills necessary to be proficient in all these areas. They were trained with a strong foundation, and with their strong pairing of retrieving and pointing skills, have become accomplished hunters of wild birds of just about any kind.

Labs are avid retrievers. Because of their degree of enthusiasm for going after birds, there must be a great deal of control introduced in their training. The pointing breeds are avid 'searchers' for birds, and for that, there is a different approach to that dog. In short, if you train your pointing retriever completely like a conventional retriever you will sacrifice the staunch and intense point. Conversely, if you train your pointing retriever completely like a pointer, you will sacrifice the control in the retrieving work. Success is based on a careful balance of two aspects to the dog, and it takes time. Two somewhat conflicting concepts will be taught to your dog: Sit, don't move, and Stand, don't move. If either is forsaken, you will pay for it in the field. Either your dog will not hold its point, or will not honor the point of another dog; or it will do that well, but will not stop when it is chasing a bird or going a direction it thinks it should be going. It is not difficult to train a good pointing Lab, but it will take time and a well-designed program so that each step makes sense to the dog.

For eleven years, we have been working with pointing Labradors. When we were initially introduced to this 'new' thing, we literally chuckled at the people who brought them to us. And we made mistakes. Eleven years and hundreds of dogs have shown us more about these dogs than we could have found reading retriever books or pointer books. As a matter of fact, we did read them. There are two different approaches to both in general. Retriever people like to start obedience and control right off the bat, and pointer people wait much longer, and never do want all the control the handling retriever does. Pointer people like enthusiasm in searching for birds, while retriever people do not always give that much thought. So the question is, how do you get a staunch and stylish point on a naturally pointing retriever, and still manage to handle the same dog to a duck 200 yards across an icy pond? And, have blast doing both?

We've read a lot of what different well-known people have to say about dog training. We've read what people who are not so well known have to say. There are several different approaches to training retrievers and pointers. It does get a little frustrating as a reader trying to get to the meat of the training system, to weed through a great deal of criticism and philosophizing regarding what the "other kind of trainers" do. There are trainers who developed methods for training on a great dog they possessed. It is pretty easy to be a good trainer when a dog has so darn much talent he looks good no matter what you do. We started training pointing Labs with some dogs who were so intelligent and so naturally talented that we looked awesome as trainers. And of course, we believed that ourselves. Only it was not true. Because, at the same time we were not as successful with the average or below-average dogs. That's a problem because there are overwhelmingly more average dogs than great or poor ones. Thousands of long hours have been spent learning how to get the most out of what was in an individual dog, and now, with our education program, what is in the handler. A sound training program should be developed so that a person not unusually gifted with training ability, training a very nice but maybe not so gifted dog, can be successful.

We've always been in the uncomfortable position of existing between several worlds. The ardent field trialers can't imagine not testing a dog to the most demanding standards because they're so capable. The hunt test fans think that just hunting a dog is not nearly as rewarding as testing against a standard, but that the artificial constraints of the field trialers are unnatural and unworthy. The hunters often think all of it aside from a good hunt is a waste of anybody's time. Now you walk into a field trial or hunt test with one of those "pointing Labradors" and people whisper about it. "There are those pointing Lab people!" Or, you go on a week long hunt in the Dakotas with a dog with titles dangling all around its name, they are thinking, "Right, but can he even hunt?" We've heard it all from every angle. Those that speak with the loudest and greatest resistance on any side of this coin are those with the least experience outside their own world. In response to any of them, we do the same thing: Smile, get the dog out and let the dog work do the talking. That usually ends the debate. A good dog is a good dog. Let's see if we can help you with yours.

Table of Contents

Chapter 1
Finding and Picking your Puppy

There is as much advice about finding a good pointing Lab as there is advice about voting in the next election. Usually the advice is either to "Buy from me" or "Don't buy from that breeder". That isn't very helpful if you are not aware of the insider information your advisor is gifted to have. It is human nature to decide this week that you want a dog, and decide you want to have it very soon. That concept works with cars, appliances and potato chips. It's not a good idea with dogs, any more than it is with finding a spouse. It should take some time and research. Finding, purchasing and owning a dog is a lifetime investment, and should be treated with that significance. We have read respected books written in earlier times in which the advice given was to get rid of any dog that does not meet all your expectations. Statistically speaking, that is not how people go about this. Right or wrong, people rarely get rid of a dog that they've chosen, so make sure your choice is one you won't regret down the road.

What is a Good Dog?

It is interesting to hear people describe their idea of what a good dog is. You will hear it's a dog with a wide head and short legs, or one with the deep yellow color, or one with a good nose. That is like describing your ideal spouse as one with short red hair or a quick smile. That leaves most of the truly important things out--not a good idea. If you could look back after the 12 or 14 years of owning a dog, what description might you give about what comprises a good dog?

A good dog, first and foremost, possesses the talents to carry out the tasks for which you are purchasing the dog. If you want a pointing

Lab to hunt upland and also hunt waterfowl, and also spend time with your kids the rest of the year, then your target traits are defined. It appears many people are unaware that not all retrievers retrieve, and not all pointers point. Not all Labs even care about birds or work, or running through fields on a hunt. Too many times we have had people bring dogs to us for training, believing and hoping that a professional trainer could make their dog want to retrieve and want to hunt. Great disappointment results when they are told the dog does not possess the basic material to develop what they want. You can train a dog with the talents they possess, but you cannot create those talents. It is your job as a 'puppy hunter' to do all you can to assure your pup will possess the desire to hunt, retrieve, and work with you.

If you want a hunting dog, look for pups from dogs that have demonstrated the traits you need. Perhaps even more importantly, buy a pup from dogs with generations of dogs that have demonstrated the traits you need. We buy dogs on litter credentials above any other single thing. Litter credentials are the proof over multiple generations that the dogs are birdy, strong retrievers, strong pointers, and healthy, athletic, trainable dogs. The fancy titles and impressive credentials often drive off prospective buyers. That is about as sensible as not buying good food because the store is well decorated. The titles are not always a necessity, but they certainly are proof the dog likes the fieldwork and can be trained. That should not be ignored because of someone's personal dislike of non-proletariat things.

Making Sense of the "Credentials"

Now you are looking for a pointing Lab with the best of credentials. What are they? "My brother-in-law's dog that is a great hunter" may not be the best credential, unless he did the background work for you with his dog purchase. People buy dogs that are conveniently located, or from someone they think they should buy a dog from, or worst of all, because they had too much to drink at a Ducks Unlimited auction. Let's break down some of the 'credentials' that are out there right now.

Pointing Credentials

There are two organizations that recognize the pointing Lab and hold events to test them. Only one of these is widely recognized, and that is the American Pointing Labrador Association. They certify pointing Labs to three levels, awarding a total of four titles: Certified Pointing Retriever, Intermediate Pointing Retriever, Master Pointing Retriever, and Grand Master Pointing Retriever. The specific requirements for these titles are available on their website, www.pointinglabs.com/apla. Currently, these are the titles that are used to show that a dog does point birds in the field, and can also do water retrieves as well. Greater titles do not necessarily mean the dog is better, but they do indicate the dog was trained to a more sophisticated level. A single lower title may mean the dog could not be trained to a higher level, or that the owner did not have the time, interest, or ability to continue the advanced training. When you don't know the dogs, the pointing titles do give you an idea the dog carries the pointing trait.

Retrieving Credentials

There are a variety of venues under which retrievers are tested for their retrieving abilities. The full gamut of these cannot be described here. There are several organizations that hold tests and award titles. AKC titles are the only ones that appear on the dog's AKC registered name, since they are the registering entity. Dogs can be registered through the United Kennel Club as well, and the UKC will recognize its own titles. There is great debate regarding the relative merit of the various titles available for retrievers, and that debate will not be addressed in this book. However, we will state that we know of no titles that indicate the dog is a robot and not a birdy, enthusiastic dog. Any dog that must retrieve in the field, whether marked or blind retrieves, ultimately has to do it because he loves the retrieve, not because someone is making him do it. People can mess up a good dog with poor training techniques, but that does not mean the testing criteria for these dogs are at fault. Field champions, when allowed to honor their natural abilities of nose and hunting, are great hunters. The very lofty titles usually imply talent and great trainability since the testing criteria are so severe, not that the dog has no ability to hunt on a natural, non-tested basis.

Now, after being given advice to look for good credentials on a litter, we turn around and tell you that credentials still do not make the dog. A pup should not be considered to be ideal because its pedigree is packed with multi-titled dogs. Your odds are probably higher that the dog has potential compared to a dog with a pedigree packed with nothing but cute dog names. Titles just for the sake of titles can backfire. There are 'fancy' dogs that can be crossed and produce pups superior to themselves, or at least as good. There are 'fancy' dogs that, crossed with the wrong 'fancy' dog, produce dogs excelling at sleeping in the yard above all else. It is not a simple or easy thing to go find a good dog. It takes some research and some effort, and usually the more invested, the more benefit derived. The best thing to do, when you are not armed with knowledge on bloodlines and pedigrees, which lines cross well and which do not, which dogs produce good dogs and which do not, is to find someone who is.

There are some simple tenets in puppy hunting you should keep in mind when talking to people about their dogs.

A responsible and knowledgeable breeder (both aspects are important) will have more to offer than "This is just a real nice dog." They should have a full explanation regarding why they even undertook the breeding they have. If they do not, they are probably generating income, or do not know enough to do this as well as some others might. There you take your chances. You might just get lucky, or not. Someone undertaking the big task of reproducing animals already in abundance on this planet is obligated to have some compelling reason for breeding these pups.

If you find a repeat breeding of a breeding that has produced good dogs, your odds of getting a good dog go up. You already know what the cross has the potential to produce.

A responsible and knowledgeable breeder will expect you to have many questions. You should have many questions. You will want to know about the sire and dam, what are their characteristics, their athleticism, their temperaments, and their accomplishments. Health issues are so important; these will be addressed in a subsequent section. The breeder must have those fully covered as well.

Because a dog is a good dog does not mean it will transfer those traits to its offspring. The female is every bit as important as the male in the breeding, and in our opinion, is the more important of the two. A National Champion bred to a female with no talent will probably result in dogs more like their mother. Do not overlook the bottom side of the pedigree. It should be strong. If you look at many of the top performing retrievers in the country today, the bottom side of their pedigrees statistically is the strongest.

Some lines cross well, meaning they produce dogs as good or better than their parents. Some do not cross well, meaning two good dogs are bred, and they produce little or nothing remotely as good as themselves. To differentiate means to research the good dogs out there and just find out which lines produced those dogs.

Some dogs have the ability to throw one or two good pups and the remainders are not so good. Some dogs have more uniformity in what they throw. Do not overlook this phenomenon. Previous breedings, if any, can shed some light on this data. We have seen litters with one or two very nice dogs, and the rest not even measuring up to any degree in the performance category. Unless you are top of the pick list, it's probably not a good idea to buy a pup from such a litter.

Talk to buyers from previous breedings. If there are none, you are an experiment. If there are some but you cannot speak to them, question why.

You have found your Litter, Now What?

It is the contention of many owners of good dogs that there is no way to tell which ones are the 'good' ones from a litter of pups. Some puppy-seekers have little interest in going through the weeding-out process and researching the litter. It is true that within a given litter of puppies, some may be slower developers than others. Those slow developers certainly will not test out as well as those who have, at least at this early stage, developed more rapidly, and appear to have more on the ball. There have been National Champions who were picked last from a litter. Even so, over many years of dealing with, buying, and selling pups, it has been our experience that, almost always, the traits the very young pups show you, in contrast to one another, do not change dramatically over time. There is something to picking a puppy, if you have the ability to see the dogs beyond just a rolling bunch of furry pups.

One of the most critical times in your career as a dog owner is this, the time when you decide you want to acquire a puppy. It is thrilling, even for the hardened dog owner, to get a fresh start with a brand new dog. The thrill and excitement can be very detrimental to your long-term interests, however, if the emotion and enthusiasm are allowed to overtake the common sense of doing the best job of selection as possible.

What do You Want from Your Future Dog?

Have you ever thought about this question in detail? Five years from now, what does the ideal picture look like? Does this dog stay home all the time, quietly and patiently, or does the dog go everywhere with you or your family? Does the dog perform a function - will he or she hunt, compete, be a companion, be a guard dog, watch children, travel? Oftentimes people get a dog and then take what comes. If the dog is good in the house, then he gets in the house. If he guards, then he protects the house. If he doesn't travel well, he stays home. If he was supposed to hunt but has no interest, he becomes a piece of lawn furniture and just 'hangs out' in the back yard. If you could have anything you want, what would that be? Here are some aspects to that picture you might want to take into consideration:

What function will this dog perform?

What is your hierarchy of 'functions'? Of all the possibilities, what is most important, and how does the list go--hunting, companion, family dog, and guard dog? Put your desires in order of priority. This will be more important than you know.

Who will be the prime caretaker of the dog? Is the whole family that 'person'?

Where is the dog expected to live, sleep and eat?

How will the dog travel, and how often?

How much time is the prime caretaker, hereon referred to as handler, willing to commit to the training and care of this dog?

Do you have a clear picture of how you want this dog to behave, now and one year from now?

Do you have a clear picture of how you are going to see to it that the dog is taught to behave now and one year from now?

Do you know why you are getting a dog?

The issue here is to determine why you want a dog, and what you expect to give to get that from the dog. It is also to decide how much of you, or whoever the handler will be, is going to be committed to work with the dog.

It is important to understand where the dog came from, because that is what made dogs what they are today. Dogs were domesticated from particular kinds of wild dogs. Those were dogs that lent themselves to working with humans, and not hunting and eating them! All domesticated dogs initially had to work for survival, and did so until the last few hundred years. These original dogs were neither large nor small, but medium sized. Large dogs could not move fast enough to escape predators, and small dogs could not defend themselves, so thin, athletic, medium-sized dogs were the survivors.

When you see very large breeds or very small breeds, understand these are in no way a naturally occurring breed of dog. Of course, there are no more natural-occurring dogs. All have been bred to fit one function or another, but some have not strayed far from their original design. The ones that vary significantly from their origins have suffered this because of human intervention. Dogs would not naturally make themselves huge lumbering beasts; it is not in their best interests. Nor would they shrink themselves through natural selection to something so tiny you could carry it under the seat of an airplane.

It is humans who, through desire for novelty or who knows what, have created the toy breeds and the huge breeds that now exist. There are good and healthy dogs that are in these extreme breeds, but there are many that are not. There is only one way to vary from any animal's optimal genetics, and that is through inbreeding. Inbreeding is how the very small breeds were created. Inbreeding is one way unusual colors are created in dogs. Of course, you will never meet any one who has done this inbreeding, but they surround you. Many may be so uninformed as to not know they are doing that.

Inbreeding is also how genetic defects that may go un-manifested or unrecognized are brought out. Dysplasia, a hip defect in so many breeds today, is rampant because of the inbreeding occurring in popular breeds. There are immune deficiency problems in breeds that have been popular for some time, and those problems manifest themselves in premature and often unpleasant endings for the dogs. The list of genetic defects in popular breeds, and Labs in particular, could go on and on. The point is to be wary of any breed that is either extremely popular or varies significantly from the original dog structure. There are ways to minimize the chances of getting a pup with some of these problems, and that will be discussed shortly.

One of the things that people overlook most often when acquiring a new dog is the origin of the dog. Remember the old saying, "You are what you come from"? That is true of dogs. If a dog comes from a line of dogs bred to guard and attack if feeling threatened, then expect that dog may tend to attack if he truly feels threatened, no matter how friendly he is to his owners. If a dog comes from a line of dogs bred to dig in the ground and hunt for rodents, then expect that dog to dig in your yard and hunt for something. If you buy a hunting dog who comes from ancestors who ran for miles and miles a day during a hunt, then do not expect that dog to sit idly in the back yard every day, watching the children play. He will most likely scale the fence and head out, not even knowing why, but driven by his very breeding to range and roam.

Understand the Labrador breed. Learn what they were designed to do, and expect what they will want to do, in one form or another. Too many people buy the beautiful sporting breeds that were developed to hunt all day, run long and fast, and go far from their handlers. They buy them because they are athletic and beautiful, intelligent and sensitive. Then they stick them in the back yard and give them nothing to do. These dogs will create something to do, and it probably won't be tending to the flowerbeds. Then the owners think their dog is a 'problem dog', when it is the very owners who are the 'problem'.

Pick a dog to which you can be fair, given the constraints of your daily life. If you don't have much time to spend with your dog, do not get a dog highly driven to perform and work. If you want a dog that can hike and run and do many athletic things with you, do not get a 120-pound dog that will break down with wear and tear. If you do get a performance dog, don't expect him to act like a toy poodle in your back yard. They are high-energy dogs, who will take advantage of every situation to do something. Have a kennel so he can be confined and not destructive. Have something for him to do, and almost every day! If you have small children who cannot be accountable for their actions, do not get a dog that has even the smallest chance of turning on them.

One final thought: consider the place you live and the conditions in which you plan to keep your dog. If you live in a place in which kennels are not allowed, or general dog activities are frowned upon, is this the best place to have your dog? If you live in an apartment, is an avid hunter designed to spend 23 hours a day inside a small room? Make sure your living conditions provide the type of environment in which your dog may remain healthy, challenged, and robust.

Picking the Right Puppy

This is the fun part for all of us. There are as many "tricks" to picking the right puppy as there are people who want to tell you about them. We have heard many interesting ways to pick up a puppy. One renowned dog trainer answered that question with, "There is no way to pick the right puppy, I just reach in and take one." Another woman said she always picked the pup that was first to the food dish. One person told us he was told to pick the pup who stuck closest to his legs. When someone goes about choosing his future hunting companion, he either has no idea how he is going to do it, or he has ideas so immutable that discussion is pointless.

It is true that there is no sure-fire way to know you are getting the dog you want. There is no positive way to know you are getting the best pup in the litter. Living things are random and unpredictable, and we cannot 'know for sure' anything about them. Just like any of us who are married realize this, it is also true with dogs. Living creatures change, and cannot be fully understood. Even so, years of experience looking at puppies and see-ing how they develop and how they might change has given us some tools developed purely through empirical data, or by just seeing a whole bunch of pups for a long time.

What Characteristics Do You Look For?

Regardless of what you are getting your puppy for, there are probably several things we all want in our dogs. One of the tops has to be intelligence. A smart dog is an easily trainable dog. Of course, it is also a dog who can easily outwit us, but that is another issue entirely. Intelligent dogs understand their role, can learn what it is you want them to learn, and do not do things for absolutely no reason, though it may be hard to understand the 'why' sometimes.

Another important aspect to a dog is sensitivity. Most of us are happier with a dog we can work with, without having to prove we are serious every time. A dog that awakens when you enter a room and is aware of your presence may be more desirable than one you have to wake up to take outside. A dog that is sensitive is easier to train to be basically obedient. These dogs you teach, and because they wish to avoid your corrections, they obey willingly. More insensitive animals do not care enough about your level of happiness, and these dogs often take more force to make obedient, because they will pay attention to little else. Sensitivity does not equate to weakness, timidity, or any other negative quality. It is a positive quality through which your dog is more aware of what is around him or her, and more willing to play a part in it.

A certain level of courage is important. It is easy to mistake courage for stupidity. Courage means the dog is willing to brave something of which he is not sure for the pleasure of the adventure or experience. This implies the dog understands there is an unknown out there, and understands there may be a risk associated with it. That is courage with intelligence. A dog with little intelligence may appear courageous, when in fact the dog is just too ignorant to realize there is a risk. A dog with courage will be one who is not afraid to get in a different vehicle, go somewhere new, is not afraid of new people or environments, new dogs or new experiences. A dog without much courage may whine and hide, or even bite if intimidated enough. A courageous dog is easier to own than one who is not.

Assuming you are looking for a dog for a lifetime, then athleticism and robustness are important. This does not mean to pick the biggest, smallest, skinniest, fattest or any other geometric outlyer. Usually, the extremes are not desirable compared to the more moderate. As opposed to picking a dog based upon its size at seven weeks, pick a dog on the basis of how easily he moves, how good his endurance is, and how enthusiastic he is going about his job as a puppy. Dogs who are very large tend to have more physical problems when physically challenged, and again as they age and arthritis sets in. For some reason completely unclear to us, huge Labradors are popular today. These are dogs weighing in anywhere from 90 to 100+ pounds. Once again, fashion and trends can destroy a good thing. There are exceptions, but in general, a physics breakdown of the stress and forces on joint and bones with a field animal carrying that much weight shows unbelievable stress where it was never intended. Nature does not create animals to run which are too big, too heavy, or too cumbersome. It is humans that create these animals through breeding. Though there is always someone around telling us that his 110-pound Lab is the best thing going, time will tell a different story. Ask a good veterinarian his or her opinion about field use of large, thick dogs. If you are fielding a cross-country track team, will you pick your runners from the defensive line of a football team? Probably not. Don't do that with your dog, either. The football players would either give out or injure themselves in the track adventure, and so will your dog.

Athletic dogs will have an easier time of it throughout their lives. If you plan on hunting with them, if they are in condition, they will hunt longer and more effectively for you because they are not limited by poor structure or movement. This will be true for any use you may have for them.

Robustness does not equate to being wild and crazy. Wild and crazy is just that, and not terribly desirable for any purpose. Robustness is the twinkle in the eye when the pup looks at you. It is the enthusiasm for walking with you, chasing a puppy dummy and playing with siblings. It is the spirit for life that will be a pleasure for you always.

For those interested in finding the best hunting dog, that is sometimes very difficult to pinpoint at an early age. All of the aforementioned characteristics are important for the bird dog. The desire to retrieve may or may not be present at the age of six to eight weeks. If it is not, that does not mean it will not appear soon. If it is there, then at least you know the dog loves to retrieve when it is fun. Many breeders will put out a bird to see what the dogs do, and certainly they must have good reasons. There are probably many breeds of puppies that would gladly chase a live bird around, so it is not clear how effective this tool is at making a good judgment. In our opinion, a better judgment of the dog's birdiness is its pedigree. Still, if the pup shows an interest in feathers that has to be a good sign. Certainly the desire to retrieve at an early age is a very positive sign, and the chances are the pups in the litter who want to retrieve at an early age will tend to be more enthusiastic later on as well.

If the pup you are evaluating walks over to a bird and launches into a three-point stance, you have a good chance that it is going to point. If your pup does nothing or just tries to catch and eat the bird, you still might well have a pointing dog. Pointing behavior when exposed to bird scent or the sight of a bird is a good sign, not necessarily an absolute sign. Often it takes multiple exposure to birds before the desire to point kicks in. Sight pointing a wing on a fishing pole is not a bad sign, but it is not conclusive regarding pointing. Too many non-pointing dogs will undertake the predator stance at a wing, or probably a guinea pig as well, if it is on the end of the line. Tests that show pointing can be misleading, and the results are often heavily influenced by the desire of the viewer. If the pup points, then that is a good sign. If it does not, it does not mean the dog will never point. This is a tough one to be definitive on.

How to Test for These Characteristics

Pups should not be tested until they are at least six weeks of age. Ideally, you should look at your pups at six, then seven, and finally at eight weeks before making your choice. There is a very good reason for this. Say you went to your breeder's place on a Saturday afternoon. It was hot; the pups had been playing all morning, except for a timid little one. Now you go out, armed with your puppy test criteria, and begin to look at the pups. They all look pretty droopy except for this one bouncy little female. She seems more alert, energetic, and just more 'with it' than any of the other pups. If that is your only time to look at the pups, you will come away with a very biased view, and probably not an accurate one. The pup that appears to be the best one is in fact the only one not tired from an all-morning romp!

Puppies develop at different rates. If the standout pup one week is still the standout pup the next week, then you may be on to something. If the emphasis shifts, weigh what you see with the dogs at a greater age more heavily. The pups can change over time, and with changing conditions. Try to pick a time of day when the pups will not be hot, tired, or full of dinner. Do not let the fact one pup had a belly full of food bias your opinion. Make every effort to watch enough of the pups to make sure you get the real picture.

Separate the males and the females. Females develop earlier than males, and usually test better. This does not mean they are better, but they appear to be ahead of the game at this stage, and so you may think you are getting the better dog. If you already know what you want, then look only at that sex. If you are not sure, look at both, but look at them in comparison to one another, males with males, and females with females. Keep in mind that, in general, the female pups will develop more rapidly and look better at this stage. There are always exceptions, but do not allow this phenomenon to cloud your opinion of what you are seeing.

Puppy testing depends a lot upon the awareness of the individual looking. Two people can look at the same litter of puppies and interpret what they see quite differently. As hard as it may be, it might be better sometimes to pretend you are looking for a pup for your boss, or your father-in-law. That way you can set aside your emotional attachments to old Shep, the dog you had as a child, who was so great. Or more commonly, if we were the kids in school who never got picked for the baseball team, we will make up for that by picking the puppy that would never make the 'baseball team'. Choices made on emotional baggage from the past are not always in the best interests of the arrangement you would like to have between your dog and you or your family for the next twelve to fourteen years.

Finally, make sure the pups you are evaluating are clearly and uniquely marked. Traditionally, colored collars or paint are put on the pups around five to six weeks, clearly identifying which is which. Any good breeder will do this so that you can make informed choices. If your breeder has not, ask if you can mark the one or two you favor. The pups will have grown so much in one week that you will be hard put to tell which one is which the next time you go to test them.

Puppy "Tests"

This exercise is not so severe and contrived as it may have sounded up to this point. With the criteria already discussed in mind, you do several things with the pups in which you are interested. The key is to remember what you see, and think about it later. First, try to evaluate your pups without a crowd around you. A bunch of people around will distract the dogs, and distract you. With three different people all going "Ahhh, look how cute the little (pink, green, red) collared pup is!"

Watch the puppies and their interactions with each other and the world around them. Who hides behind his or her littermates when you come in? Who notices your presence first? Who is curious? Who is asleep all the time? Who appears to be the most mobile, the most spirited? Who takes off all by himself? Who ignores you?

Take the puppies, if you can, to an outside location. It is most preferable if you can take them somewhere unfamiliar to them. A field or

Head out into unfamiliar territory

place they do not normally romp and play in is very important. It is under these circumstances that you can tell something about courage, curiosity, athleticism and spirit. In the confines of a very familiar backyard, the outgoing pup may have so thoroughly explored his world that he no longer needs to explore and you can misread his disinterest.

Take off walking with the pups in tow. Some will follow, some will hang back. The ones who hang back may be fearful, or may just be tired. Just keep track of who goes and who does not. If a pattern develops each time you test them, and little blue collar never comes out with you, you might believe little blue collar is somewhat timid, or does not feel well. Similarly, if a pattern develops, and three of the pups always come out with you, you might believe those three are rather robust. Continue walking, calling the pups to go with you. Watch who has the physical ability and desire to keep up with you. Watch who tires or becomes bored with the activity. So many times we have seen the desire to keep up, the physical ability to keep up, and a lack of boredom translate to a dog with a high level of interest in working and training.

Here is a place you can gauge something about courage. Find something like a steep incline, a stream, some difficult terrain, a sticker patch, anything that is quite challenging to a six-week-old puppy. Watch the puppies' reactions when confronted with this 'challenge'. Let's say you encounter a precipice that cannot hurt the pups if they tumble off, but that is a little frightening. Of course, never put the puppies at any real risk, just a perceived risk. You head down the precipice and on, encouraging the pups to go with you. Watch closely. Is there a puppy that just headlongs right over the side and never gives it a second thought? Is there a puppy that encounters the edge, stops, looks at it, decides it is a risk worth taking and proceeds? Is there a pup that sees the edge, stops, and will not consider proceeding? How do you read these reactions?

It is customary to think the pup that just jumped down the edge without thought was the 'brave' one, but is this true? More likely he was not smart enough to take time to consider the risk. Often, lack of using the brain is construed as courage when it is not. The pup that would not consider taking any risk, if consistent in that reaction, is most likely not

Watch pups face a perceived risk

31

a very courageous dog. The pup who took notice of the risk and then opted to take the risk is likely a courageous, thinking dog, particularly if that pup tends to repeat that kind of behavior when presented with other 'risks'. Courage without thought usually winds up as a frequently injured dog, or a dog who may be a little harder to work with.

A bold, confident pup

On your outing with the pups, take your time. Plan on more than a couple of minutes. If possible, walk with them for ten minutes or so. This will definitely tire out a six- or seven-week-old pup, but this will give you more insight into the little ones. Go over the hard stuff, across the water or stickers, up a steep hill, down a steep hill. As time goes by (within reason, of course) keep an eye on who sticks with you, who has an efficiency of movement and innate strength. These dogs will tire less readily and are more athletic, physically and in spirit. Often, a pup you may not have paid much attention to earlier will show up at this point. This will show not only athleticism and physical ability, but may indicate courage, tenacity, and spirit. A dog that consistently shows the ability to withstand difficult rigors is a dog you may want as your hunting companion.

Perhaps since we are trainers, the sensitivity of a dog is very important to us. It is easier to train, work with, and live with a dog who is more tuned in to those around him or her. A dog that can pick up clues and signals more quickly takes less discipline, and less time to grasp certain concepts. A dog that is more aware probably finds birds with less effort as well. Watch for a pattern of behavior in the pups that shows a continual and heightened level of awareness. Who is the first dog to notice your presence? Who is the first dog who awakens after a noise? Who is the first dog to notice you changed directions, or that you called? Who is the first dog to run after the bird wing you tossed? Who watched you the most intently? There are many ways to assess sensitivity. Mostly, keep your eyes open.

Intelligence is important in a dog, no matter what you plan to do with him. Although many times we have seen dogs that constantly outwit their owners, intelligence should be desired and channeled appropriately in a dog. The signs of intelligence go hand in hand with the aspects already described in the early sections. An intelligent dog is one who thinks before taking a risk, a dog that watches you closely, looking you in the face. An intelligent dog sees what goes on around him or her, watches birds in the sky, notices action on a television screen, looks toward a strange noise, has a high level of curiosity about everything. An intelligent pup senses when to pick a fight, or when best to leave it to the others. Look for the pup that looks for you.

Spirit in a dog is one of the things that make him or her most memorable over your lifetime. We all remember the one dog we had who went with us everywhere, protected us, explored with us, or who was the most prolific and joyful hunting companion. Though it is hard to qualify in a pup, it can very often be sensed on the part of those to whom it is important. In this way, dogs are very like humans. Some exist in a lump-like state and are quite satisfied in doing so. Others have the ability to experience pleasure in the smallest things, making them all the larger. Spirited dogs anticipate any activity with you. They have the ability to relish work. They appreciate challenges. Life

Spirit is important in a dog

Does your pup like you?

for that type of dog is something they do, not what describes their existence. It is something to think about as you watch your prospective litter.

Spend some one-on-one time with each pup you find interesting. Take him away from the others. Interact with the pup. Does the pup pay attention to you, or everything but you? Can you get the dog to look you in the eye and focus on you? If the pup has no interest in you, read that accordingly. If you find one that watches you and knows what you are doing and likes you, that is a big positive. You'll want that in the dog you train, so look for it now. Toss a rolled-up sock, a glove, or some other easy, tempting object and see if the pup shows any interest in retrieving. Some pups retrieve right off the bat. Others have no idea what you are doing. Play and entice them to get interested in what you have, and into running after it. This is by no means a definitive test, but if the pup does like to

Will the pup retrieve?

retrieve, you will often find that is directly proportional to the desire to hunt birds.

People buying a potential pointing Lab want a test to determine if the pup is a natural pointer. Based upon the data gathered over about ten years of looking at pointing Lab pups, we offer the following observations. Some pointing Lab pups sight point a wing on a fishing pole, while some that will point later do not point that same wing. If a seven-week-old pup points a live bird to which it has been exposed, that is behavior you may also see with a non-pointing Lab puppy. Many breeds of dogs will 'point' things. If you see a pointing Lab pup point a bird or a wing, that is a positive, but not a definitive thing. If you see that same pup repeatedly point, that is far more definitive. As often as not, you will see a future superstar pointing Lab wish to eat a live bird as much as any other dog.

Summarizing the "Choice" Process

There is often a great deal of emotion associated in picking a puppy. Too many times we have seen someone let his daughter pick the puppy so she would feel a part of the process, or they pick the one that looked just like their old dog did. This is a kindness to the people involved, but it may not be the best thing for you or your puppy! If space allowed, dozens of stories could be told here regarding the results of poor puppy choices. One avid hunter we knew was a very large man. For him, large was good. When he picked a puppy, he always chose the biggest one in the litter. That would work well if they were eggs in a carton, all basically the same thing. Since puppies are like children, and for those of you who have had children or siblings, you know what a huge differences can exist between identically bred humans. What this large hunter wound up with was a dog who ate twice as much food as the regular dog, constantly tore tendons and ligaments because he was so large, and was not much of a hunter and ultimately underwent multiple shoulder surgeries to repair repeated damage. Perhaps if he had chosen the pup that exhibited the characteristics that would eventually yield an ardent and capable hunter, his sizable investment might have netted him more.

As mentioned before, there is no such thing as a 'sure thing'. The dog that tests out the best may not be the best dog. However, if you had to pick ten dogs from ten different litters, going through a thoughtful and deliberate process will net you the best dog the majority of the time. We have seen that borne out time and time again in our own kennels.

• Separate males from females. Usually, the females look better because they tend to develop earlier. This could bias your opinion.

• Test the puppies somewhere other than their own yard. Do not let familiarity with environment bias your judgment. It is best to take them somewhere new.

• Test the puppies in a location that will provide physical challenges and perceived risks to the dogs. This allows you to evaluate for courage, intelligence, and athleticism.

• It is not advisable to pick a pup based on one evaluation. The pups may be tired, not feeling well, or some other thing that masks their real character. Test a number of times so that you may see the pattern of behavior. When you see a consistent behavior in the pups, then you can have some comfort level in the validity of your assessments.

• Watch the pups in general, during all their activities, including in their whelping box or kennel. Notice who sees everything first, who is most aware, who is most curious. Watch for the dog that thinks.

• Physically challenge the dogs so that you may see who is the athlete, who is tenacious, and who is lazy or weak. Look for the one with good movement and stamina.

• Look for the dog with an interest in retrieving. A dog that does not have it at six weeks may acquire it later on. The dog that does have it at six weeks definitely has the desire to retrieve.

• Look for the robust dog--the dog that enjoys playing, sleeping, eating, and interacting with littermates and with you.

• Look for the pup who believes in himself or herself enough to take some risks, but understands that what they are doing is a little scary. This is courage.

• Expose the pups to bird smell in some real form and see if any genuine pointing behavior appears. Believe only strong pointing behavior that is repeated. If that is not so apparent, it doesn't mean the pup is not a natural pointer.

• Look for a pup you genuinely like.

Health Issues

The retriever breeds can be fraught with genetic problems. Hip dysplasia, eye defects, immune system problems, thyroid problems, elbow defects, etc. are pervasive. It is not possible to be absolutely certain the dog you are buying will never have any of these problems. You can go a long ways to reduce your chances of getting a dog with these defects.

Deal only with a breeder who is aware of these problems, and who breeds dogs that have proof of not possessing these defects. Dogs two years of age and older can be rated for hip dysplasia. Dogs younger than two years are not mature enough for a final judgment, but preliminary x-rays can be taken to determine if the dog should be bred, or spayed or neutered. The x-rays are sent in to one location where they are evaluated by a team of board certified veterinarians. This team assigns a rating of Excellent, Good, Fair, or Poor, and an "OFA" number (Orthopedic Foundation of America, www.ofa.com) goes with it. This number goes into the dog's registration and is permanently assigned. (Dysplastic dogs are not rated at all, and receive no OFA number.) Your breeder should have the OFA certificate and rating on both sire and dam of the litter. A rating of Good or Excellent is the only kind of dog to reproduce. If you have ever seen a dysplastic dog, it would make you wish to prosecute those who have allowed them to reproduce and pass on the pain and suffering. There are continuing developments in the evaluation of hips, and more than just OFA certifications. Make sure you and a knowledgeable vet discuss this so you make very informed decisions before buying a pup.

Both sire and dam of a litter should possess what is called an "eye CERF" (Canine Eye Research Foundation). This is an annual examination done by a canine ophthalmologist, the results of which are sent to a central location in Ohio. In this examination, the eye is closely examined for cataracts and retinal defects. If the eye shows no detectable problems, an eye "CERF" is given with a CERF number and certificate assigned. This is the only evidence you will have the dogs you are evaluating are likely not to have eye problems. In addition, it is now becoming standard to have the eyes of pups be evaluated prior to being sold. Even with both parents passing CERF, pups can still have eye problems. Increasingly, breeders are having the pups checked by an ophthalmologist prior to releasing the pups.

Any breeder who truly cares for the animals he or she is producing and for the breed as a whole will go to these lengths to assure the quality of what he or she producing. It is strongly our recommendation to purchase only from individuals who have invested the time, money and care in the animals they are breeding. In the end, this type of dog will be the least expensive to own. You are far less likely to be constantly running to the vet because of various problems. Nor will you have to put your beloved pet down at an early age because of problems he is having or pain he is enduring.

The ticket price for a puppy should not be the criteria for buying a pup. It is easy to tell someone that the money is not important, when to all of us, money is very important, and some do not have a large puppy-buying nest egg saved. It is not cheap to breed a litter of pups if the breeder does all the things he should to assure a good, healthy, robust litter of pups. Regardless of how much you spent on your first dog and how much you wish to pay, the purchase price is a small portion of the money you will spend on the dog. A pricey pup that lives for 14 years with nothing but shots and dog food for expenses and that hunts for ten years is far less expensive than a cheap puppy that racked up five thousand dollars' worth of vet expenses and/or disappointing hunting trips.

Conclusions

You want a puppy. You most likely know the type you wish to buy. Do remember that you cannot deny your dog's genetics; runners run, protective dogs protect, dogs with a purpose need to have a purpose in their lives. No matter what puppy you take home, if you purchase a dog who is bred to do something, then you will have a much better time of it if your dog gets to do that something. Most of the behavioral problems we encounter between people and their dogs stem from the fact they have never given their dog the purpose and the outlet it needs. Running behind your vehicle in a field is not an outlet. Dogs with a function need to be mentally and physically challenged, just as you do.

Pick a dog that is right for you, for the 10-15 years you expect to own that dog.

Be prepared to provide the health care and daily care required in responsibly owning a dog.

If possible, work out ahead of time who will be the primary 'handler' of this dog; who will feed, exercise, train and work with the dog. When, where, and how often?

Plan for future needs. Puppies chew, puppies can be quite destructive. Do you have a place for your pup when it needs to be confined, a place in which it will be safe while you are away? Where will the pup sleep, will it need to be housebroken, how will you do that?

Find the right litter of pups. If it takes months, the wait will be worth it. Try never to go look at a litter you do not want to buy from. There are no unattractive puppies!

Find a litter from breeders who will guarantee the health of the sire and dam, and guarantee to replace your pup if there is a genetic problem. That is standard in the reputable section of this industry.

Buy only dogs with sire and dams with OFA hip ratings of Good or better, and eye CERF's. There are no justifications for not having those. If the dogs do not, move on.

Once you have found a breeding and a breeder you really like, plan on taking some time to pick the individual you will own for a lifetime. Pups can change between five, six, seven, and eight weeks. If at possible, plan on doing two or three evaluations over two or three weeks' time. This is not always possible, but if it is, you will not regret it.

Make sure the pups are marked so you can tell who is who. Watch the dogs in an environment in which they are comfortable. Test the dogs in an environment that is new to them, or as unfamiliar as possible.

For the outside tests, find a place if you can that has obstacles, challenges, weeds, stickers, water, hills, etc. Use these to gauge the pups and their reactions to the world.

Look for a dog that is sensitive, aware of his surroundings and what is going on. Look for a dog who is intelligent and who appears to think about things.

Look for a dog with some courage. Remember that courage can be confused with stupidity. Courage is assessing a risk, and then taking it if it is not truly unsafe.

Look for a well-built, proportional, athletic animal that moves easily.

Look for a dog with spirit in his or her heart, and a spirit in his eye, in his movement, and in his way of living. Look for a robust animal. They are usually healthier and more fun to be around.

Look for an animal that you like, not one that reminds you of something else, but an individual who on his or her own merits is appealing to you.

Enjoy this process. It is fun, and should be approached as such. You are not assessing lawn mowers or robots, but little living things.

Open your eye, your heart and your mind, and usually the choice becomes quite obvious to you.

Choosing the right pup is not purely a game of chance. Nor is it a sure thing. By using common sense, your intuition, and making your choices from the kind of animals you would want to own yourself, you can increase your odds of getting your 'perfect dog'. Be patient, set your emotions aside. Take the time to watch, and you will begin to see the pups tell you their story. You can often easily see the one you want after a while.

Once you have your pup, plan on making your investment truly pay off. Plan how you are going to 'raise' this pup. Do not let it run wild for six months, and then decide to work with it. Make every day count, and develop a rewarding relationship of respect between the dog and you and your family. Give your dog a purpose, one that includes physical and mental challenges. Enjoy your dog and have fun with the ownership.

Chapter 2
Starting a Puppy

So, now you have your new pup coming. Whether this is your first or your fifteenth, it is always a time of anticipation. Puppies are such fun, so lovable and so very entertaining. They are also a mixed blessing, to be sure. That adorable little bundle possesses teeth like a razor, with no idea of the damage that can be wrought. Body functions mean nothing, nor do most of your words! After having lost, too many times, one of a pair of expensive boots, or the edge of a cherished antique, or any other valuable thing that you might never expect them to go for, out of necessity we have learned how to deal with these little ones. Though they are as cute and lovable as anything you would ever want to see, it is a mistake to let that blur your perspective on why you have the dog, and what his ultimate purpose in your life is. You can have fun with your pup, enjoy the puppy stage, and still work toward saving your valuables, your guest's clothing, and eventually developing the kind of dog who is a pleasure to own.

The concepts will sound simple, and indeed, they are simple. In applying them to your own circumstances, often the apparent simplicity gets lost. It may be easier to remember the bottom line when this happens: You are the human, the pup is the dog. People are the bosses; dogs are the cherished employees. You decide the rules, and those remain the rules. It is your dog that must learn to comply, and not the other way around. Remember this sometime when you feel you are not in control of a situation. Also, keep your sense of humor--sometimes that is the best you can do.

You can read a variety of books with warm, enchanting methods of puppy raising. Over the years, we have heard so many entertaining things people have been advised by 'experts' to do with their pups. Usually what you find are methods and ideas that make you feel good about what you are doing. It is much easier to take your money when you feel good about it. It is a business concept utilized globally with great success. Show a beautiful woman near a man shaving with Razor "X" so he will want to buy it. Does that mean a beautiful woman will suddenly be drawn to him because earlier that day he shaved with that special razor? Of course not, but it sure feels good to think about, doesn't it? So it goes with dog training methods, classes and books. Give someone something that makes him or her feel good about themselves and they will buy that preferentially. We do not see the respect for either book buyer or dog in that, only for their money.

Does this mean that the methods and philosophy we will outline in detail here are not warm or are brutal or unkind? Absolutely not. It is premised, however, not on you and how you will feel (perhaps our mistake of being dog trainers before business people), but on what is most fair and most effective with your dog. The single biggest challenge we have had over the years in working with dogs is the dogs' owners. People believe what they want to believe, period. If someone believes a dog is the same as an infant, then it is in his or her mind. If someone likes to assign human motivations and reasoning to a dog, then they will. A brief trip into the natural world of animals would cure people's misconceptions, but most folks aren't willing to do that.

Let's Talk About Dogs in General

A dog is a dog. That seems so obvious, but it is one of the biggest problems people have with their animals. So often, family dogs are treated like one of the children or in some form as another person in the household. It is wonderful to love and care for your animal. However, it is not so effective if in doing that, you ignore the fact he has a canine brain, canine motivations, and canine ways of receiving and processing information. Dogs are not humans, they do not think like humans, they do not have the emotions humans have nor do they do things for the same reason we humans do. Still, because we have no sound understanding of how a dog thinks, we conveniently attribute the reason we would have done what the dog did and figure we understand what has happened. Usually this is very far from reality. It takes some mental discipline, but it is important to put aside traditional thoughts you might have had about dogs and begin to look at them as realistically as possible.

Dogs are generally simple. They need water, food, shelter, a purpose for living, and positive human interaction. The order listed is probably the hierarchy of those needs as well. The first three are easily taken care of, but those will be discussed briefly in the next section. It is the fourth item that is the key to your dog, and the most overlooked of them all. The purpose for living and the positive human interaction should be intimately linked. When they are, there are few problems with having a well-behaved, pleasurable animal. When they are not, the problems are numerous. It is the purpose of this book, and the ultimate purpose of our overall educational program, to teach dog owners how to establish this critical link and use it to create the right kind of relationship with their dogs, and to help shape the kind of dogs who are a pleasure to own.

The First Three Needs of a Dog: Food, Water and Shelter

Food and Water

A dog is a dog. That means they do not view consumption of food and water like we humans view it. Unfortunately, we often transfer our perspective on eating and drinking to our animals, creating big, fat, lazy, or picky dogs. Dogs, by nature, do not eat to savor and enjoy; they eat to stay alive. They do not need to eat frequently nor do they need to have variety in food or yummy, delicious meals. A mature dog should have clean water available 24 hours a day. A mature dog does not need to eat more than once a day. If you wish or are advised to feed more often, feed less when you do, but frequent meals are not usually necessary. If a dog sleeps in the house at night, feed in the morning so his digestive tract is emptier at night. Use common sense regarding your lifestyle and the feeding of your dog.

Usually, people over-feed their dogs because they love them so. This, of course, is not love, just as over-feeding a child is not love. If you love your dog, give him just what he needs, no more and no less. Dogs should not be overweight, even if spayed or neutered. Give them enough to have all the energy they need, but not so much that they have rolls or bellies. Food should provide the nutrition necessary for development and maintenance and the energy for the day's activities. That is all. You should be able to feel ribs and hips but they should not protrude. Fat animals suffer far more health problems than fit animals; they do not feel as well, and they do not respond to training as well because it is hard for them. Be fair to your dog. Give him all that he needs, and nothing more. Puppies should not be overfed either. Follow a veterinarian's direction on puppy care, but do not overfeed a pup. They suffer just as an overweight adult does.

Many people believe in 'on-demand' feeding. This is rarely advisable and it does not lend itself well to very many dogs. Most dogs will overeat because they are bored. If you own more than one dog, one will eat more than the other, usually resulting in one fat dog and one skinny dog. Another downside of this type of feeding is that when a dog is not conditioned to eat when the bowl is set down, they do not eat well when they travel. If your dog has learned to eat when the bowl is down, then he will eat when the bowl is down whether at home or on the road. Continuous feeding allows them to be picky about the conditions under which they will eat and often they won't eat if things are not just the way the dog would like them to be. It is just easier to own a dog that eats when you want him to.

Very often, no, actually very, very often, we find people transfer their own unhealthy relationship to food directly to their animals. People who use food to feel better or fill some void use food to make their dogs feel better as well. And then the dog adopts the same unhealthy perspective on food. It is sometimes so difficult to separate our own emotional baggage from our canine friends', but if the dog is truly valued we can find the means to do what is actually best for the dog.

Shelter

Housing a dog is very much personal preference. A dog's housing does enter into the training and ownership of that dog very significantly. Many times we have told caring dog owners they need to have their dogs outside more, and in a confined manner. They look as if we have told them to torture their dogs every afternoon. Though it is hard for the owner either new to Labradors, or new to serious training of a dog, to understand the concept of confining the dog for periods of time. Without exception, every owner who has done it has stated that it was the right thing to have done. More detail will be given in following sections, but we state strongly that every owner of a sporting dog (and maybe any kind

of dog) should have a dog kennel outside. The kennel does not have to be large, because it is not where the dog should be expected to get its exercise. It is the place the dog goes to relax, be quiet and just "mellow out". Kennels run normally from four to six feet in width and 10 to 12 feet in length. They should be high enough for the dog to walk comfortably, and preferably high enough for people to walk in and clean. Females who come in heat or dogs that jump should have a lid on the kennel as

Kennels are very useful

45

well, for obvious reasons. The kennel should have a house so the dog can get out of rain, wind, and cold.

A kennel is an excellent place to feed your dog. There are no distractions, and nothing to draw the dog away from his dinner. It also serves to make the kennel a positive place, since that is where 'dining' occurs. A water bucket can be easily hung from the kennel wires, so that it does not get knocked over or stepped in. Ideally, kennels should be chain link. They are inexpensive, easy to maintain, and your dog will not feel like he or she has been totally isolated since kenneled dogs can readily see their world around them.

Obviously kenneling or not kenneling is your personal choice, but please read on about the use of a kennel before making a decision. It is a tool we would absolutely never do without, for a large number of reasons.

Crates

We emphatically endorse the use of a dog crate. Dog crates are the containers in which dogs are shipped or housed at the veterinarian's. They are just large enough for a mature dog to turn around or lie down in, and

Safe transport and restraint

no larger. A dog crate is absolutely invaluable for the dog owner. They should be used anytime a dog is transported, whether to the vet, the neighbors, the next state, or the next country. They serve several very significant purposes. First, they are exactly like a child safety seat. If you are in a car accident, your dog will not go through a windshield or flying out the back of a truck. They also prevent your dog from damaging the inside of your vehicle, or at least filling it with dirt, dog hair, saliva, or mud. Next, if your dog has been injured or had surgery or some medical procedure, a crate is the best place for the dog to sit quietly with little movement. This can be mandatory with some medical conditions, and if your dog is crate-broken, keeping him or her in the crate will be easy to do.

Perhaps most importantly, a crate is a tool to establish control with your dog. Whether traveling or having guests at your home, it is a good thing to be able to put your dog into a crate and have him safe and out of the way. This way he conforms to your rules, not his whims. You may not wish to use it often, but it is a nice option to have when necessary. If you train your dog to crate without having him feel he is being perse-cuted, you have an excellent means of controlling your dog when needed. In fact, many dogs enjoy going into their crates as a kind of denning behavior. We will go into how to train a dog to use a crate shortly.

Bringing Your Puppy Home

Usually, the first few days are the toughest. This is the time your pup must make the transition from its mother and the only world it has ever known to the new world that will become its home. The first couple of puppies we ever had been coddled and kept close by and there was constant worry about how they were adjusting. Now that our need for feeling like we were being good puppy parents has been satisfied, we do things a little differently. If the puppy coming to our house is healthy and sound, we do not worry about its 'adjustment'. For those who have not gone through this process, they will need to be concerned and need to feel like they are doing the right thing. Please understand it is your needs you are addressing more than the needs of your pup, because the pup's needs are few and are easily met. Puppies adjust rapidly and well almost all of the time, provided the environment in which they are placed allows them to do this.

You should already have a plan for where your pup will stay during the day, at night, while you are gone, and when you are home. Plan this with the future in mind--do you want a dog who will always sleep in the house, or do you want a dog who can sleep inside or outside, or do you want an exclusively outdoor dog? It is our experience that the more flexibility you have, the easier it is. This means, why not have a dog who can sleep outdoors or indoors, depending upon whether the dog is traveling, being boarded, sent off for training, on a hunting trip, or at home? There is a certain 'robustness' associated with dogs who spend a good deal of time outdoors instead of indoors, just as there is with people.

It is usually easier to first teach a dog to sleep outside and then later teach them to occasionally stay indoors than it is to do it the other way around. Unless your pup is absolutely going to be a house dog and nothing else, then consider starting him outdoors. The obvious exception to this is if you live in northern Minnesota and get your pup in January. Common sense is the greatest factor at this point. Consider these factors: where is the pup coming from? If your dog is being shipped from Florida to Canada, the temperature adjustment may take a few days or weeks. Similarly, if your pup is coming from a cold climate and you are in south Texas, the temperature adjustment will be equally difficult. Perhaps you can house him in a garage or basement until he can acclimate. If it is below freezing outside, and the pup is not accustomed to that temperature--and few pups should ever be accustomed to that low a temperature--then leave him in the garage or basement until he is old enough to withstand colder temperatures. Wait until the weather warms up enough and then put your pup outside safely.

If you bring your new pup home and set him next to your bed, you can expect your next attempt at moving your pup to more distant arrangements to be difficult. It is easier on the pup (though not so easy on you) to put him where he is going to be. If not the first day, move him within the first couple of days. If you plan on kenneling your dog, then have a good doghouse, good bedding if necessary, water, and put your pup to bed in his kennel. Again, if it is too cold, crate him in the garage or somewhere that is not your bedroom but as close to the ultimate destination as possible. It is always entertaining to watch the dynamics between the individuals in a family when a pup comes home. Someone has to be the "Mom" and baby the poor thing as if it were actually human. Someone else has to be the "bad cop" and always point out why what everyone is doing is wrong and how they will regret it. Pups are very often the focal point of marital problems and each spouse blames the other for all the pups' faults. Rarely do those arguments have much to do with the actual dog, but the certainly open a vent for problems between two people. Ah, what our dogs must endure sometimes...

Outdoor Dogs and Housing

For those dogs that will be outdoor dogs, at least in sleeping arrangements, it is extremely useful to have a kennel. As mentioned earlier, kennels are where dogs are confined and not where they are expected to exercise and interact. Therefore, kennels do not have to be large. Four feet by 10 feet is enough, and six feet by 12 feet is common. Kennels are also places your dog can be safely kept away from the possibility of theft, harassment or even attack from other dogs. It also prevents your dog from roaming. A kennel can be bought in panels from local home-improvement or lumber stores. Chain link is desirable because it is strong, allows full vision, and is not terribly susceptible to chewing. The greater the gauge of wire, the more impermeable the chain-link kennel.

Kennels placed on concrete almost completely prevent your pup from digging out. Concrete is easy to keep clean, but it can be hard on a dog's paws if the dog is in it for extended periods. It is not natural for a dog's feet to be on a hard surface constantly and can occasionally cause problems. Pea gravel is a good surface and yields when dogs walk or lie down. It is less expensive but you will have to replace gravel occasionally. Dirt is not as easy to keep clean, can smell very bad in a short period of time and dirt does allow for digging and escape. Early investment in a good kennel set-up will pay for itself very quickly in the continual cleanliness and security of your dog.

Dog houses are very important for outside dogs as a place where dogs can escape the weather conditions. We have very strong opinions about dog houses, and will offer what we have learned over many years of kenneling dogs. A series of studies was done on dogs and housing to determine what geometry of house dogs actually preferred. This study was done with working stock dogs which endured harsh weather conditions of every extreme. Almost to a dog, all the animals in the study preferred the rounded barrel geometry to any other type of house. We have found this to be true in our kennels as well. Depending upon the weather conditions in your location, an open-ended barrel elevated off the ground may be adequate, and is inexpensive compared to manufactured doghouses. We live where the summers are very warm and the winters can occasionally be quite harsh. We have found an industrial plastic barrel with the doghouse barrel kit (known as the K-9 Kondo, available in all the hunting magazines) is the most useful dog house we have had. They come with a vent system (so there is no condensation in the winter months inside the barrel), and a door flap that can be held open during the warm months, and can swing shut for cold months. It is elevated off the ground and comes with a fixture to place a piece of plywood on the top for the dog to lie on, if desired. It can easily be picked up and carried for movement and cleaning. It is also guaranteed chew-proof and we have yet to replace one. In the summer months we leave the door open and put nothing in the barrel. It is rain-proof and very comfortable, even for very large dogs. During the cold winter months we fill it with grass hay--not straw--and then close the swinging door. The dog burrows into the grass hay and literally builds a nest. The house is warm and dry, even if it is blizzarding and very cold outside. The grass hay has proven for us to be the best bedding possible. It does not pack down and slide out like straw does, it is not harmful if chewed and it makes the dogs smell very good after nesting in it. Blankets do not lend themselves to nesting the way hay does and are never as warm. Plus, dogs very often chew up and swallow pieces of a blanket, which is an expensive habit that can also cause severe digestive distress.

With a good kennel and a good dog house that effectively keeps out wind, rain and snow, a dog can comfortable stay outside in all but the most severe conditions. Unless it is below freezing, we put our new pups in their kennel the first day they are home. If it is winter, we put the pups in the kennel during the day and crate them in the garage at night until they are old enough to withstand the outside nights. This usually occurs around 12-16 weeks. This way, they develop good winter coats and become very healthy dogs from the beginning.

Indoor Dogs

If you choose to keep your dog in the house, you should still plan on as much outside time as possible for your dog. Dogs are naturally outdoor animals, particularly the working and sporting breeds. You will find a dog crate to be one of the most valuable tools for dog ownership you can own. It serves many purposes. Introduce your pup to the crate from day one and you will never have a problem using it and having your dog actually like the crate. Put your opinion of dog confinement aside, if possible, and do what is truly best for your dog.

Have your new puppy sleep in the crate the first night home and for all the nights thereafter, when the dog is in the house or garage. In the very beginning when accidents may occur, fill the bottom with shredded newspaper. This will absorb any urine or feces and will also supply nesting material. Although we hear time and time again about people getting up every few hours the first nights home with their pup, we no longer do that. This policy arose from having small children, with their demands more immediate than puppy-crate-tidiness. It has turned out to be the quickest route to crate breaking and housebreaking a new puppy. When we go to bed, we put the pup into a clean crate containing shredded newspaper. The pup stays there until we get up and let the pup immediately outside. In a very few days the majority of pups will learn to sleep through the night and not relieve themselves. Some may take longer.

The shredded paper will allow your pup to stay out of any urine or feces he or she may initially and unavoidably put in the crate. Most pups that spend a few hours that way work very hard not to do that again. If your pup sets up a howl or cry you have a choice to make. We have chosen to teach the dog that noise is not an option. When a new pup sets up a ruckus we will bang or hit the crate with something that makes a resounding noise and say "Quiet!" If the pup continues, the repercussions become more unpleasant until the pup learns that the noise gains him or her absolutely nothing. If you give in and let the puppy out, you have just successfully taught him or her that the noise works well. Be careful what you do at this stage, because it sets you up for all the training you plan to do in the future.

If your pup is a tenacious howler, put the crate as far from your sleeping quarters as possible. We have put crates in barns, basements and outside in trucks when it became necessary. Be creative, but try and teach your pup from the very beginning that his job is to abide by your rules and that your rules do not bend to suit the pup's whims. We rarely have trouble with new pups because we have learned not to succumb to puppy cuteness. We just get them going on the track we want them on from the beginning. If you think about it, it's the fairest thing to do for your puppy. If in the beginning you treat him like a toy poodle, and then at some magical point down the line decide it is time for him to become a hardened field dog, that is changing all the rules in midstream. That is not in the best interests of your dog.

Feeding Your Puppy

First and foremost, follow the guidelines of your veterinarian, and not some well-intentioned "expert" down the block. Beware of over-feeding your puppy. Most commonly we see little roly-poly puppies that are so loved by their owners that they can hardly get around in the field or when playing. Puppies do not have to be fat any more than children do. Feed them a top-quality puppy food and feed them frequently and in smaller amounts. If possible, try to feed them more in the morning and less toward the end of the day, so their little digestive tracts are emptier. This makes it easier to learn to get through the night without relieving themselves.

Just like people, some pups will have a faster metabolism than others will. Some pups will require more food, some less. Use the appearance of your pup to gauge how much you feed him and not the instructions on the back of the dog food bag. Always have fresh water available, except in the crate. In the crate they learn to rest. The kennel and the yard are the places for eating, drinking and relieving themselves.

Puppies and Health Care

Puppies should have already had their first round of shots by the time you take yours home. They will need a series of shots between then and the time they are six months of age. You should plan on taking your pup to your veterinarian and get the shot program planned out. Ask your vet about worming, feeding and the eventual heartworm program your dog should be on. These are not recommendations--these are life-threatening issues. Talk to your vet about all of them.

One important aspect of new puppy ownership that is often overlooked is the exposure of very young puppies to other dogs or other sources of bacteria and viruses a young pup is not yet equipped to handle. The immune system of an eight-week-old pup is not developed enough to handle exposure to many 'bugs' that mature animals can easily overcome. As much as possible, avoid subjecting your new pup to many other dogs and even other people and places. Let him mature before a tremendous us amount of exposure occurs. Though this is not often a problem, you surely do not want to be one of the cases in which it is a problem.

Activities and Training of a Young Puppy

Puppies are intelligent little creatures and they begin learning the day you bring them home. When referring to the 'training' of a very young pup, please understand that does not mean they are put on a leash and given commands. What this does mean is that you begin to acquaint your pup with the concepts of respect for you and what his role in your life is going to be. You begin to help in the development of muscle and strength by taking him on planned walks. You teach him to focus and listen to you on these walks. You do not teach commands or basic obedience. This will be fully described in the next chapter.

If your dog is going to be a working dog, you begin to show him what great fun his work is. For retrievers you throw little puppy dummies without a bunch of rules or regulations. First they learn what a blast retrieving is and then later you begin to impose stricter behavior requirements on them. There is a real science to early dog training, but the difference it can make later on is beyond estimation. When we get young dogs in for training who have gone through a good puppy-training program, the progress they make is limited only by their natural abilities. Dogs that come to us with no grasp of their relationship with people or knowledge of what their job is take a great deal of time to just get started. It is some time before we can begin the work of retriever training when first we have to teach them how to be a functional and respectful dog. Ignoring the difficulty on the trainer, it is hard on the dog when they have to unlearn all they have been taught through not being brought up correctly, and relearn how to be a pleasant, functional, obedient dog.

Plan your puppy's upbringing. Without any heavy-handed tactics, teach him to listen, to enjoy life, and above all that you are the center of his universe. Give him a job from the beginning. You will be surprised in the difference that makes in an animal.

General "Puppy" Guidelines

Puppies do not have to be attended to like human babies, no matter how enjoyable that is for many of us to do. Unless you plan a lifetime of continual attendance to your dog, don't set up that pattern now. Granted, you will have to spend more time now than you will later, but save your parenting for any children and be a dog owner with your pup.

Use what you want your adult dog's life to be like to set up the guidelines for your puppy. If you want an outdoor dog, then if weather allows, start your pup as an outdoor dog. This does not mean he cannot spend time in the house with you, but allow him to spend the majority of time outside.

If your adult dog is going to spend periods of time alone, then let your pup spend periods of time alone. We have read veterinarians who advised 'spending as much time as possible with the new pup'. If you do that, then as your real life begins to require your presence, what happens to the completely entertained and spoiled pup? You have a BIG problem on your hands as you now teach your dog you are not a minute-by-minute part of its life. And it suffers more than if you showed it was an important but not all-consuming part of your life right from the start. If you do not have an enclosure of some kind to protect your dog from other dogs or from running away or into the street to get hit, then you should not own a dog. The days of the old farm dog hanging around the house are over--that is irresponsible pet ownership. It is strongly our opinion that every dog should have a kennel and a crate. The kennel is the place where an outdoor dog sleeps and spends time when he is left home alone. The dog will be safe at all times there. The crate is what your dog is transported in and confined in for medical purposes or house training.

Often people perceive it is inhumane to confine a dog in either crate or kennel. That is a very naïve idea. Because it would be inhumane to confine you to a crate or kennel, in no way means it is the same for a dog. Dogs by their very nature enjoy conforming to clearly established rules, they enjoy 'doing their job' and they truly enjoy having their own 'place'. Every dog we own, train or kennel for any reason spends a good part of its time in its kennel and travels in a crate or dog box. They do not have to be made to get in either of these and they are dogs with a purpose who enjoy their lives very much. Kennels and crates also save you from the damage of a destructive puppy.

Young puppies should have a great deal of social interaction so they learn how to be good companions, but they do not need what a human baby does. Pups should be fed only puppy food and no people food. This goes for the lifetime of the dog if you truly care about the health of your animal. They do not need your food or your handouts. Teach him now that eating is a kennel activity and that they eat their dog food. Then you will not have to contend with a dog hanging his head on the dinner table or a fat, unhealthy adult dog with physical problems.

It is natural in the world of the dog for a young puppy to be physically active. Your pup needs exercise on a daily basis. Use common sense and do not over-tire your dog, but allow him to develop physically and mentally by giving him the job of exercising every day. It is better to use the exercise time to simultaneously develop the relationship between you and your dog by going on a walk alone together, than to just let the pup romp and play by him or herself. Your investment of time now will pay itself off ten times over in the future with the enjoyment you will get from your controllable, pleasant companion. Do not exercise on a full puppy-tummy, make sure water is available when you return, and once your pup is tired from your session together put him or her away in the crate or kennel. This way he comes to appreciate it even more.

Plan on instilling the basic obedience skills on your pup once he becomes mentally mature enough to teach. You will never regret the time spent developing an obedient, happy dog.

Developmental Milestones in a Puppy

Young puppies should be able to eat dry puppy food, but occasionally they require puppy food softened with water, not milk. Dairy products are not good for a dog despite what you might always have believed. Dry food helps when baby teeth begin to fall out, but it might also be painful to eat at that point. Dry food is better for dogs in terms of plaque formation on teeth. Canned food usually contains more fat and forms deposits on teeth more readily. Discuss this with your veterinarian.

Puppy teeth begin to fall out, in general, at between four and six months of age. During this process your docile pup may turn into the "great chew monster." This is not a behavioral problem, but his way of assisting his tooth transition. This is another reason a kennel is good. You can deposit a chewing puppy in a kennel with a Nylabone or other object he can chew without hurting himself or your valuables. Never give rawhide chews--they can bloat inside a tummy and have been known to kill some dogs. This is often the point we hear from people that their adorable little puppy has turned into an outlaw. Puppy teeth can be a big factor in puppies' behavior at this stage. Keep an eye on his mouth. If your pup is retrieving, it may be too painful at this point to carry his dummy. Do not make an issue of it. If that is the case, just wait until he shows the desire to retrieve again.

Pups in general should be house-trainable with the first few weeks. Some take longer to train, others less time. Just be patient and consistent. Use the crate to help you. When you take your pup out of the crate, the first place his feet touches should be the outdoors where it is OK to relieve himself. Praise him for doing what you want him to do. If you cannot catch him in the act in the house, you are not going to be able to correct his behavior. Dragging a puppy back to the scene of the crime usually teaches him to avoid you when you are upset instead of teaching him not to go in the house. If you see a puppy committing the act of going in the house, then you can give him a severe "No" and put him outside. You need to establish an association with going outside for 'pottying'.

Puppies of any age can be expected to get along with the members of your household. This includes children, adults, other dogs, and other pets. From the beginning, establish the relationships you want to have. If you do not want your dog to bite people, even though they are doing it playfully, do not let him bite. If you do not want your 75-pound adult dog to jump on people, do not let him jump now. Stop him when he first begins, and do whatever your pup requires to have him stop. For some dogs a firm "No" may be sufficient to stop him from jumping, biting or chasing. For others, it may take a slap on the side of the nose with the firm "No". For a few others, it may take a stronger physical intervention. You are not the one to decide how much discipline is enough--your dog will tell you how much it is going to take. You may own a sensitive dog that requires little disapproval to alter his behavior. You may also own a dog who has a greater interest in doing what he or she feels compelled to do than in complying with your wishes. Then you have to raise the level of correction until you find the point at which your dog is willing to alter his or her behavior.

That is the secret of good dog trainers. They do not have one way of getting a point across to a dog. They find out what method is mean-ingful to a particular dog and then use the method that will generate the desired results. This is an important concept. Find out from the start how to get your pup's attention and correct his unacceptable behavior in a manner that permanently stops it. It is not necessary to engage in a continual conflict with your pup. Fix the problems before they begin. Of course, never abuse or hurt your animal--which is absolutely never necessary. If you ever find yourself losing your temper, put your dog away and remove yourself from the situation. Only interact with your dog when you are calm and in complete and rational control.

By the time your pup is around four months of age, you can and should leash break him. He can learn to walk at your side, at your pace, at this age. From the beginning, do not let him learn to tug and pull you. If you allow this now, you will fight it from now on.

At around six months of age, you can begin to instill the basic obedience skills more formally. These skills include heeling, sitting on command, and coming when called and remaining in place. Do this early in your dog's life, though never before he is physically and mentally capable of doing it. This is the best 'problem prevention' activity you can undertake. Get help, do it right, and you will have an easy time of it from this point on in your dog's life.

Between six months and a year, you can switch to feeding an adult dog food. When your pup begins to gain weight from the puppy food, it is usually time to switch to the lower-calorie adult food. You can also go to one feeding a day if you want. Discuss this with your vet. At six months your dog will get the first permanent annual series of shots. Somewhere in this 'teenage' stage of dog life your males become capable of fathering puppies. In general, retriever females come in heat around one year of age and continue, on the average, every six months after that. Do not let unplanned breedings occur. It is not necessary or good for your dog or the dog population in general.

For people who plan on carrying out responsible breeding of their dogs, eye examinations and subsequent certification of eye soundness (CERF) can be done after a year. The certification of hip soundness cannot be done until a dog is two years of age (OFA). Please learn all you can about these certifications before even considering breeding your dog, and for many reasons, females should not be bred until they are at least two years old.

Summary

• Draw up a plan for your pup before you bring him home. Think about what kind of dog you want one year from now and five years from now.
• Be fair to your new dog--do not start him one way and change all the

rules later. If he is to be outside, start him outside if weather allows.

• Put up a puppy-tight kennel outside to protect and house your dog. They do not need to live only in the kennel, but it is a valuable dog-management tool.

• Buy a dog crate before you go to pick up your puppy. It should be large enough for the adult dog to turn around and lie down in. Bigger is not better in the case of crates.

• From the first day, carry your dog in the crate any time he travels. Puppies in laps can go through windshields more easily than a human infant can.

• Protect your young pup from the germs that other dogs, people, and certain environments may carry. This is only for the first weeks or months, but be careful.

• Select a veterinarian for your pup and start the shot program immediately. Ask about worming, heartworm and feeding.

• Feed only a top-quality puppy food and skip human food altogether.

• Do not let your adorable tiny puppy acquire habits you will not want in your adult dog. Stop him from biting, jumping, barking, and other bad behaviors before it can become a habit.

• Use the level of discipline or correction to stop your dog from engaging in unacceptable behavior that works with your dog. Do not be abusive or cruel, but be effective in your corrections. Stop poor behavior before it becomes a habit. Get professional help if necessary, but do not let poor behavior continue. If you cannot correct a 12-week-old pup, you will never handle a mature dog with problems.

• Dogs tend to be healthier if they spend more time outside. If your dog has a kennel, install a good dog house in the kennel. Protect your dog from the elements of all seasons.

• Always have fresh, clean water available.

• Give your puppy a 'job'. In the beginning, it should be your daily walk together and a few fun puppy retrieves. Dogs need mental and physical challenges just as we do. Never forget this aspect of your dog. Later the job should be learning and carrying out basic obedience. For the hunting dog, it will be developing the hunting skills and doing the actual hunting. Give your dog a purpose and a reason for living.

• Give your puppy that loves to chew, your teething pup, and your adult dog something to chew on that is safe for him. If he runs loose all the time, he can choose what he wants to chew. If you kennel him, you can provide Nylabones or some other safe material for him to chew on whole-heartedly. He will need to chew. Be prepared.

• Leash breaking can begin around three to four months of age. Leash breaking does not mean he pulls you around on a leash--it means your dog walks with you. Be firm.

• Formal obedience skills begin around six months, when the dog is physically and mentally ready.

• Housebreaking begins right off the bat. Use the crate and common sense. Do not feed and water right before bedtime. Air your pup and put him to bed for the night. In the morning, take him from the crate directly outdoors. Create an association between going outside and relieving himself. Let him sleep with his mistakes, provided he is not sick or in danger of any harm. That teaches him most rapidly.

• Use a good sense of humor with your puppy. Things will never go perfectly.

• Have fun with your pup! Establish a shared joy of life and the work you share, and the rewards of this relationship will be endless.

Chapter 3
Beginning Your Serious Puppy Training

The Fun Part: Establishing the Right Relationship and Attitude

The easy part of responsible ownership is the food and shelter aspect. The part usually neglected is the developmental part of dog ownership. Little puppies are clean slates, eager to understand and adapt to the environment in which they find themselves. When new pups are ignored or allowed to do whatever they wish for the first six months of their lives, you have taught them that they get to do whatever they wish. This may include barking, biting, ignoring you, and chewing important things. Unless that is your intent, it is easiest instead to teach them the way of life you would like to have with them. This does not mean, however, that you must have a little four-legged soldier who will follow any command given and behave like an adult dog. This is where your advanced human brain must balance two somewhat conflicting concepts.

A pup is just a baby and cannot understand things the way it will a few months down the road. Still, the pup is taking in and processing information continually. There are books and advice in abundance out there giving you techniques to get good obedience started, including whistle training and even force fetching (??!) at an early age. This is a mistake, particularly with a pointing Lab. As we will mention repeatedly in this text, plan your training program for the long haul. Do not teach your pointing retriever to "sit" above all other behaviors, or to stop and sit while on a retrieve. This is so counter to what you want it is not funny.

These are babies and they do not understand that when you blow the whistle on a retrieve they should stop, but continue again with great passion shortly after. You are telling them to retrieve and then to NOT retrieve. Is that what you want? Because you can understand the concept, they cannot. Do not do counterproductive, stupid things like that. Drum the "sit" into a baby dog and it will learn to sit to relieve any pressure from you. That is not what you want on a pointing dog. That is why many pointer trainers rarely teach sit, or do not do it for a long time.

Your new family member is going to learn through meaningful repetition. What does this mean? It does not say through repetition, but through meaningful repetition. That is, by setting up a pattern your individual pup can understand, a pattern that repeats itself when appropriate, and rarely varies. This concept will be illustrated shortly. The first concept described above is to teach through establishing patterns of desired behavior. The second and equally critical concept is the development of enthusiasm for the dog's role in your life. You probably learn more and retain more that you have learned when you had enthusiasm for what you were doing. Think about that. If you sat in a classroom and were being taught the great works of Shakespeare by having a monotone reader sitting up front and reading all of Hamlet, Hamlet would have seemed so very long and so very boring. Your mind would have drifted to the activities outside or to your game that evening, right? But if you watched some passionate and animated actors play out the murder drama, you would have found Hamlet fascinating and you might have eagerly looked forward to the next reenactment. It is no different for your dog. So how do you develop that enthusiasm in a tiny puppy?

Developing Enthusiasm in Your Dog

Dog work can be very much like Shakespeare: both dry and boring or passionate and exciting. You make the difference. When interacting with your dog, your pup will reflect your attitude. If you are businesslike and dull, eventually you will make your dog the same way. If you are energetic and a little crazy, your dog will ultimately reflect that as well. How would your ideal dog look to you? Enthusiastic but controlled? Obedient but happy? Then think about that and behave in that manner yourself. We get a great many dogs in to us for training, and within the first couple of training sessions we can tell a great deal about the personality of that dog's owner. This is done just by seeing the dog's attitude toward work, the dog's response to the trainer and to those people and dogs around him or her.

It is easiest to create enthusiasm and positive attitude in a dog by doing what that dog loves to do. Using the dog's natural inclinations is the most effective way to get inside the dog's head and create responses you want in that dog for a lifetime. Retrievers usually love to retrieve. If you have one who does, this will be a valuable tool. All dogs love to move and they love to accompany you, so use this to begin teaching some important concepts to your pup. Take your pup on a walk--every day if you can. We have preached "The Walk" for years now to new puppy owners, and people who undertake this activity come to swear by it as well. It is the single most important thing you can do with a new pup. This walk is not in the park, the backyard or the neighbor's driveway. It is in an unfamiliar place with natural foliage. The walk goes across the terrain, up hills, down hills, over reasonable obstacles, through cover and across ditches and 'icky' stuff. This should be time just for the new pup; it is his or her 'training session'. If you take all your dogs, or even one other, your new pup will view this as gang-time and pay attention to the other dog and not to you. This defeats the purpose of this exercise.

The pace is such that the pup is truly challenged, but still capable of keeping up. The duration of the walk is enough to really tire the pup, without hurting or over-tiring the pup. Generally, you should start with about ten minutes, and within a couple of weeks, go to half an hour. As the pup grows, the pace quickens, so the pup remains challenged to keep up. There should be no danger to the pup, like cars driving too close or a dog that might attack the small pup. Most folks new to this process stop and entice the dog to keep up, or try to lure the pup away from a tempting smell. Don't. Keep walking. Get the pup's attention if you must, but do not stop unless there is some potential harm to the dog. You will find this may be necessary the first time or two, and never again. Ideally do this every day and you will not believe what you have accomplished.

A walk seems so...boring. When we tell most first-timers to do this, they are a little disappointed. First, they aren't barking any commands or making the dog sit or anything. Then, it takes time and energy, and not just a little bit. It isn't a convenient little drill in the back yard or the hallway. These are all reasons that some people just don't do it. We will go on record saying it is the single most important thing you can do for your young pup. It is the greatest concentration of training and conditioning you can provide for a developing dog. Here's why.

Let's say you take your new pup out every day after work. You either load him up and go to the nearest open space or you cross the back fence and head into the fields behind your house. You set the pup down and head out at a puppy-fast pace. You cross the stream and the ditch, and make it through the weed patch. After a day or two (if even that), your pup begins to make every effort to stick with you, and he does. Every couple of days, you increase the distance and the pace and even the degree of obstacle to which you subject your new pup. You might even stop once or twice along the way and toss the puppy-dummy whatever distance the pup can retrieve. You wind up back at the car or back fence, praise the heck out of your pup, put the pup up and go back to normal business. Training over.

What have you done in these daily sessions? You have made your pup physically strong and fit. The walks have served to develop good, strong muscles, ligaments and tendons. It also contributes to good bone growth and general health. The heart and lungs are developed and will be suited for athletic endeavors in the future. You have taught your dog that you are the center of his universe. You've taught him that watching you and staying with you, no matter what other distractions or temptations prevail, is what your dog does as a way of life. He never learns any alternative. Your pup learns to be brave and bold, and that the world is interesting and exciting. He learns he can negotiate any obstacle, developing skills to traverse any kind of place he may find himself. He learns not to fear new things, but certainly to think before leaping or diving or chasing. He learns to use his nose, his eyes and his head. He learns there is a start and a finish to this, and when it is over, it is over. He learns there is a time to be quiet and to settle down. He learns to get out of the car or house, and look to you for what he is going to do. He learns to watch always for your movement, your turns, your stopping. And he learns nothing else. He learns you are the source of its greatest activity and reward, and he learns that he does this with you, not in spite of you or without you. He learns your actions are the ones to respond to, not his own whims or inclinations. He learns to have great heart for life.

Do this for four months, and preferably, all of your dog's life, and you will circumvent so many problems. Have you ever seen those dogs that BOLT when the front door opens or the car door opens? That is a learned behavior. These pups will never know to do that. Have you watched someone's dog that completely ignored the "handler" if there was a nice smell, a squirrel or someone more interesting around? Another learned behavior. For hunters who do not want a dog to follow them or stare at them constantly, this does not teach a dog not to go out front and hunt. It does teach them they must watch their owners and respond to them, not run off on their own gleefully.

This simple exercise of walking every day is usually too boring for most people to do. The difference it will make in a dog later on is incredible. It is one of the biggest 'problem prevention' efforts you can undertake. The important points to this early training exercise are these:

• Begin walking and don't stop and wait for your pup. Make your pup work to stay with you. Teach him to think about where you are instead of what looks like fun to explore. If he stops to investigate, keep going. Use your enthusiastic voice to lure him on with you--talk with your pup, get him excited about the activity. This teaches him to pay attention to you.

• Do not be afraid the ground is too difficult or the weeds too challenging. Teach your pup not to be afraid or to avoid obstacles. Give him the opportunity to learn he is brave and strong. Let your pup learn to negotiate stickers, thorns and rocks. He'd certainly better be able to do that if he is going to hunt, hike or go somewhere other than the back yard. Teach him to overcome those things now, and he will never be a problem in the future. Only help your little one if there is potential harm of a serious nature.

Let your pup learn to handle tough cover and keep up

• Walk at a pace that makes your pup hustle. This is not a stroll, it is an exercise. Walk until your pup is truly tired, not just winded slightly. Increase your distance and speed as your pup grows and becomes stronger. Increase the degree of obstacles and challenge over time. Let your dog learn there is nothing he or she cannot do.

• Use your voice to encourage and reward. Do not give commands--you cannot enforce these early on. Let your tone and excitement communicate to your pup how fun this is and how much you approve of his or her willingness and effort. Make it fun. The more fun it is, the more your dog will look forward and relish these 'training sessions'. This is the groundwork for creating the super attitude toward more serious or difficult work in the future.

• Stop when your pup is tired. Give water and put your pup in his crate or kennel. Let the dog savor the activity and rest. This only serves more to generate enthusiasm for the work. Allowing the dog to immediately run free and play in the back yard will dilute the effects of your 'training session'. There is no need to do that now.

Beginning Retrieving for the Retriever

Whether you got your puppy for a hunting companion, family pet or any other use, the art of retrieving is a valuable tool for the retriever. It is so important for several reasons. One, like the exercise above, it gives you a tool using the innate desires and talents of your dogs to establish the relationship you want with your dog. You rarely have to teach a retriever to retrieve, though poorly bred or just unusual ones will sometimes have no interest. Some pups are enthusiastic about retrieving at the age of six weeks, some not until a couple months after that. You cannot make your dog love to retrieve any more than we could make you love to interpret Egyptian hieroglyphics. What you can do is take the kernel of desire to retrieve and feed it so that it grows and becomes a big part of your dog's life. This gives you four things: the ability to create enthusiasm, love of work, respect for you and focus. It also allows you to teach your dog that you are the source of all good things, that working with you provides the greatest reward and satisfaction.

There several important concepts when doing the retrieving work with your dog. Never let your enthusiasm or excitement induce you to overlook these factors:

1. At this stage you are working with a baby. Do not use strict discipline or regimentation. Get your dog excited, make him stay with you, but let him be happy and anxious.

2. Use a soft, appropriately sized retrieve object like a rolled-up sock, burlap bag, or a bumper designed for pups. It must be soft so he never learns to chomp down and small so he can easily carry it.

3. Make sure he sees you and the object you are going to toss. Use your voice to get him excited and focused on you.

4. When he is looking, while you are talking or otherwise verbally attracting his attention, toss it somewhere he can see and easily get to. If he runs after it, as soon as he picks it up, praise the heck out of him and begin to move away so he tends to come toward you. Do not chase him. If he does not return it, try to induce him to come to you. Be crazy, loud, silly, anything it takes to get him to want to come to you. Be inventive. You would be surprised what you would see professionals do in this case, but they will get the pup to want to come back. The critical thing is not that the pup brings the object back, but that he returns to you. If the pup runs back to you without the object, praise the dog for the return. Shortly he will learn to bring it with him. You want the dog to go out and come back, so be happy with that to start.

5. If your pup shows no interest, stop. Wait another week or more and try it again. When your pup does show a spark of interest, praise him furiously. Do not praise the lack of interest. Instead, just put away the retrieve object until interest is shown.

6. Do not make the mistake of expecting your dog to naturally do the right thing. Take the beginnings of the right thing and enhance it with praise and enthusiasm. Heap it on.

7. When your pup will retrieve, do no more than three or four retrieves and stop. Let us repeat that; do no more than three or four and stop. Do

not let your excitement about your future champion allow you to overdo this exercise. If you let your pup retrieve enough to have fun and understand what he is doing but stop soon after starting, you will generate increasingly greater enthusiasm each subsequent time you do it. Never allow your pup to get tired or bored with it. That creates negative associations you do not want and do not have to have if you use good judgment.

8. When your handful of enthusiastic, silly, fun-filled retrieves are complete, put your pup in his or her kennel. Do not dilute the effects of your 'training session' with more play. If you allow a pup to develop the ability to focus on his work, it is an immense help. Later take him out and resume his normal activities.

9. Do these puppy retrieves in different places. You may have heard to begin them in your hallway so your dog can only return to you. This may be necessary. When you can, do it in the field away from other playmates, dogs, or tempting distractions. Set up the situation such that your pup will focus on you and the retrieving and nothing else. The ability to focus sets trained, exceptional dogs apart from dogs that are neither.

Encourage the pup to deliver the bumper, not spit it out

10. Encourage your pup to hold on to his retrieve object until you take it from him. Under no circumstances do you want the dog to learn to 'spit out' what he has retrieved. Do not make this an issue of correction, but encourage the "hold" if possible.

Introduction to Live Birds in Brief

Don't start your retrieving with birds. That being said, a good percentage of first-time dog trainers will go out and use birds, because, after all, "That's why I got the dog." True, but no more than you toss a toddler into the deep end of the pool because he needs to know how to swim, do you give a pup a bird to retrieve. This is an important concept. A good retrieving bird dog will retrieve birds when the time comes if he understands fully the expectations for retrieving. First teach your dog what fun retrieving is, and then gradually teach him he is supposed to wait to be sent, run directly as possible to the object, and bring it directly back to you. It is easier to instill this behavior on a dog with an object appealing only by virtue of its retrievability and not by its potential tastiness as a dinner morsel. A good dog does not need a bird to enjoy retrieving. When you have the tools to control the dog's behavior, then you introduce birds for retrieving and will not have to contend with bad habits taught early on by a premature introduction to feathers.

For a dog to become an accomplished upland hunter, introduction to live birds at an early age is very helpful. It is not absolutely mandatory, but it does assist greatly in developing the same passion for hunting for live birds that the dog possesses for retrieving. For those dogs with only a moderate interest in the demand of upland hunting, an early introduction to birds will bring out the interest that is there. Waiting too long may result in the dog never getting terribly excited about running around for extended periods of time.

In our experience, we like to introduce the concept of a live bird hiding in the field around three to four months. Before that age, the pup is usually too young to know anything except play and will view the bird as a toy or a snack. Once the pup is mentally mature enough to become excited about a live bird and know there is some compelling reason to get excited, though he is not quite sure what that is, the time is right.

To introduce a pup to live birds requires live birds. Bird scent or feathers tied to a plastic or canvas bumper is not the same. And, when introducing your pointing dog or potential pointing dog to birds, you don't want him to learn to run in and grab whatever it is that is 'hiding' in the cover. As will be mentioned a number of times in this book, do not lie to your dog. If you want to teach your dog to hunt live birds, do not think you are fooling it with a scented object or an old wing. The purpose of exposing a young pup to live birds in an upland situation is not to train your pup to do anything. Instead, what you are doing is giving your pup an opportunity to learn the magic of a bird hidden in a field. He learns that these exciting little things are out there and if he uses his nose and eyes, he might find one. At this point you need to make sure he doesn't learn to run in and eat it. The next chapter will address how to do this.

Attitude is everything.

Chapter 4
Starting the Early Pointing Work

When a pup is between about three and four months, it should be introduced to live birds in the field. The purpose for this activity is not to teach the dog anything aside from the glorious fun of looking for and finding live birds in his natural environment. It is also the place your pup will most likely tell you how much of a pointer it is. It is so hard for people not to put too much emphasis on this stage, or worst of all, actually go hunt birds with their baby dog and figure that is the best way to teach him. You can go hunt birds with a baby, and sure enough it will learn about hunting them. It will also learn about 12-gauge shotgun fire, bird guts (if you are any kind of a shot), retrieving and eating freshly shot birds and running wild and out of control, while you are busy with the serious business of hunting. This works every now and then, but usually it creates a problem you or a trainer has to spend a lot of time trying to figure out or fix. It isn't a wise thing to do if you are working on a long-term training program.

Take a baby dog out and let him learn the great joy of looking for and finding the exciting feathers and subsequent flutter and flight as the bird flushes wild. Give him the opportunity to get what is often referred to as "bold on birds" so he has the spirit, desire, and relatively concrete idea of hunting for birds. The good pointing dogs will show you points after a few birds. Some will do it on the first scent, though they really have no idea what they are doing. Some will chase and flush and act crazy and wild and then on the magic 'eighth' one, or whenever, lock up in a sure-nuff point. Do not confuse the hesitation of pup searching for something as a point; a point is a point and you will know it when you see it.

There is not one way and only one way to do this, but there are some things you need to make sure happen and do not happen.

Remember that this is not a 'training' session. It is a 'learn how fun this is' session, tapping into your dog's natural desire to hunt birds. Don't bark out commands and demand control and responses out of your pup. Don't do this in a location at which your pup may encounter road traffic, other dogs, or some game you do not want it to learn to hunt. The ideal place is a hunting preserve or lodge where there are birds left over from hunts. Do not have a crowd of people with you all watching for the greatly anticipated point. The purpose is to turn your pup loose on his own volition to learn to look for and find wild birds. You do not want him tuned into the people around or other dogs. Give him this time for himself completely.

Most new pups are not going to have any idea what they're doing, so don't expect them to. It is your job to entice the dog to run out and have a blast. You need to make sure there are some birds to stumble upon. Often, that is what the pup will do the first time or two. The reaction is funny to watch. Some will stand there dumb-founded at what just happened as the bird flies away. Others will give chase. Some will want to chase but turn to look at you to make sure you are okay with what is happening. Whatever happens, relax; just make sure your aggressive pup

Dog hunting, finding and flushing first wild bird

can't chase the bird into a dangerous area for the dog. You may have difficulty getting your pup to forge ahead of you, but this is not really a problem, though most first-timers perceive it to be. It is a good thing your dog likes to stick with you. The discovery of birds and their escape will entice the most tightly bound pup to go ahead and look for more. Let time and boldness take care of teaching your dog to hunt ahead. Do not make great efforts to make the pup do it right out of the box. Once he figures out he can find those delightful birds out there, you will have the new problem of trying to reel him back in. Do not make a big issue of either thing; your goal is boldness and passion for looking for live feathers

You want the birds your pup will find to be able to escape. If he can go out and catch all the birds he finds, he will learn that is what you want him to do. If a dog learns to rush in and catch birds, it will never want to stop and point, since that will only delay the gratification. Allow the dog to learn that finding the birds is exciting, and when he does, the bird flies up and away. Do not shoot it. If you do, your dog will still learn it 'gets the bird' and may even enjoy eating it. That is extremely undesirable. No matter how much fun it would be for you to shoot the bird and watch your pup go find it again, you may be creating more problems you will have to address down the road. Most died-in-the-wool hunters find this contrary to their natural inclinations. That's why they are hunters, not dog trainers. To have a staunch, intense pointing dog you need to have one that doesn't think it can or should go get the bird. Begin that now by not teaching your dog to get the bird. That said, if your dog does actually catch one, don't make a big issue of it, just get the bird away from him and proceed with the planned activities. A few mistakes like that will not ruin your ultimate objective. Consistent mistakes like that will.

If you don't have a game preserve full of game birds down your block or close enough to utilize, then find some birds, preferably game birds, to buy and toss out in a remote location for your pup to learn to look for. In the beginning we use quail, primarily because they are relatively inexpensive. Since we are usually returning them to nature or the return pen, we don't want it to be more expensive than necessary. Be wary of utilizing the local meadowlarks or robins, as those are not birds you will eventually want your dog to pay much attention to. Be cautious about deciding to use the big, exciting game birds like pheasant, because if your dog becomes accustomed to the big enticing birds it will not always think much of the smaller game birds or it will be frightened by something seemingly larger than it is. That is another reason we use the smaller quail, which is awfully exciting to the new dog. When the day comes that they do get a pheasant, they just enjoy it all the more. Do not dizzy or tie the birds either, because this will make the birds catchable.

This activity should be undertaken ideally with just you and your dog. Anything more serves as a potential distraction. Don't talk a bunch with your dog. Don't constantly try to direct him out and make him behave a certain way. Encourage him to loosen up and get out there, and beyond that leave him to his own devices. When you speak, you pull your dog's focus onto you. That is not what you want in a dog learning the passion of hunting. Do your best to set up the opportunity for your dog to figure out for himself that there is something wonderful out there and it is up to him to find it. This takes time.

Often the first few times someone does this, they return home disappointed. The dog never left their side, never looked for a bird, or found one and ran away from it…. We've had Grand Masters who at this young stage thought we were taking a stroll, and showed no interest in anything. Time, patience, and staying out of their way soon found the spark that grew into a fanatical hunting dog. Take what you get and go back another day.

The Point

Let's say it's the second or third time you've tossed birds out for your pup, and the pup has gotten the idea when you say "Hunt 'em up" that good things happen. If your dog is going to point, this is often the place you will see it. If you do not, it doesn't necessarily mean your dog will not point. If he does point right away, then you know what you have for sure. Most folks, when they see this the first time, want to immediately intervene and make sure their dog doesn't do anything they don't want it to do in the future. If you see your pup point a bird or a place that held a bird recently, don't do anything. Just watch. Do not speak or interfere with your dog's focus. Some pups will hold the point for a few seconds, some longer. Just let your dog do what it is going to do. Eventually most pups will tire of waiting for something--though they have no idea what--and go in after the bird. This is natural. In fact, this means you have a dog that loves birds and loves hunting, all of which is a good thing. What you are doing now is letting what is in this pup come out without your interference.

As the upland free-for-all sessions go on, if your dog only flushes birds, then that might be what your dog is: a flusher. If your pup does show some point--it doesn't have to be rock solid or for very long--you have your next job cut out for you. The question at this point is "How long do I wait to see point?" "However long it takes" is the only answer. We have experienced a few dogs that didn't point at this stage that did months down the road. Looking back now, it was likely because we put too much early control training on them and never let the natural point come out in the exuberance of the hunt. What we repeatedly see is that the dogs that point will show point within a few weeks of this initial intro-duction to birds, perhaps only slightly longer than that. Always keep in mind this is a no-pressure, big-time fun activity for a pup, nothing more. You also incidentally are showing the dogs what great fun this is and how much they will love it. Later, when you implement in their upland-hunt-ing behavior some controls you have taught elsewhere, it will be straight-forward and simple for the dog and for you.

The Pup that Points

Once your pup has learned what "Hunt 'em up" means, loves to run out and boldly look for birds and has shown you that it will point the birds, you stop doing the upland hunting exercise. Now this frustrates the hunter anxious for the season around the corner. However, since the objective of this whole endeavor is to train a superb hunting partner, that is what we are going to do, frustrating or no. As a matter of fact, it is at this point that many people believe their dog is actually ready for hunting since it knows what its job is and will most likely retrieve. Nothing could be further from the truth. That would be akin to having a child who has just figured out phonics enough to sound out words, being sent to a National Spelling Bee. There is a whole bunch more before they are skilled enough to succeed and feel competent in even undertaking the event. Remember, if you want a dog that quarters within your desired range, finds birds well, holds the point until you are ready to flush the bird or take the shot, and then waits until you are ready to release the dog for the retrieve, you have much work ahead of you.

For dogs three to four months of age or a little older, if necessary, it is important to allow them to become as bold as they possibly can on birds. They should develop as great a passion as their genetics allow for looking for and finding birds. They should be allowed to have their natural tendency to point live birds come out strongly and without interference. They should believe, without a shadow of a doubt, that this is the most fun thing ever, ahead of playing with the kids or having dinner. When you have accomplished this with your dog, you are ready to proceed in developing a superb pointing retriever.

Key Point: Do not try and make your pup hold a point. Do not mess with your pup at all while it is pointing. It is so tempting to want to get in there and start managing the situation and 'train' that great pointing Lab you just found out you had. If you interfere with a pup pointing a bird, you teach it that when it finds that delightful treasure, bad things start to happen. If you grab onto a rope and yank the dog in place, or start barking whoa commands at it, the bird becomes a negative thing. Do it more than a time or two and when the dog finds a bird, it knows it will get yanked or hollered at, so it will quickly turn away or avoid the corrections that will be coming. The pup can't figure out you just want it to stand still, it thinks it's the finding the bird that brings all this bad stuff on. None of that is necessary. Your pup is too young to be made staunch or under control, no matter how 'Type A' you may be. Let it be. With good whoa breaking in the yard, you can enforce a lifetime staunch point when the dog is actually ready for it.

No cheating, either!

Chapter 5
Beginning Training

Before you begin your training program you should have the "what's, when's and why's" thought out completely. That approach is pretty helpful in every aspect of life, but when it involves another living creature it makes things much easier. There are books, videos, seminars and television programs abundantly available telling you how to train your dog. They will show you little tricks with the leash or the kind of collar to use or how to walk. That is appealing to the person looking for a quick and easy way to get the job done. The best way to train a dog is to understand how to get into his mind and how to create the kind of thoughts and responses you need or want in the dog.

We are asked hundreds of times, "Do you train with positive reinforcement?" or "Do you train with punishment?" "Do you ever hit your dog, or do you give them treats?" We probably have a deer-in-the-headlights look when that happens because the answer is not yes or no. There isn't an answer to those naïve questions.

Dogs should be trained so the training results become a way of life, not a quick behavioral adjustment while visiting relatives or hunting South Dakota pheasant. Recall observing a seeing-eye dog in action. They are not praised, not punished, not hit, nor given any treat. They do what they are supposed to do to keep their persons alive and well and going where they need to go. When they reach a curb they stop. They don't stop because someone praised them each time they did it and ignored them when they didn't. They don't stop because someone pounded them when they didn't stop or gave them a dog biscuit when they did stop. They stop because they have been conditioned to stop when they encounter a curb, no matter what else is going on. That is not a reactive kind of dog training, but a proactive kind. Teach the dog what you want, condition him to do it, and then don't do anything stupid to ruin it.

Dogs trained this way are great to hunt with. They hunt with great spirit and passion because they've never been shown the alternative.

They also respond to your directions without deciding whether they feel like it at the moment. If they are ranging too far, you can bring them closer in. If they want to chase rabbits, you can stop them. If they want to chase birds across a road busy with truck traffic, you can call them back. If you want them to wait until you send them on a retrieve, they do. If they need to hold a point while you load your gun, they will. Dogs are not intimidated or beaten into that kind of behavior anymore than the seeing-eye dog is. They are merely taught what their job is and then conditioned to carry it out.

It takes some thought to learn how to teach and reinforce a dog in this manner. The small details of your interactions are important. You must actually consider how and what you are going to do before you do it. After enough training and enough dogs it becomes second nature. Until that time, you must think out your interactions and what your goals for each training session are. This method of training dogs is that used when dogs must carry out the jobs for which the dog is present. Seeing-eye dogs are trained this way. Advanced fieldwork for dogs is trained this way, because dogs must stop on a whistle at 50 or 450 yards. You will find when you talk to people who train dogs and must have the dog perform as intended, that this is the way they all approach it. You will also find they will not necessarily engage in arguments about dog training, since they need only point at their dogs' performance as their proof.

Getting Started

The training of a young pup should be designed with the long-term goal in mind. Too many times we are terribly excited about the new pup and listen to what everyone has to say, we read five books--all with different tactics--and begin the project with those things isolated from each that are most appealing to us. That is about as sensible as choosing a college because it was where you were driving when you decided college was for you. A bit more thought must go into a lifetime decision. In training dogs for a living, we have learned that the process is most expedient and most reasonable for the dog if the project is designed with the ultimate goal as the driving force for the components.

What is the 'ultimate goal'? For the overwhelming majority of us, it is a dog that is an enjoyable companion. It is also a dog that willingly goes hunting, stays under control, works with us at each step, and has great love of the whole activity. It is a dog that is birdy, loves to look for birds, loves to find birds, loves to show them to you, and loves to bring your shot or mostly shot bird back to you no matter where it landed. For a few more, it is that same dog with enough of the 'bells and whistles' that it can compete in any of the various venues available for competition for the hunting dog. If this is what you want, then keep that in mind as you enjoy your rolling bundle of energy and cuteness.

For the pointing retriever, things can be a little confusing to the reader looking at all the different ways pointers and retrievers are trained. Pointers are not usually drilled on sitting and looking into your face for direction. Retrievers are. For retrievers, the "Sit" command is the power command and is used in everything the retriever does. Pointers "whoa" and remain in place standing. So does the pointing retriever. So here you have a dog that must ultimately sit with pressure, and stand with pressure. These can become confusing to a dog not introduced appropriately to these two conflicting behaviors. Be aware of this as you begin to work with your dog.

Obedience training can begin around 12-16 weeks. At this stage, it is not a strict discipline but an introduction to the concept. As the pup matures, depending upon the development of the individual dog, increasing levels of obedience should be required. You must 'read' your dog and determine what he or she can handle and what may be too much.

Introduction to the Leash

Started correctly, leash breaking a dog is not very difficult. There are always some exceptions, but those are quite rare. When a pup becomes physically strong enough that he will not be hurt by it, we put a small choke chain on him. This is one that fits, not one he can step on or get his mouth around. It should not be too tight so that any constriction can affect his breathing. Normally this is started around 12-16 weeks of age. Attach to this choke chain a cord made of thin cotton rope or nylon boat rope. The diameter of the rope is not more than half inch. It should be about three to four feet in length. It is okay if the pup picks it up and carries it in his mouth. As you take your pup out for his daily walk with you, and whenever you go out to do your 2-4 retrieves of a training session, put the chain/cord on the dog's neck. Remember to put a choke chain on a dog's neck so that the end attached to the leash comes

First chain and leash

from over the top of the dog's neck toward you and not from underneath his neck. The reason for this is because a choke chain pulled from the bottom does not release its constriction when you release tension on the leash. When it comes from over the dog's neck toward you, it releases constriction as soon as you release tension. Choke chains are the only tool used in obedience training. They are not cruel and they don't hurt dogs when used correctly. They do allow a quick and meaningful correction when necessary. When dogs pull on a conventional collar and you pull back, you don't make much progress on making them decide to honor your request. Serious training is always accomplished with use of a choke chain.

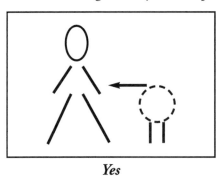

Yes

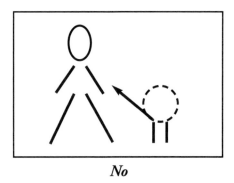

No

Place the choke chain with short cord on your pup correctly and proceed on your normal activities of walking or retrieving. Ignore any contortions or interest your pup may have in his or her new 'attire'. Once your pup learns that the chain is part of the deal and nothing he does changes that, he too will learn to completely ignore it. Usually this happens within the first few minutes of wearing it. Make sure the cord is short enough that it doesn't hang up too much in weeds or other things. Too short and the dog will not grow accustomed to something hanging from his neck. Soon your dog will associate putting the 'leash' on to getting to work and he will be quite excited when he sees it.

Carry out your daily and brisk walks with the 'leash' on. You don't need to pick it up yet. Remove it when your dog kennels again or is put back in the crate. Don't just leave it on for him or her to 'get used to.' You want the association of work and leash because they learn to want the leash and what it brings. When you do your daily three to four retrieves, do this with the leash on as well. You can now use the leash to hold on to your pup or keep him in place. Do not yet use many commands, not while taking your walk or while retrieving, except the dog's name when you send him on a retrieve (or whatever you plan to use in the future) and "Here" when he is already coming to you. Structured introduction of basic commands will occur separately. Now that you have learned how to introduce the leash, we will go into beginning the basic obedience and how to begin to tie in the different training activities you have been working on.

When training a dog at any level, it is important to remember to always keep things simple.

"Heel"

Regardless of your great ability to grasp and interpret many complicated things at once, dogs do not have that ability. Put aside completely what seems logical to you, and learn how your dog thinks and processes information. An entire book could be written on this subject, but there is not room to go into great detail here. When teaching a dog, teach one thing at a time. Have your goal of that training session very clear in your mind, and stick to that. Starting a young dog on obedience should be simple and relatively short. After a few weeks of walks and retrieves with the choke chain and short cord, exchange the short cord with a longer cord or a standard six-foot leash. The leash should be strong enough so that it will not break or tear, but not so big that is carries a great deal of weight. Decide on the first day of 'training' that the goal is to have the dog walk at your side (traditionally the left, but that is personal choice). The dog must walk at your speed, in your direction.

Be prepared for anything. The gentle little pup you have come to know in the last few months may now become a wild animal. Or nothing may change. The first time out on your obedience training sessions, and every time after, have the dog walk with you. You may have to keep giving the command "Heel" as your pup runs forward, backward, turns upside down, lies down, sits down or who knows what. Don't let the dog get out of the work, no matter how creative his avoidance measures may be. In the beginning, the "Heel" doesn't have to be perfect, but the dog must generally walk with you. The command "Heel" is to be given as you begin the walking, and each time you must correct your dog for not heeling. Common sense should prevail at this point. Your dog will most likely try initially to avoid the heeling, but saying "Heel" 25 times as you continue to bring your dog quickly back in place is overdoing it.

Start with the "Heel" command, and use it with obvious corrections, but not every couple of seconds. Walk briskly and with conviction. If your dog senses you are not sure of what you are doing, he will reflect that lack of confidence. If you head out with every expectation of having

the dog heeling with you, your dog will sense that and conform much sooner. Do not allow your pup to alter your speed; maintain your speed and require that your pup stay with you. Corrections should be quick and effective. This is not a tug-of-war where the stronger creature prevails. Keep this good-natured, no matter how trying it might become in the beginning. This is not life and death, and your dog should perceive some fun and some enjoyment of this. At the same time, if you

Walk side by side

say "Heel" and begin to walk, the dog does have to walk with you.

If your dog tries to rush ahead, say "Heel", bring him back in place, and end the correction with the command "Heel" again. If your pup tries a more drastic avoidance, make your corrections increasingly severe so he quickly learns that avoidance never works, and that he pays a price for trying. It usually takes only a handful of corrections before your dog realizes there is only one avenue, and that is one of compliance. They will test you, so be prepared to require compliance.

When your dog is sitting in front of you and you give the "Heel" command, the dog must return to your left side (or whichever side your dog heels). It is advisable to have the dog move to your left and turn around in a direction towards you and sit facing straight forward at your left side. You do not want the dog walking around behind you and reappearing at your left side.

This is important, because if your dog walks to your left and turns around heeling at your side, you are in control of everything the dog does. You don't have to switch hands with the leash, the dog cannot walk too far behind you, and you can see everything the dog is doing. If the dog disappears behind you, you are not in a good position to manage the situation. The dog could drop a bird if returning from a retrieve and you wouldn't know it until the dog sat beside you 'empty-handed'. If a dog goes behind you, it can continue to go until you turn around to look. Teach your dog to sit in front of you. Give the "heel" command. As you do, take a step back with your left foot, enticing the dog to move that

"Heel" means return to your left side

83

way. Bring the dog back a step, and then turn him in towards you and forward into the sitting position.

If you need to take a few steps forward in the beginning, do so to get the dog forward and straight.

This sounds very simple, but its execution can be amusing in the beginning. Sometimes dogs just sit there and look at you. When you try to pull them forward when you are not moving, they don't understand.

You may have to back up a few steps to get your dog moving, then go forward a few steps to get him forward and straight. The goal is for you to give the dog the "heel" command and it will quickly circle around at your left side and sit straight and square with you.

Dogs that like to make it a challenge to heel while walking along with you can really use this to make you earn your trainer's pay. Other dogs will use this as an opportunity to run way behind you and maybe avoid a little work for a moment. Don't allow

Step back to bring the dog to heel

this habit to develop. Remain calm but insistent, so that all your dog learns to do is calmly place himself at your side with as little wasted motion as possible. Later, you will teach this as the logical conclusion to a retrieve. A dog will be sent on a retrieve and return to you, heel around to your side without going

Your dog must be lined up forward and straight

behind you, and sit down waiting for you to take the bird.

Do the heeling exercise once or twice a day at most. Use motion to your favor, instead of fighting or barking commands. If your dog lunges ahead a lot, then change direction more often to counter the dog's desired direction. If your dog tends to drag, pick up your pace so it is more difficult to hang back. Think more like a dog here; if your dog tends to do one thing, counter it with the opposite so the dog learns it has to do what you ask, and cannot creatively avoid it. Outwit your dog as opposed to intimidating him into the desired action, at

least for now. Of course, that is not always as easy as it sounds. You may have to think a little on this one. End it, as with all training sessions, on a positive note so your dog feels a sense of accomplishment, and you do too. Do the heeling only for five minutes and not much more. Your dog should be worked long enough to have learned something, but not so long as to wind up dreading the next session. Start each session on a happy note, and end each on a happy note with praise and affection.

"Sit" with "Heel"

When you begin heeling with your dog, you begin sitting as well. This 'sit' occurs whenever you stop your motion. "Heel" is given as you begin forward motion, or when you are instructing your dog to be at your side. Remember, "heel" means to walk at your side, at your speed, in your direction. No tugging or pulling. "Heel" also means to maintain the position at your side. "Heel" in the mind of your dog needs to be a position, not an action. In other words, whether you are standing, sitting, walking, running or turning circles, your dog is to be at your side. "Heel" should be that in your mind as well.

Use the "heel" exercise to reinforce this notion of proper position. Remember to use quick, effective jerks on the leash to maintain your dog in the heel position. Do what it takes to maintain your dog in the correct position, but do it quickly, smoothly and consistently. If your dog likes to pull forward, jerk him back crisply into the heel position. If the response is to pull forward again, make the correction more severe and crisp. The key is to make your dog quickly understand that resistance is pointless--the more resistance, the more severe the consequences. This is how you get past the resistance stage.

The timing of command and correction is important. Always bracket your correction with a command: "Heel"--quick jerk back into place--"Heel". You by no means need to hurt or frighten your dog, but you do need to do what your dog requires to enforce the command. This will vary with animals. With some it will take very little, with some it may take a strong person to accomplish. DO NOT think there is only one 'right' way; to be a good trainer, you need to find what your dog takes to believe in your commands, then be very consistent. Let your dog learn that you mean business 100% of the time. For dogs who have learned already that sometimes you are quite serious and sometimes you are not, you must re-teach them. Of course this requires that you remain consistent. And consistency means you are serious during training sessions and any other time as well! Never again give a command you are not prepared to enforce.

The "sit" must be as responsive as the "heel". Anytime you stop, or any time you give the command "Sit", your dog must sit. Here is the part most people miss: "Sit" is not the goal--response is the goal. If you tell your dog to "Sit" and the process takes seven seconds to execute, your dog is giving you an opinion of the whole exercise, and it is not a favorable one. The sit must be immediate. The timing is critical for this reason: To create a conditioned response where your dog does what you ask under all circumstances, he must learn he cannot consider how he feels about your commands. He just carries them out. Set this up with the basic obedience in a situation in which you are in complete control. Later, at a distance when you tell your dog to sit, he will do just that, without thought. Through repetition, consistency, and requiring crisp responses, your dog will become conditioned to respond immediately.

As mentioned above, bracket any correction with the command: "Sit"-- pull up on leash and pop the bottom down--"Sit". This firmly entrenches the command and the desired response in the dog's mind. There are a variety of ways to enforce the sit. To begin, always pull straight up sharply on the choke collar. Simultaneously push down on the dog's bottom. Do it with enough force that you make the dog sit the first time. You should get past this with the first couple of training sessions, and just a jerk up on the leash should initiate the sit. The top of your foot from the opposite side of the dog can be used, but this can teach your dog to 'flare' away from your feet if he suspects you will use them. This is employed normally if there is nothing else to use, a situation you should not be in during a training session. We do not use whips on dogs. They can actually break skin and do muscle damage. To enforce a crisp sit, we often use a child's plastic whiffle bat. It makes a popping noise on the dog's behind, but does no damage and actually does not hurt at all. Try it on yourself to see. It is the sound and realization of the 'pop' that your dog wishes to avoid. If you do decide to use a tool to enforce the sit, do not carry it anywhere but on your shoulder like a rifle. If it swings around and is plainly visible, it can intimidate your dog and keep his mind on avoidance of the bat instead of the work at hand. Say "Sit" and almost simultaneously pop the bottom, then "Sit" again, and your dog will quickly learn to sit immediately, without there being any harm or real force used. Do not be slow in this exercise such that your dog has time to avoid any correction. Your timing must be enough that once your dog is told to sit, he has to sit before he has time to avoid it in any way.

The key to effectively introducing and using commands is to never give a command you are not prepared to enforce. If you do give the command, make sure the dog's next action after hearing the command clearly is the execution of the command itself. This is the secret to conditioned response. You are actually programming the dog so that consistently carrying out a command upon hearing it becomes second nature. Begin that thought process now. At the same time, remember you have a puppy, not a fully mature dog. You cannot expect the same level of understanding and response you would in a mature dog. Above all, be aware of the impact of your timing and enforcement. Manage to enjoy this as well. If you do, your dog will.

The Use of Praise in Training a Dog

Do not use treats for rewards. That is a negotiation between you and your dog: "If you do this, I will give you that." What if your dog doesn't do it? Then what? What if something more enticing than the treat comes along? Then you lose. This does nothing to help in creating the conditioned response that may save your dog's life someday, or make your interactions with your dog any more rewarding. Forget the gimmicks and tricks. Teach your dog the reward of working together.

Use verbiage to reward your dog. It is much easier to train a dog with which you can communicate your pleasure with a word or tone of voice. How else will you praise your dog when he does something spectacular at a distance from you? You do not necessarily reward your dog when he or she does something right, you reward him for trying to do the right thing. Let's clarify that: Remember, the response is the goal more than the action. When your dog is responding as much as he can, reward that. If he is not, then require that he does respond.

We had a dog in for training for a couple of months when its own-ers came out to visit and begin to learn to work with their dog. As always, we started the session with some basic obedience. Next, the owner took the dog by the leash and began the ever-familiar heel and sit exercises. The first time the dog sat, the owner enthusiastically praised the dog. The dog sat again during obedience, and was again met with vociferous praise. That brought about a discussion of when and why to give a dog what we like to call 'praise'. In fact, praise probably serves the giver more than the dog, but it should do one thing only--communicate approval with the action.

Think about yourself. What would your reaction be if each day as you arrived to work, you were met with great praise for having made it?

First reactions are often "Oh, I'd love to have my boss appreciate me!" Well, think a little bit more about it. Your boss praises you for finding your way to work. Does that mean there was some recognizable risk that you might not find your way? Does it mean that he or she loves you so that they cannot find enough ways to show it? Or, maybe you are such a klutz that you should be rewarded for something so trivial as finding your way to your daily job?

Let's take it further. You have a boss who praises your daily appearance, your choice of shoes, your good taste in lunch foods, and your neat handwriting. Now, let's transfer you to another boss. This one does not praise your daily appearance or handwriting; he or she in fact assumes you can do that, and expects something more out of you. This boss even asks you to step out of your normal routine, and reach for a higher level of performance. It is hard, and you are not sure you can deliver, but you give it a real try, staying up late, working extra hours, and suddenly, you deliver a job performance you never believed you could. Now this new boss walks into your office and says, "Boomer, that was one excellent job! You exceeded my expectations, I could not be more pleased, take the afternoon off!" Would you feel differently about that praise, as opposed to the daily reinforcement for finding your way to work? Would you make even greater efforts for this boss who has actually improved your sense of accomplishment and value?

And so it is with your dog. Praising your dog for doing something it knows how to do, and should be a part of its routine behavior, including obedience, response to known commands, retrieving, etc., is like praising someone for having matching shoes. Of course you can match shoes, or find your way to work! Praising you for something that is part of your natural actions eventually convinces you the praiser is an idiot. The praiser that utilizes the judicious use of praise earns your respect and loyalty, in part because they recognize something of real value, and not something trite and stupid. It is more than that. They also earn your loyalty because they bring the best out of you, and actually make you more than you were before.

When we tell good-hearted owners to stop praising their dogs for doing mundane, 'should do' things, they first think we are awful tough on their little Bowsers. However, when they see Bowser work to do anything we ask, and get extremely pleased when we give a heart-felt "Good Dog!" they begin to understand. In short, praise is most valuable when it is given to reward a good effort. Outside that, a dog will begin to ignore you because you can't tell the difference. Even if a dog does not completely deliver, but is doing his or her best to try, that deserves the greatest praise. A dog that knows well how to deliver should not be praised, but certainly respected for his accomplishments.

Praise should be a consistently used phrase like "Good Dog!" Your tone of voice should reflect your pleasure. Teach your dog to respond to your tone of voice, positively and negatively. Limit the physical interaction until you are finished with the training session. It is too distracting to your dog. A pat or reassuring touch should be enough during training.

Ultimately, you want to completely control your dog with words and tone. Later, whistles or alternative commands can be used in place of words. Use this entire exercise to create that conditioned response to your words and tone. Develop it so that you do not have to physically restrain your dog. Your words must eventually carry as much weight as a leash or plastic bat.

Key Points to remember
in teaching beginning obedience commands:

• Keep things simple. Teach one thing at a time.
• Start on a happy note, end on a happy note.
• Accept only compliance with commands. No avoidance techniques can be allowed to be successful.
• "Heel" is a position, not an action. It is the dog at your side, whether you are walking, running, skipping, or going over obstacles. Install that concept in your dog's mind as well.
• "Sit" is an action. It means to drop the bottom upon the command. More advanced obedience, when your dog is more mature, allows for sitting while you keep moving, on the whistle, at a dead run, etc.
• Your goal is the creation of good responses in your dog. To have a dog sit on command is only minimally useful. To have a dog that believes he or she must do whatever you ask is extremely useful. Use these basic obedience commands to begin to create that conditioned response in your dog.
• Use the basic obedience exercises to teach your dog to respond to your voice. Use primarily verbal praise, but limit physical interaction. Do not use praise to release your dog from work, but to communicate your pleasure with their response. This is an important distinction.
• Keep things simple.

Use of Crates in Training

A dog crate is absolutely invaluable for the dog owner. They should be used anytime a dog is transported, whether to the vet, the neighbor's, the next state or the next country. They serve several very significant purposes. First, they are exactly like a child safety seat. If you are in a car accident, your dog will not go through a windshield or flying out the back of a truck. They also prevent your dog from damaging the inside of your vehicle, or at least filling it with dirt, dog hair, saliva, or mud! Next, if your dog has been injured or had surgery or some medical procedure, a crate is the best place for the dog to sit quietly, with little movement. This can be mandatory with some medical conditions, and if your dog is crate-broken, keeping him or her in the crate will be easy to do.

Perhaps most importantly, a crate is a tool to establish control with your dog. Whether traveling or having guests at your home, it is a good thing to be able to put your dog into a crate and have him safe and out of the way. This way, he conforms to your rules, not his own whims. You may not wish to use it often, but it is a nice option to have when necessary. If you train your dog to crate without having him feel he is being persecuted, you have an excellent means of controlling your dog when needed.

Crate training is simple. Put your dog in the crate with whatever command you plan to use for that action, shut the crate and you are finished training. You can throw a dog biscuit in to make it more positive, but we never do that. Someday, you will not have a dog biscuit--then what? For an adult dog that has been allowed to develop some fear of the crate (which should never happen), a biscuit may be helpful. For the young pup that may not wish to be confined but has no great fear, skip the enticement and teach him his job is to honor your command. Do not be concerned about how much the dog likes being in the crate. You probably do not like paying taxes, but you do it anyway.

The Use and Enforcement of Commands at this Stage

For the young pup, there should be very few commands used. The little puppy brain has much development to do before you can introduce more sophisticated commands or conditions. Simple is always better at any age. Strive to be simple, consistent and fair. Give no command you are not prepared to enforce. When you do give the dog a command, give it once. If you are teaching the command, after giving the command the first time, make the dog follow the command, and give it again. Once the dog knows the command, give it once, and reinforce it if it is not carried out. Bracket the correction with the command: "Sit", pop on the bottom so he sits, "Sit". This will rapidly develop a good response in your dog. Remember that response is your ultimate goal, and these obedience commands are the means to that end.

The following is a complete list of recommended commands. You do not have to use these particular words; they are traditionally used. The important concept is to always use the same command. Early on, your pup will not be ready for all of these commands.

SIMPLE COMMANDS:

• "NO" - This means "Stop what you are doing." That is all it means.
• DOG'S NAME - This is used to send your dog on a retrieve. "Fetch" comes in later.
• "HEEL" - This means to be at your side, regardless of what you are doing. It is a position, shoulder to shoulder, facing the same direction as you.
• "SIT" - This means to put the dog's bottom on the ground and quit moving. It also means remain sitting until directed otherwise.
• "HERE" - This is used to get the dog to come to you, or to get closer to you if he is by your side. It is not usually formally taught until the dog is around six months old, but it can be used to begin to teach the dog to come to you. There are methods to teach that command, and it should carry as much weight as the sit or heel command.

Giving a dog a command seems pretty easy, but there are some mistakes commonly made that end up creating problems the owner never understands. Then some trainer comes along and tells the well-meaning owner that he or she created the problem, and that never goes over well. A command must mean exactly what it means. That is, if you tell your dog to sit, and he sits on your cinnamon roll, the tendency is to say "No!" rather loudly. What has been communicated to this dog? "Sit", or "No"? What should the dog have done, read your mind and sat in the exactly correct spot? No, you said "sit" and the dog sat. You were in error giving a command whose results you would not want.

Another example: if you tell your dog to sit and he sits, only to get up again, what command do you give then, "No"? Absolutely not. Here is one of the Cardinal Rules of Dog Training: Give the command for the desired action. If the dog should be sitting and is not, give the command "Sit". If you send your dog on a retrieve and he goes but picks up the wrong thing, you never say "no", because he retrieved as directed. If your dog tries to chase a squirrel while heeling with you, you do not say "No." You give the command for the desired action, and that is "heel". If a dog breaks on a retrieve later, you give the correction "sit" because that is what the dog is not doing. When you remain crystal clear in the commands you give to your dog, he or she will become very clear on what is being asked of him. If you fuzz it all up with confusing directions and corrections, you cannot create a good conditioned response in your dog.

The whole point in training a dog for anything is to create a conditioned response. Conditioned responses are how dogs learn to sit on a whistle from a dead run at 300 yards while they're in hot pursuit of a bird. Conditioned responses are how dogs are called away from running across a busy street. Conditioned responses are how dogs are sent from your side to retrieve something they have not seen that is 400 yards across a lake. Conditioned responses stop a seeing-eye dog at an intersection. Create the right kind of a response now in your pup, and the future is wide open for you and your little one.

As an informational note, a dog can be sent on a retrieve on any sound or command you want. It is convention to send the dog on its name for several reasons. One, if you plan on force fetching the dog, the command "Fetch" becomes all important as a force command, and not a fun 'go get it' type command. It means business. Secondly, if you are hunting with a friend who uses the same command to release the dog, then one command will release both dogs. If the dogs are released on their names, then only one will be released when the name is given. Keep things very simple. It also makes things easier if you have more than one dog, or hunt with more than one.

Retrieving

Once your pup understands what you want in the retrieving game, you can begin to draw in the lines on his behavior. You should have created an enthusiastic desire to run after what you've thrown, and with luck, most of the time your pup will bring it back to you. Now you begin to acquaint the pup with a few concepts that will not come entirely naturally. First, the dog must wait for a moment before leaving, and leaving should be in conjunction with hearing the command you have for retrieving, ideally his name. If you want your dog to be steady as a finished dog, then give him a command on which he is to retrieve. It should be simple, not easily confused with any other command ("Nit" or "Speel" would not be good commands to send a dog.) The dog's name is conventionally used in retrievers, because each dog can have its own unique command, not confusing for any other dog.

The pup now learns to look out for what may be falling, to wait a second with restraint before being released, and should come back and let you take the puppy bumper from him. This sounds good, and often it even works out this way. Other times, it is another America's Funniest Videos session. People get so upset when their dog does not do what they want them to. Remember that this is where you take the time to teach what you want. Retrievers aren't born knowing the rules; they just like to have fun. This is also where you can introduce the gunshot. If your pup has learned to love retrieving, then when you pop a .22 blank pistol and throw something for him, he will still love to do what he has already been doing. It really is that simple. The gunshot, in fact, just makes it more exciting. Very soon, the dog will learn to look in any direction where he either sees a gunner, a gun, or hears a gunshot.

Do not introduce more than one new thing at a time. If you're going to have a thrower besides yourself for the first time, don't introduce the gun the same day. Some dogs adjust instantaneously to the bumper being thrown by someone else, and some are dumb-founded by it. Some pups are accustomed to the bumper coming from your hand and from a source near them. Change those two things and they don't know what to think. Outthink this situation. Have your thrower get their attention while standing right next to you and tossing the bumper. If the pup retrieves that, slowly move your thrower further from you until the pup easily retrieves what someone else has thrown. If your pup wants to return to the thrower, which is what he's done with you throwing alone, use the same logic. Have the thrower standing close enough that the pup returns to you even if he's returning to the thrower. Or, you can have the thrower run back to you once the pup picks up the bumper so that no matter what the pup thinks he's doing, he's still returning to you.

When the pup is to the point where he will watch your thrower, watch the bumper as it is thrown, run out after it and bring it back, then introduce the gunshot with the retrieve. Your thrower might throw one retrieve for the pup, and on the second, shoot the .22 blank and then toss the bumper. Regardless of what your dog does, treat it as if there had been no gunshot. Unless you have a naturally fearful animal, you will rarely see much except heightened excitement as a result of the gun. Don't look for gun-shyness, and don't expect it. Of course, don't shoot a 12-gauge off over the head of your unsuspecting pup, either--that would frighten you as well.

When you have a thrower in the field, hold your young pup up so he can clearly see the mark in front of him and so that you control the pup. Do not ask the pup to be steady--don't make the pup be steady. Steadiness is far easier to teach than it is to recover an enthusiastic attitude. Instead, prevent the dog from going before you send him, and hold him so he cannot gyrate out of your hands and perhaps entirely miss

Hold your pup

watching the mark fall. Generate enthusiasm in your pup with great energy and enthusiasm in your voice: "Watch it, watch it, mark..." Once he learns the game, all you'll have to do is hold on.

The thrower should not interfere or interact with the dog. He must be far enough from the bumper that the pup ignores him and returns to you. Encourage the pup to come directly to you, even if it requires your running backwards, tossing another bumper, encouraging in a high pitched voice, whatever it takes. Create the enthusiastic return. If the dog is lackadaisical in the return, it can be because you've never developed a good return, because the mark is too far or too hard to find, because the dog is tired or bored, or because the dog is not that interested in retrieving. You can fix all but the last one.

Your dog should focus where you focus

Encourage the enthusiastic return

Strongly encourage the delivery to your hand. This is what you will always want, and if you plan on force fetching your dog when it is older, this will be very helpful when you begin the hold concept. Reach out, back up while the dog is coming in, and do what you can to keep the dog holding on to the bumper. You should not be barking any hold or fetch commands--take what you get here. This should be imminently fun for your dog, not a nagging chore. At the same time, you do not want to teach

Encourage the delivery to hand

your dog that returning equates to dropping. Teach just that returning merits great praise and often another retrieve.

Do only three or four retrieves, as always, and end on a successful note. If you must end on a short retrieve, do it. Leave the last taste in your dog's mouth a positive, happy one, and that is how you will begin the next time.

Praise the retrieve with great enthusiasm

Teaching the Whoa Command

This section is put at the very end of the chapter, separate from the obedience. This is because teaching a dog what the "Whoa" command means should also be separate from heeling and sitting. In the upland field, you do not want a dog sitting and heeling, unless it is to and from the truck, the hotel room, or while running a blind. You will want a dog to hold a point in the upland field, however. When you are teaching your retriever to walk at your side responsively and to sit as a default when you stop, or whenever you direct, the "whoa" command does not fit in 'mentally' to the youngster. Conventional obedience training certainly does teach the "sit" and "stand" command at the same time or under the same conditions. Obedience dogs do not have to execute their "stand" command while the most excruciatingly exciting thing in their world is looming ten feet in front of them in the cover. Dogs being dogs, when trained with reasonable obedience, will find that sitting is the best way to relieve pressure from you, and so will automatically sit whenever they are anxious or concerned. This is not what you want your pointing dog to do.

The "Whoa" command means only one thing to the dog. Do not move your feet. It does not mean "don't go get the bird", "don't chase the bird", or "stop moving, you $#! dog!" "Whoa," when being taught, should have absolutely nothing to do with birds. Just as the force fetch you will read about later on is never done with birds, neither is the whoa. You teach your dog a conditioned response to a command in a manner and place in which you can completely control everything. You make it become second nature to the dog. Then when you go out into the field with your dog fully prepared, you then use the conditioned response you have created in your dog to control his hunting behavior. In this way, you do not have to fight with the dog, get mad, train the dog or do much of anything besides reinforce what he has already been clearly and thoroughly taught.

It takes a long time to teach a good, staunch whoa. Not weeks, not even a few months, but many months or more. It is imminently worth it once you have a solid pointer, and one that will back another dog, but it does not come overnight, particularly if you have a dog with a lot of boldness and aggressiveness towards birds. It will take time, patience and maturity to get it right with that dog, but once it is there, it is worth great bragging rights.

Whoa training evolves as your dog evolves. At this early stage, all you want to do, or maybe all you can hope to do, is acquaint your dog with the concept of standing still when asked. You want to make this teaching exercise simple and clear. There are a number of ways to accomplish this, and the pointing breed people have a variety of techniques. We like to approach this with a positive attitude and initially using what we affectionately refer to as our "GRT Board". The dog is introduced to whoaing when he is worn down a little from previous work. We could have been on America's Funniest Videos often if anyone had videotaped some of our whoaing of young exuberant retrievers. They either thought it was a smooching session or something that required great wiggling and movement on their part. We have had to remind ourselves that we are competent dog trainers, and can prevail over these little bundles of energy. And we do, and so will you, given enough patience and humor.

Take a piece of plywood about two feet by three feet. Set it down someplace where there are not a lot of diversions, at least in the beginning. Sometimes it is easier if your dog faces into the wind, which is the position in which they will be pointing ultimately. Make sure your pup has not just come from some other more rigorous training, but has some of the edge taken off, if necessary. Their little minds should be relatively free of earlier work or pressure. Put a collar and long leash on the dog. Place your dog on the board, put him in the standing position and give the 'don't move your feet' or "Whoa" command. This is where it gets funny. You will have your hands on the dog because you have to, so any red-blooded retriever pup views that as love or playtime. Standing still is the most remote concept. Use the collar to hold his head in one position, and if necessary, loop the leash under his belly to hold up the back end. Hold him in place and give the whoa command again. If he wiggles or moves, lift up on the collar and the leash circled around the belly and enforce the original position with the command again. You will find the less you physically contact the dog yourself the better, since that is a release to him.

There are some pointer trainers who use a table and harness or similar means to hold the dog. We do not do that because in all of our training methods, we stay as close to the final application as we can. It may take a little more time and a little more effort, but the dogs seem to be less devastated by the natural on-the-ground method than by being hoisted or otherwise unnaturally constricted. It is personal preference, but the dog's state of mind should take precedence over convenience.

When your dog will begin to stand in place, release the belly leash if you can, and release the pressure of holding his head up. Your goal is to have him relaxed and standing in place. Make this a positive thing for him. Tell him quietly and calmly he is doing well, but do not release him from the task. When you can, run your hand along his back and tail while giving the whoa command so he gets used to your touch, but knows it does not release him. Do not pet him--that has nothing to do with this--but reinforce with touch. Stroke the long back and tail of a pretty point. The whoa exercise should be viewed by your dog as a nice, positive thing to do. It will make little sense to him, but it will teach him the pleasure and reward of standing perfectly still for you.

In the beginning, it may not be reasonable to expect your pup to stand still for longer than a moment or so. Push it as long as you can without making your dog think this is torture. When you are ready to end the session, or the whoa for that time, tap your pup on the head and give a release like "Okay." Encourage your dog off the board so he can relax and be a pup again. You may wish to do it once again, or not, depending on how your dog views the whole thing. Do not overdo this, so your dog learns negative associations with the whoa command. That will haunt you later in the field. Once your dog will stand still on the board such that you can drop his leash and he will honor the 'do not move your feet' command, begin to do this in different places. Do it in the field before you take your walk or do a set of marks or before you load up your dog for a trip to the vet. Begin to acquaint him with the concept that when you ask him to stand still, he does it and it is not an unpleasant or force-filled activity.

It may take weeks to reach a point where your dog will actually stand still for you without your assistance. When he does, then walk slowly out in front of him. If he moves to follow, or even takes a step forward, go back firmly and put him back in place with the whoa command, and then walk out again. Now you are teaching him to stand still, no matter what you are doing. At first he will get it with you by his side. When you start moving, all bets are off. Now teach him it applies if you walk in front. As you can, begin to kick the cover in front of you, as if there was something in there. Calmly walk back when he has stood still long enough, run your hand along his back and tail, primp him 'pointer style' a little, walk away, come back, and finally, release him with a tap and an "Okay".

At the early stages of whoa training, when a pup is a pup, your goal is to teach your dog to stand still, allow you to move about in front without moving, walk back and forth, and do it consistently no matter where you ask him to. It may take weeks or months. Because a dog is smart and understands what you ask does not mean he would do it in the field when a bird was actually there. Take your time and condition your dog in a manner that will make it second nature when you do go to the field. Take whatever time is necessary. Do not rush it. Above all, no matter how tempting, leave birds out of this at the early stages. There is more to the whoa exercise and this will be outlined further along in this training.

Chapter 6

Continuing Retrieving for the Retriever

By the age of four to five months, your pup should love retrieving and understand the exercise completely. This is the stage at which you begin to hold your dog in the heel position for a second or so before sending him on his name to retrieve. Your pup is too young to be steady, and in your efforts to have a trained dog, be careful not to quell the enthusiasm for retrieving by trying to make him steady at this stage. You will have to read your dog and treat him accordingly but do whatever it takes to maintain the enthusiasm and desire. That is what is important right now. That will change in just a few months, but let your pup be a pup right now.

It is best if you can have someone else throw your training bumper now. Generally don't use birds at this stage. That is frustrating when you want a hunting dog, but you do not want any association with birds and obedience corrections or any other negative thing. The use of birds too early can teach your pup to stop and have lunch instead of bringing the feathers back to you. The pup may learn to chew, toss and generally play with the tasty bird. That is not what you want in a hunting dog or competing dog. Use bumpers now. Once your dog reliably goes out and comes back without dropping or chewing, you can switch to birds if you have them. Never use live birds on a pup. That is too tempting to bite or eat. Frozen birds work most easily, and can be re-used for a long time. Frozen birds can be thrown with great accuracy as well.

You will not hunt or compete in a park, so make every effort not to train in a park. Use natural fields and environment as much as possible; a park is better than nothing, but your dog should be acquainted with as many new smells, nasty stickers and bushes, wildlife and other things that occur during hunting or competition as possible. So many times we have gotten dogs that people have worked diligently in their back yards or neighborhood parks that became so entranced with the natural outdoors they looked as if they had had no training at all.

Your Training Scenario:

You will need help--someone else who can throw and shoot a blank pistol, if possible. You handle the dog, they handle the throwing. Before getting your dog out, decide where you want the 'falls' to be and place your thrower as far from your intended falls as their throw distance allows. The thrower should never interact with your pup. They are the source of the bird (read that as training bumper), and nothing else, although your thrower must be ready to help if your pup needs it.

Place thrower and fall as shown below:

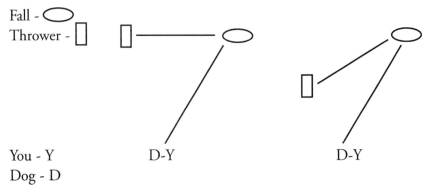

Fall - ⬭
Thrower - ▯

You - Y   D-Y   D-Y
Dog - D

Your thrower can throw at right angles to you or angles back from you. Do not have your thrower throw toward you. This can serve to teach the dog to run toward the thrower and not focus on the bird. The throw should be as far from the thrower as he or she can throw. Ten or twenty feet is too close. Ten or twenty yards is better. The fall should be close enough that your dog can get to it without becoming disheartened, but not so close that it is effortless.

Placement of the fall is important. Do not have it go into bushes or stickers; your pup will learn not to try. Start with throwing it where he can see it once he gets out there, but eventually you can throw into cover so he learn to use his nose. Use common sense. If your pup is weak on coming back to you, make the throw such that shrubs or vegetation prevent anything but a return to you. Have the return be downhill so it is easier. Use the natural terrain to your advantage in this way. Try to challenge your pup frequently, but also mix the falls with ones that build his confidence in retrieving. More rules on setting up retrieves will be listed later on.

Your thrower can make you or break you. He must clearly understand his job before he begins to throw for your pup. Put your thrower in position before you bring your dog to the line. Have him practice some throws first so he can place it where you want it. Placement is important in training. We often take a dog off line if a fall does not go where it needs to go, but this is not usually a good idea with puppies. If the fall goes severely awry, have your thrower pick it up and do it again. The jobs of the handler and thrower will be clearly defined in the next two paragraphs. Read these until you can recite them, they are that important.

The Handler

This is the person training the dog. The handler should be in control of the dog at all times. Air your dog before training so the need to relieve himself is diminished. Take him out of the crate; put his choke chain and short cord on. If he wears a collar, leave it on. There is no need to generate any concern about what is around his neck. If you are going to be an electric collar user, put the inactive dummy collar on during all training so the dog assumes it is part of his training regalia and nothing more. Make him heel to the line with you. There is no need to let a dog run wildly about, visiting your thrower or other interesting sites. In the early stages, squat down with him, facing him in the direction of the fall, not the thrower. You do not need to be severe and tough--keep him happy but make him behave. Do obedience training elsewhere, and reap the benefits of that training here. Hold on to the dog and get him to look out at the thrower. Traditionally, handlers say "mark", which means mark or watch the fall. Use excitement and enthusiasm in your voice to generate that in your pup. Make him sit still to look out. He may stand up when the fall goes down, so use the next couple of months to teach him to remain seated. You can hold his collar with one hand and his bottom down with the other to indicate how you want him to do this. Tell him to sit. The thrower should be ready.

If the dog does not look out towards the thrower, have your

Point dog towards where the mark will fall

thrower get his attention by excitedly saying, "HUP, HUP" or something to catch the dog's attention. Your goal is to have your dog learn to look out without any help and find the gunner on his own. When the dog looks out, be ready to give the signal to throw to the thrower. When the handler gives the signal by nodding or making some agreed-upon movement, the thrower should shoot the blank pistol, if he is using one, and immediately throw the bumper into the air. The throw should be high enough to represent a bird, maybe two or three human heights, and reach the area of the fall. In the beginning, the handler should release the dog when the bird is in the air. Over the next couple of months, slowly work on backing that down until the bird can hit the ground for a few seconds before the dog is sent.

If the dog struggles and tries to go before being sent, he may be looking backwards or up, or otherwise not see the fall. If this happens, ask the thrower to throw again, and do what it takes to make the dog watch. Eventually, he will learn this is the only way he gets to go. If for any reason the dog cannot find the bird (bumper) or does not stay in the area to hunt, your thrower needs to be ready to help. If the dog begins to come back to the handler, the thrower must be ready to give another "hup, hup" and throw another bird, thereby drawing the dog back. How to do this the right way is outlined in the next section.

Once the dog has picked up the bird, the handler must get them back to the line, or at least to the handler. Early work done on a pup usually prevents this from being a problem, but if it is a problem at this stage, put a long, lightweight rope on the dog and let him drag it. Then, if he chooses not to return, you have a long rope to grab and bring him back to you. If he drops the bird while being pulled back to you, that is okay. He needs to learn that his job is to return to you. The later force fetch allows you to go after the problem of dropping a bird. There is not much you can do now but generate enthusiasm for coming back to you with the bird.

To get your dog back to you, you can use the command "here!" with great enthusiasm to entice him back. You might mix that with the 'toot-toot' of a whistle. Right now, just get him back. The return commands become something you can enforce after more advanced obedience work. Now, you may have to trot backwards or use all kinds of verbal encouragement, but do what it takes to get him to return. Do not become intimidating or mad, because then you give your dog every reason NOT to return to you. Do not forget a teething dog is in pain, and may drop birds or not even pick them up. If your normally enthusiastic retriever stops retrieving, check the teeth. This is almost always the reason. Wait it out, try something soft if necessary, and soon your dog will be back better than ever. Strongly encourage the delivery to hand. Get down on the dog's level, if necessary, and encourage the dog to come all the way to you with the bumper. Take it from the dog before the dog learns to spit it out and wait for more. You will be glad you did later on.

The Thrower

Your thrower is very important. Sometimes, well-intentioned spouses or friends who cannot throw outside a ten-foot range, or who cannot watch the dog and be ready to assist when necessary, are more of a handicap than help. Your thrower must already know what to do in different cases that come up. Ideally, your thrower should have a bucket or bag of bumpers or birds. These should be contained and held up out of puppy range. If they are set down or dropped, your pup will run over to the thrower and retrieve the dropped bird and so learn just to run there instead of marking the retrieve. Five-gallon buckets with lids are handy; they can be set down and sat upon.

The thrower should have a bird in one hand and a pistol in the other. In all our years of introducing young retrievers to retrieving, we have not encountered gun-shyness. Don't worry about gun-shyness. If you have generated enthusiasm in your pup, he may be surprised by the noise the first time or two, but he will very soon learn to love it. If your pup has not learned to look out at him, the thrower must "hup, hup" with enough volume and enthusiasm to draw the dog's attention. When the dog is looking out, the handler signals. When signaled, the thrower shoots the pistol and throws the bird to the appropriate spot. The throw should be plainly visible to the dog. It should not be two feet off the ground, nor should it be 40 feet off the ground. Make it reasonable.
If a pup shows some alarm over the sound of a gun, don't let that worry you too much. By all means do not respond and reward the behavior.

Make sure your pup adores retrieving before it hears the pop of a blank or starter pistol. The gun will not create any enthusiasm where there is none, but do not let it detract from the low-desire dog. When your dog really enjoys the retrieves, then remotely introduce the blank pistol so the pup learns to associate the noise with the joy of the retrieve. We have never banged pans over dogs' heads or shot guns around the kennel because it has never been necessary. It might impress a puppy buyer, but it does not impress a dog much. Teach him to love retrieving, then associate the gun with that great activity. You are not going to fool a dog.

Once the handler has sent the dog, there should be neither noise nor any movement on the part of the thrower. He is no longer a part of the picture. If the pup comes over to him, he should ignore the dog. If the pup stays there, he can throw another bird out and draw the dog away. This must never become a habit or the dog will learn to give up and wait for another bird to be thrown.

Here are some general help guidelines for the thrower:

• Do not interact with the dog.
•   If another throw is necessary, make every effort so that the dog does not see the throw come from the thrower, but only sees it in the air. When the dog is looking away, give another "hup hup" while throwing. This way, when he turns to look, the bird is already in the air.
•   If the dog begins to hunt distantly from the area, draw the dog back to the area of the fall with an excited "hup hup hup…". If that does not work, "hup hup" and throw.
•   If nothing else works, walk out to the bird, pick it up and toss it again so the dog sees it.
• Do not let the dog give up and return to the handler. Get him back out there no matter what contortions you must go through. You do not want a dog to learn it can give up and come home empty-handed.
•   If the pup brings the bird back to the thrower, the thrower must stoically ignore the dog, and it becomes the job of the handler to draw the dog back to him.

Once the dog has successfully retrieved the first mark, which may take one or two repeats, the thrower should move away from the fall far enough that the dog will not be tempted to run back to the old fall. That will teach him to go back and hunt where he have already been, not a good habit. If possible, throw with the wind. That way, if the dog runs to the gunner, he will not wind the bird and be rewarded. He will only wind the bird away from the gunner (thrower).

Move into the wind, away from the old falls, for the next marks. Do only 2-4 successful marks and quit. Tempting as it may be with a talented dog, do not overdo it. Go back tomorrow and do more. Be careful not to bore the dog or allow any bad habits to develop. Try to keep the terrain, fall visibility, wind direction and distance of marks in mind each time you set up the marks. These are major considerations for your dog, though they may not be to you.

With time, stretch your distances, degree of difficulty, and length of training session. Read your dog. Start on a good note, and end on a good note, even if it means running a little bitty short mark your dog can do well. Keep your dog's attitude in mind all the time. Be demanding, but be fair. Reward effort, keep him challenged, but keep his confidence up. By doing so, you are creating a great hunter or competitor.

Do not throw your marks in your backyard. Don't do them in the same place every day. If at all possible, avoid throwing them in a park. As much as a dog may love retrieving, familiarity is boring. It does not create improvement in marking ability. When a dog knows a field or an area intimately, there is little challenge in finding the mark. Your dog will learn to find 'birds' by just knowing where they are, instead of having to actively watch, remember, and work to do the job. The better you want your dog to watch and retrieve birds, the more effort you will have to make to find new areas in which you can work. People who train dogs for competition will drive hours for a new place to train, and have dozens of places they use. If you train in your back field or the community park because that is all 'you have time for', then don't be disappointed when you take your dog hunting and it has no idea how to look for a bird in unfamiliar territory. If you want your dog to hunt in a new environment, give it the skill of knowing how to hunt in new environments.

Run marks of different distances. One day you may set up marks of 50, 75 and 90 yards. The next day you might have marks of 150 to 200 yards, ending with a short 40-yarder. You want to teach your dog to mark the area of a fall and go to it. If you set up marks routinely of 60 yards, then you effectively teach your dog to run 60 yards and start hunting. We got a very talented dog in for training one time that always ran about 70 yards and started hunting, no matter where the mark was actually thrown. He hunted a 25-yard mark out at 70 yards, and he hunted a 300-yard mark at 70 yards. Turns out his owner was at one time on his way to becoming a professional baseball player who took great pride in throwing the bumper as far as he could, every time. It took about two months to teach this dog to hunt where the bird actually went down.

This stage in your dog's life is so extremely important. This is where the foundation is laid. Let him do nothing but hang around and play and eat, and you will have created a dog with no purpose and no focus. Do this basic obedience and retrieving work, and you are well on your way to having a well-trained, enthusiastic, and controllable dog which can handle any hunting condition or be ready to move on the more advanced training. These dogs are happier, healthier, and more appreciated by their families. They are useful, easy to handle, and a great pleasure to their owners. In short:

• Work every day if you can. Do some obedience. Away from that, do some retrieving. Whoa your dog daily as well, but separately from the obedience.
• Use conditions that most duplicate those for which you are training your dog.
• Keep things simple. Teach one thing at a time.
• Get good help for retrieving.
• Do not use a dummy launcher at this stage. When shooting one, you are not in a position to fully control your dog. If possible, always have good help so you never have to use one.
• Be demanding, but be fair.
• Start happy, end happy.
• Challenge when you can, build confidence when you need to.
• When training, vary the locations, conditions, cover, terrain and distances.
• Have fun while you are doing this. Your dog will reflect your attitude.
• Train with the future in mind. Always have a goal, each day.
• Respect your animal.

Introducing Birds to Running Marks

The premature use of birds in retrieving can create lifelong problems with a dog. For most pups, retrieving itself is great fun and the use of feathers is not usually required to make it more appealing. Once a dog has gone through the force fetch program and has learned what is expected, the use of nothing but birds for marks is ideal. When a dog will bring a frozen bird back as reliably as he returns a bumper, then using frozen birds is more fun for dog and owner. The introduction of birds for retrieving to a dog can be an entertaining endeavor. For some dogs there is no transition problem at all--they will run and scoop up a frozen pigeon, duck, pheasant, or chukar as if they had every day of their life. Other dogs will act as if you had tossed a road-killed skunk. It is not terribly important how your dog initially reacts to a bird, but it does matter what you do and what attitude you create in your dog.

The use of frozen birds is extremely advisable. A warm tasty bird will entice the young dog (or dog new to birds) to explore the body. There are wonderful smells and tastes with a warm bird body. To make the whole endeavor work smoothly without creating any new behavioral problems to tackle, we begin with a bird that is smaller in size and quite frozen. Chukars seem to be a bird that dogs enjoy. Pigeons work well also. In the frozen condition they don't weigh too much and they're easy to pick up even for the dog with a very small mouth. Now some folks are wondering how they are supposed to get their hands on a dead, frozen chukar or pigeon. Frozen birds are going to be pretty necessary for dog training, so this is an important issue. Birds from previous hunting trips can be sacrificed and left feathered and in the freezer. This does not always go over well with all members of the household, so a freezer in the garage or a good friend's freezer may be useful. Volunteering to rid the local farmer or warehouser of excess pigeons can be a source of birds as well. Bottom line: you need the real thing when your dog is ready.

When you have located a few birds that are now in the whole but frozen form, introduce them to your dog as you have done everything else--make it fun. Put your training gear on your dog and walk out to your training area relaxed and ready to 'happy' your dog. Get him excited with the tone of your voice and your actions. Do not make him sit or comply with any rules right now. You're having the 'happy' fun first. Get the dog very excited and then, just as you would the happy bumper, toss the bird out for the dog. One of several things will probably happen. Your dog will run out and pick it up and bring it back to you. Or, your dog will run out and stand over it, not sure what to do. Don't view this as a refusal or a bad behavior. You just changed the rules of the game and the dog is not sure what it should do. If the dog does stand over the bird or mouth and drop it, just walk out to the dog in a very non-threatening manner, and pick up the bird, tease and excite the dog and toss it again. Entice the dog to pick it up and when he does, back away and praise the heck out of him. Get the bird and toss it again, all as a big, fun game. In short time your dog will run out and pick up the bird and run back to you. When he does this, calmly enforce the rules already well understood; bring the dog back into the heel position and have him release the bird to your hand.

Occasionally, for the very sensitive dog, you may have to put the bird in the dog's mouth and walk back with the dog holding the bird. Then praise him a bunch and toss it out again. Teach your dog what you want and that this is a great time. Do not create any negative associations or get mad at your dog so he will dread the sight of a bird. If it takes a few days to convince the dog, it takes a few days. This does not happen too often if you approach it correctly, particularly if the dog has a reasonable desire to retrieve and is birdy. Your earlier bird work in which you created a boldness and excitement should translate well here.

Use birds when you can in running marks. Bumpers are better than not doing any retrieving, but birds are what these dogs are about and you will see a difference in dogs accustomed to the real thing in their training. Training with bumpers is like teaching dating and courtship with cardboard cutouts. It just doesn't translate the same. Birds are never used in force fetching or drills, which is what training bumpers are for. Just make sure you wait until your dog is reliable and controllable before you do introduce your birds.

Teaching Steadiness

One of the biggest questions people ever have is how to make their dog steady to the retrieve. We have heard about tying dogs to the bumpers of trucks or putting cords around their waist (ouch!)

Steadiness to retrieving is not some hallowed ground that only Master Trainers or people with a lot of rope know. It is a common-sense thing once you have done it with a dog. To avoid the constant breaking of their older dog, people frequently make the mistake of making their young pup just start out steady from the get-go. There is nothing worse than taking an enthusiastic little pup and teaching it to sit still instead of experiencing the joy of the retrieve. Attitude is first. Let the little guys get terribly excited and keep them that way. As a pup begins to mature, depending on the relative enthusiasm level of the dog, you can begin to make him wait. If a dog shows only a moderate interest in retrieving, don't detract from that further by making the disinterested dog even more disinterested. If you have a four-month-old pup that tries to rip your arms from the sockets to leave, then you have a little leeway in making the dog sit for a moment before releasing it. There is not a hard-and-fast rule regarding when you begin to make a dog learn to wait. You do not sacrifice attitude and enthusiasm for control. If you can begin to make the dog wait for your release without detracting from his desire, then you need to make him wait. If you let the hard-charging dog go whenever it wants, you are teaching it to go whenever it wants and exert no control over its own actions. You will regret that in the field.

As your young dog or dog new to training becomes accomplished in marking and retrieving, you begin to make him control himself. From the very beginning you should send your dog on its name (or whatever cue for going you plan to use). The tiny pup can have the puppy bumper thrown and hear its name as he goes after it. He will learn to associate the command with the action. As your pup's excitement grows, you will hold him beyond the time he wishes to remain in place and then send him with his name. You can hold your dog either just by holding on the to the cord, or if you have a socket-ripper you can squat down with one hand at the back of the head and the other on the rump, holding each straight and in place.

You may have a dog that naturally sits and waits for your cue. That is rare, but they do show up sometimes. More often, the dog will remain seated if it knows you will hold the leash and make it stay in place. Use the "Sit" command to communicate what you want. You can say "Sit" before the bird is thrown and again after it hits the ground to let the dog know what you expect. Some dogs will turn themselves inside out to get out of your hands and to the bird. This does not necessarily mean you have the greatest retriever ever. It does mean you have one that really likes to go. You will have to teach the dog it has to watch the mark before it can go. If you loose grip and the dog is looking skyward when the mark falls, have your gunner pick up the bird and get ready to throw again. This time, make sure you hold your dog enough that it has to watch. Use the pressure of good obedience to make your dog settle down and think about what it should be doing instead of going completely crazy. Again, high enthusiasm is good only if it is controlled. If it is not controlled, it is of little value since your dog won't learn to mark; instead it will run wildly until it stumbles upon the bird or by chance goes downwind of the scent. Don't teach your dog to do that unless that's exactly what you want.

Win this battle when you begin Never let your dog learn it can wear you down, out-wrestle you or that you will not be consistent in what you ask. When you decide your dog should wait for a second or two, then from that point forward, make your dog wait a second or two. Once you start making your dog wait and your dog understands the concept, increase and vary the time. Be careful not to get into a pattern of waiting for a count of three and then sending your dog. Your dog will learn to wait for a count of three and then go, whether you have sent him or not. Teach your dog to listen for your signal and that nothing else releases him.

Send your dog with a tone that is proportional to distance. Do not beller the dog's name for a mark twenty yards from you. If you consistently send your dog quietly for short marks and increase the intensity as the distance then you can ultimately use your decibel level to assist the dog. When a bird falls a considerable distance from you while hunting, and you send your dog with the appropriate 'cue', your dog will know to get on out there. Conversely, if a bird drops just outside the blind you can use the very quiet cue to let your dog know the bird is not very far away.

Because your dog knows you want it to be steady does not mean it will, especially when things get exciting. You will need a conditioned response to remain in place despite great desire to run. It is far easier to proactively teach your dog it has no alternative but to be steady and then continually enforce that behavior than it is to react to the dog that always breaks if given half a chance. Use your obedience tools to enforce steadiness with the maturing and mature dog. When the wrestling match is over and you can remain standing when the marks are thrown, you will use your leash and heeling stick or whiffle bat to enforce the steadiness. Give the "sit" command, tell your dog "Mark" and signal for the bird. Make sure you have a good hold on the leash and the heeling stick in your left hand. View any movement as the start of a break. Remember, your dog doesn't think in these gray areas the way you do. If you let the dog move an inch, then the next time it will move two inches. Two inches becomes six and pretty soon the dog learns it might as well take the whole distance. If you do not want a dog to break, teach him to sit still until you release him. When the dog moves or lifts its bottom, it is no longer sitting. Correct the dog for what it is not doing--sitting. Give the "Sit" command, pop the bottom pretty severely with the stick and give the "Sit" command to reinforce. If the dog moves very much, correct him and have your gunner pick up the bird and start over. In no way ever let your mature dog learn it will get the bird when it moves or tries to break. This should not happen much because you should do a good job of enforcing the sit on the line.

Some dogs resist the bottom popping and still wish to move forward or stand up. If the sit pressure doesn't work, then use reverse psychology on the dog. If your dog is so bent on moving forward during marks, instead of fighting it to stay in place, make the dog heel backwards for four or five feet. When the bird goes down, walk backwards with the command "Heel". When the dog does not immediately move backwards with you, correct the dog severely with the choke chain and heeling stick for not moving backwards with you. You have to get your dog more concerned about staying at your side than it is excited to break on you. Don't make a pattern out of walking backwards five feet every time a bird goes down, but vary it so the dog tunes in to you and what you are doing. Be consistent and never let your dog creep or stand up on you. Sacrifice time and retrieving to make your dog learn to be steady and that there are no options, once the dog is ready for that level of control. If you do your basic obedience exercises thoroughly, you will use them as tools to steady your dog. Test your dog's steadiness when you think it's pretty solid, giving another dog's name or another word at the time the dog expects to hear its name, or whatever cue you will use to send the dog. If your dog's name is Abbey, say the word "eight" and see if she starts to go. If she does, correct her for breaking. You are not teaching her to go on vowel sounds, but on her distinct name. Teach your dog to go only the single cue you plan on using. Steady dogs are far more fun in hunting, and are a must in most competitive ventures.

Honoring

Not only should a dog be steady to marks, it should be steady to the work of another dog. In competition this is called honoring. In pointing, it is called backing. For some dogs it seems reasonable to remain steady until released. That same dog may find it almost impossible to let another dog go get a bird it wants but knows it is not supposed to have. When you have taught your dog it must be steady until released, you may also want to teach it to honor the work of another dog. The only way you can do this is to actually honor the work of another dog. You can begin by setting yourself and your dog behind and off to the side while another dog runs a set of marks. You should restrain your dog in exactly the same way you do while your dog is actually running the marks. It must sit and not move or stand up. Correct the same way as you do on the working dog.

As your dog gets the idea of honoring, move up until you sit beside the working dog without interfering with that dog. Require the same level of steadiness in your honoring dog as you do when it is the working dog. Use the backward "heel" sometimes, even if your dog is doing everything right. It never hurts to drive a point home and the more a conditioned response of doing as you ask you create, the more chance you have your dog will do as you ask when you are not in a position to enforce it.

The upland hunter will most likely want a dog that will remain at point and in place until released to retrieve the shot bird. If there are two dogs in the field, only one will be able to retrieve it. It will be invaluable to teach your dog to honor both the point and the retrieve of another dog. That way you can avoid the tussle for a bird between two determined dogs. When your dog is mature enough teach it to honor and you can via the presence of other people and dogs, reinforce the behavior as often as possible. Honoring does not come naturally to birdy dogs, and does not remain with them as a skill unless it is continually reinforced. Make honoring a part of your training if you have enough people to set it up.

Chapter 7

Introduction to Water

This could be the humorous section, if we could fill it with stories of how people go about introducing their pups or young dogs to water. Most retrievers are bred to enjoy water retrieves. As always, there are some that are ambivalent about going into the water, and some that flatly do not like the feel of water around them. Most dogs can be shown, with time and patience, how enjoyable water can be, at least to some degree. Each dog is unique, and what is offered here are some guidelines to consider with your dog. For those planning on going into upper-level competitive endeavors, there is more to the required water work than you will find here. This section serves to introduce your dog to water and demonstrate how to bring about the best attitude toward water that you can. There will also be advice on how to prevent problems like bank running or avoidance of the water. Water should be a blast for your dog and for you; just plan on taking the necessary time to achieve that attitude.

The "First Time" Guidelines

Common sense is the single most important thing to employ in this endeavor. Think about things before you begin. Of course that seems obvious, but it is amazing what people think is reasonable or appropriate to do in water introductions. We have witnessed large, macho men put on hip waders and walk out into a lake, encouraging their pup to accompany them. Chuckles aside, they were asked if they planned on doing that in January when the duck fell in the icy water. Assuming you did not teach your dog to retrieve by running out first and picking up the puppy bumper with your mouth, neither must you swim to show your dog how to do that. Use an approach that enables your dog to learn himself, again contributing to your dog's ability to do things on his or her own. Before beginning, do take a few things into account as you plan your first introduction:

• The water should be warm and comfortable. Cold water creates negative associations you may never overcome.
• The water should be calm and inviting. Whitecaps and waves may be too intimidating, again creating very negative associations with water.
• If possible, the body of water should be small enough that it does not appear to be an infinite hole, capable of overwhelming the young, small or frightened pup.
• If you need to use a large body of water, find a small cove or quiet area that is less intimidating to a small pup on an eye level to the water.
• The water/land interface needs to be as smooth and uneventful as possible. Ledges, sharp rocks, steep drop-offs, stickers, heavy cover can be frightening to a young dog.
• If possible, introduce your pup to the water when the sun is overhead.

When the sun is on either horizon, it reflects off the surface of the water and directly into the eyes of anything on the surface. For some dogs, this is no big deal; to others, the blinding effect is frightening. Verify this effect yourself at sunset or sunrise by lowering your eyes to the water level. You cannot see at all on or near the water's surface. This is an important factor to keep in mind when training your mature dog in the water. Dogs running into the reflection of the sun off the water cannot see what they are trying to see, and often can't tell where they are going.

Having Fun with the Water

Running through water is one thing, while intentionally swimming can be another. It is always a good idea to acquaint your pup or young dog with the idea of running through a stream, water puddle or other shallow water. Do this when you can on walks and on retrieves. Don't make an issue of it. Just make it a part of the whole fun, running after the bumper through whatever water is present. Similarly, don't avoid some running or standing water if it is chilly or cold. Let your dog work that out on his or her own. If you make a big deal out of water, then your dog will think it is something to worry about. If your pup runs through a stream in the winter and gets a little cold--fine. He'll learn to be more careful the next time. Let him learn about the world when he can, and give him the opportunity to think and react. At the same time, don't walk right by an iced-over pond that your pup could run onto and then fall through. Common sense can save a life as well.

Assuming the air temperature is warm, the water is sufficiently warm, and you have located a pond or body of water that is quiet, with a gently sloping bottom and not filled with other people and dogs, plan your first couple of water introductions. We will give you the insider secret on how we introduce the young pups we have to water. It's called the "Punkin Method".

The first time we introduce a little guy to water, we get out a regular training bumper and our female Labrador named Punkin. Punkin doesn't mind young pups, and she's fanatical about the water. With pup, bumper and Miss Punkin in tow, we head to a quiet, private piece of water. The bumper gets tossed into the water, and in a flash, Punkin is diving into the water. The pup watches in amazement. Sometimes they turn and run the other way, sometimes they just sit and watch, and sometimes, they consider following her in. Not too much attention is given to the pup. We're just throwing 'happy bumpers' for Punkin. The bumper is repeatedly tossed out for Punkin. If during this frenzy of water retrieving the pup shows no interest, that's perfectly acceptable. At least the pup has gotten to see a dog that passionately loves the water, with no pressure on the pup itself to get in. This is important. Don't put pressure on the pup to do something it doesn't feel ready to do. You could create a whole bunch of negative connotations here that you just don't need to at this time. If the pup never shows any signs of thinking about getting in, we quit after five or ten minutes and put Punkin up. Then we let the pup explore the water edge without the splashing and action of the older dog. Sometimes the older dog knocks an inquisitive pup under the water or backwards, and then they become more afraid of the water. Ultimately, a dog that likes the water will not let that keep them out long, but it can scare a timid water dog. Again, use common sense and don't let the older dog do more damage than good in the presence of the young pup.

Let the pup examine this new world on his own terms. Do not search for signs of your future water champion, or otherwise put pressure on the dog to be something you want it to be. Sit back and see what the dog is or may be. Let the pup splash and walk in the water if it wants.

Toss a puppy bumper six inches out in the water. Don't toss it so far that if the pup doesn't retrieve it you have to fish it out yourself. If the pup brings it back, toss another out a couple of feet. Watch the pup, and that may be enough, or even too much. Do not push this as far as you can. Quit and go on home or on to other activities. Leave the first introduction with the dog not wanting to leave yet, so that the next time the dog is perhaps a little more excited to play.

Getting a Little More Serious

After the first time or two you may have one of several things: a pup that dived into the water and loves it, a pup who shows some real interest in the water but not enough to get in, or a pup who ran the other direction and would not come near the water. None of these means the dog will or will not be a great water dog. Obviously, the first option gives a little more hope that the dog will love water, but some dogs take more time than others and some never will love the water. Your job is to make the most of what it is you have in your pup.

If you did have the little water monster that ran in until the water was over his head, then your next step is to develop a dog that loves the water, has no fear and doesn't begin to learn habits you won't want as a mature dog. This will be discussed first:

The Pup who Loves Water

You will need a puppy bumper that floats well, with a rope on it for tossing well. You may also need a handful of rocks to toss at the bumper if your pup loses sight of the bumper and needs some help. You will need the rocks, so keep some in your pocket during these early stages. Don't employ steadiness or other obedience commands in these teaching stages. Your first objective is to get your dog to have a great attitude about the water. You have plenty of time to refine the control and behavior, as your dog is older or more experienced. Attitude first--always.

With no other distractions like other pups, dogs, or well-intentioned family members, take your puppy bumper, pocketful of rocks, and pup with no choke chain or cord on it to the water. Do not have a chain, collar or leash on your pup. If the collar or leash hang up on something in the water, you will have to rescue your pup, or worse. We have seen the dire consequences of a dog getting hung up. Don't take that risk.

Get the pup's attention and toss the bumper out an appropriate but short first distance. This may be two feet or six feet, but try to make it so the pup doesn't have to swim at first. Encourage a return directly to you. Meet your pup at the water's edge so you don't create a game of 'chase me along the bank'. If your pup will come out of the water and up the bank to you, continue to encourage that behavior. If your pup leaves the water and begins a game of running around, then meet him at the edge and prevent the development of any games. The force fetch will teach your dog at a later stage to come out of the water and right to you, delivering to hand. Until you have that tool, do what it takes to have your dog bring the bumper to you, even if you must stand right at the water's edge.

Continue to toss the puppy bumper out a little further each time, far enough that you are increasing or at least maintaining the distance, but not so far that you overwhelm or tire the pup out. As with land retrieves, do not do more than three or four or so, then stop. Now you must control your stage-parent desire to see how far your pup will go and how great a water dog he is. Save that for a few weeks down the road. Structure each water session with your pup to end successfully, extremely fun, and not nearly enough for your pup. This maintains and expands the positive attitude toward water. Particularly if you have plans for competitive ventures in the future, or more advanced training, your greatest priority should be attitude development and not showing off the young superstar.

Now that you have a pup that likes the water and will swim out and bring back the puppy bumper to you, you must keep a number of things in mind to prevent problems or bad habits:

• Throw the bumper only into the middle of the body of water. Make sure the shortest route back to land is towards you. If you throw near an edge and your pup does the intelligent thing and goes to the closest bank, you have successfully taught your dog to cheat and get out as early as possible. This is a VERY difficult thing to overcome. Even if you have no plans for competing, still do not teach your dog to always look for the easiest way. Instead, first teach the dog to go directly to the bird and directly back to you. You will always want the businesslike, no-nonsense attitude in any working dog. When hunting, if you want your dog to go the shortest way, he'll do it without your having to teach that.

- If you inadvertently throw the bumper so that the dog will go to a closer bank, then go over to the location so that your dog is still returning to you. Do not let your dog begin to think he can go anywhere he wants to. He needs to always return directly to you.

- If the pup cannot locate the bumper, or the otherwise gives up the hunt, then use your rocks to toss at the bumper, making a splash right where the bumper is. Make every effort to make sure your pup does not return without the bumper. Keep a backup bumper ready if the rock tossing doesn't work. Do not allow your pup to learn that giving up is an option.

- If for any reason your pup does give up or quit, stop right then. Don't give him more opportunity to learn that quitting is acceptable. You have overdone the work, the water is too cold, or there is some reason the dog has given up the fun. This cannot become a routine. That routine effectively teaches your dog that quitting is an option when he doesn't like the way things are.

- If your pup drops the bumper when he lands and then runs joyfully towards you, that is not a good habit. It is not acceptable in hunting or competition if your dog drops the bird and comes back to you without it; do not let that seed of an idea germinate now. Instead, meet your pup at the edge so that you take the bumper from his or her mouth.

- If your pup will bring the bumper out of the water to you, then just as on land retrieves, encourage the delivery to your hand.

- Do your best to encourage the pup not to shake until you have gotten the bumper. Until force fetch, you don't have a way to enforce this behavior, but do what you can to encourage the businesslike approach of delivery before hygiene.

- Start close with retrieves, and end close. Go as long as the dog can reasonably handle in between.

- End before you or your dog wants to. Keep the "Ah, just one more" attitude strong. It will serve you well in the future.

- End with a land retrieve to help dry your dog off and remind him of what he does the rest of the time. Your pup may swallow a lot of water.

Give him ample time to empty himself if necessary. Walk for a while if possible to dry him and give him time to relieve himself.

The Pup Who Is Unsure or Doesn't Like Water

Some dogs that initially appear to dislike water can become great water dogs. Some remain that way. Don't jump to any conclusions too early. You will know what type of dog you have by the time he is eight or ten months old. Before that, different things can show. For the dog that is not so sure about the water, there are several things to try to encourage the enjoyment of the water. Some work with some dogs, and others work with others. Within the abilities and options you have, read the following list over and do what you can with your pup:

• Try the Punkin Method a number of times. It can be very encouraging to a dog to see another gleefully playing and enjoying the water. If the first two or three times it doesn't coerce your pup into the water, don't quit trying. This peer pressure has worked more for us than any other method. It can be quite difficult for even a fearful young pup to not at least try to go out where the other dog is having so much fun. If your pup does like to retrieve, then after you have thrown the bumper for the big dog, toss the puppy bumper out for the pup, even if only a few inches. Try to not get frustrated and just toss your pup out into the water. This usually makes him avoid you at the water's edge from then on. Be patient. Understand it may take a couple of months to get your dog truly open to water retrieves.

• If the season allows, use temperature to your advantage. If you have a hot day, and particularly a hot afternoon, have your pup do several land retrieves so that he is almost a little too hot. Then, go to water. Unless you live in the Deep South, where the water is as hot as the air temperature, the water is quite inviting, even to dogs that don't think they like the water. Toss the bumper into the edge. Your pup may drink first, but that's okay. What you want is the desire to get into the water, for whatever reason. Play with the dog and the bumper near the edge. Praise any water play or retrieve. Don't overdo it. Leave it so the experience was truly pleasant for the pup. If it worked, plan on using the temperature to your advantage another day.

• Another method that can sometimes be successful when a dog is not so positive about getting into the water is to pretend the water really is not there. This means have your dog do some land retrieves near the water. Then, just as casually as can be, when your dog has momentum about retrieving, toss the third retrieve into the water a couple of feet and send your dog. The momentum established in the first two retrieves may carry your dog right into the water after the bumper. Don't take the initial small success here and begin to throw big water retrieves. Read your dog and decide what is best; either quit right then or maybe do one more small water retrieve. One of the biggest mistakes people make in their earnest desire to train the dog in the water is to take a little success and kill it with too much work or repetition. Err by underdoing here, not overdoing.

• Be patient. In the end, if things still are not working out well, get out the waders. You and your pup can head out together.

General Water Training

Be quite patient and realistic in introducing your pup to water. If it's a major thing in your mind, then it will be in your dog's, and that's usually not a good thing. Go about water training like everything else. Take what comes, and be willing to take the time necessary. If your pup learns that you can be upset by the water work, he may opt to use that to drive you crazy. If he learns that, like everything else, this is a teamwork thing you both do and both enjoy, he will take it on with a good attitude. Getting a young pup to become a 'water retriever' may take one day, or three months. Some pups like the water when they are eight or ten weeks old. Some are not ready until they are three or four months old. Read your dog. If he shows no interest at ten weeks and it is warm and nice, then hold off for a month and try again. By the time your pup is three or four months, you can and should begin the water-attitude development, provided the weather allows.

If it is November and your pup is just coming of age to begin water work, you are out of luck. Does this mean you will lose out and your dog will not be a good water dog? No. It does mean that when the season and weather does allow, you need to begin your water work and be quite diligent about keeping at it, even if you must drive a ways each day to do the work. If you have just started your water work and then winter comes, you can start up where you left off in the spring. Use the land work you can do to continue to develop your dog, so when you do start the water work again, your dog will go farther and have a great attitude, even with the layoff.

Understand, because you go out for a few weeks and your dog does wonderful water retrieves, that does not mean that work will carry for the rest of the year and you don't need to do any more water work. It also does not mean that your dog can do any water retrieve. Just because you can grasp the concepts of retrieves in cover in the water, or retrieves through water and back on land, or even retrieves thrown at the land/water edge, does not mean your dog does. There are concepts in the water that mystify people when their dogs cannot carry out apparently simple retrieves. This is not because the dog is dumb, or blind or obnoxious. It is because dogs think differently and perceive differently than we do. There are some very important things to be aware of in water retrieves with dogs. The following section will outline some of these.

Water Concepts Important to Understand

Because a dog will run into water, retrieve a bumper (or bird) he can see and swim back to you does not mean he can do most water retrieves. Water retrieves required in real life hunting situations or competition are set up to test the dog's real ability to carry out water retrieves. First, you must have a dog that will willingly go into the water, pick up what is there for him to get, and return to you with it. Young pups--dogs under six months of age--should be expected to go into the water, swim, retrieve and get back to the water's edge at least. This is trained with no pressure, no correction and no means of enforcing very much besides just doing it. Once your dog has its adult teeth, the force fetch must be carried out, and this is fully outlined in the Force Fetch chapter of this book. Once force fetched, your more mature dog will pick up what you ask him to, bring it all the way back to you, and wait for you to take it from him. It is this skill that will give you the ability to demand that your dog come out of the water and all the way to you without dropping the bumper or bird, sit beside you and wait for you to take it. Once you take it, then the dog can shake. The following discussions will be premised on the assumption that the dog is now old enough to be force fetched, has been successfully trained as such, and now the tools to enforce more strict behavior are available to you as a trainer.

Any intelligent dog will opt to get out of the water as quickly as possible, since that is the fastest way to the bird and back to you. (The term "bird" will be used but refers to either bumper or bird.) Understand right up front that that is what a good dog will do, and be prepared to deal with that behavior. In hunting, it may be most desirable to have the dog in the water as little as possible. Still, train the dog to go as straight as possible, since that is what you are doing in all your other work. It is a respect issue more than anything else. For dogs that will run competitive events, going straight is very important. Dogs in competitive events are not judged on how they return from retrieve, but they are judged on how they go out. Bank running is reason for dropping a dog from a contest. Even though a dog is not judged on his return, a very important concept is this: if you teach your dog he must do what you say, and going straight is part of that, then make him go straight both out and back. If you allow a dog to decide how he will return from a retrieve, then you give him the option to decide things for himself. Once he knows he can do this, you can be certain he will decide sometime on his way out on a retrieve, most often after you have driven all day to one very important, very expensive event. Dogs are not sophisticated enough to know they must do things one way one time, and another way another time. Be consistent in your demands on your dog. If he must go straight, then make him go straight ALL the time, out and back on any water retrieves. In hunting, set your-self up so he goes the smartest route, and do not put your dog at any risk for hypothermia or ice dangers for the sake of some training concept.

Noncompetitive hunting dogs are taught to go as straight as possible, merely to maintain the issue of control and respect. If a dog is sent on a retrieve and the handler sits back and lets the dog go any old way he wants to the area of the fall, then you detract from the businesslike approach to the work, which is go straight to the area, hunt the area, and come directly back. Because this is what is desired on any land retrieve, it is taught on water retrieves as well. The difference in training is that hunt-ing dogs are not trained on retrieves set up to correct them for cheating very much, while competitive dogs are literally set up so that they will want to cheat, and can be corrected. While both dogs are required to go pretty straight and get right to the business at hand, it is the mark itself that is different. Keep this in mind, depending on what your training objectives are. Let us break down the different concepts in water retrieves you will want to introduce your dog to, regardless of whether you are training just for hunting or for competition.

Cautionary Note: Before ever training in a body of water, personally check the water for hazards you might not readily see. A dog with a great leap into the water may impale itself on a submerged branch. There may be equipment or metal beneath the surface that could slice a leg or entangle a dog. There are a number of things that are in water that can harm a dog if it jumps or swims through or by it. Always take the precaution to check for hazards both where you expect your dog will be, and places your dog may be you never intended. That is a lesson that should never be learned the hard way.

Middle of the Pond

A dog must be familiar with retrieving a bird that is in the middle of the pond, floating in the water. This is easy to accomplish in training, by throwing the bird into the middle of the pond, such that the dog can see the splash and the bird once it is lying there. This should be started with the dog sitting at the water's edge, and graduate to the dog sitting at some reasonable distance from the water, still where he can readily see the fall and the splash. This process takes weeks or months, not a day or two. As with all marks at this stage, the dog should be made to sit at the heel position and watch the mark. He must also wait to be sent on his name. Young dogs will have to be restrained with the command "Sit" and the check cord. More advanced dogs must be made to be steady with the same means used on land retrieves, whether this is a check cord or collar.

Into Cover in the Water

Once a dog understands the simple water retrieve, the dog must then learn to retrieve in water in cover, just as he must do on land. Cattails or other water flora can be used, as long as it is reasonable and the dog can't get caught up or hurt in any way. Use common sense. Start with a simple retrieve, not too far, with the dog close to the water's edge. If possible, throw so that there is a visible splash, so the mark is easier to see. Be prepared to have your thrower help with a rock toss if the dog gets lost or is prepared to give up. You will have to teach your dog, with time and repetition, to go into cover while swimming and use his nose to find the

#1

#4

#5

#7

#9

#10

#11

#12

#13

#14

#15

#16

#17

#18

#19

#20

#21

#22

#24

#25

23

"The Pointing Labrador"
COLOR PHOTO CAPTIONS

Cover:
GMPR HRCh Blackdog's Bonkerjohn Kate MH points a pheasant
for owner owner Jim Bonham.

Photo #1:
GMPR HRCh Blackdog's Bonkerjohn Kate MH, owner Jim Bonham

Photos #2 and #3:
GMPR Barnone's Snake River Otter JH, co-owned by Gary Buys and Kevin Hollern,
points a quail for Paul Knutson

Photo #4:
GMPR Grits of Black Forest SH points a pheasant, owner Kevin Hollern

Photo #5:
Larry Morgan tracks a rooster pointed by Barnone's Snake River Otter,
co-owned by Gary Buys and Kevin Hollern

Photo #6:
CP Goose Creek's Black Rose hunts with Paul Knutson.
Owner: Paul Giesenhagen.

Photo #7:
CP Joli of Black Forest, owner Paul Giesenhagen.

Photo #8:
GMPR Gumbo of Black Forest MH points a pheasant.
Owner: Kevin Hollern.

Photo #9:
Jennybelle from Spinney holds a mallard. Owner: Dr. Dick Bell.

Photo #10:
GMPR Star's Casanova, owner Larry Morgan,
ready to retrieve from the duck blind.

Photo #11:
GMPR Gumbo's Smokin' Harley JH delivers a goose to
Paul Knutson. Owner: Rex Eaves

Photo #12:
Harley and Rex Eaves sharing a day of goose hunting

Photo #13:
CP Jacks The Duke, National Hunting Dog Association Pointing Retriever AND
Amateur Pointing National Champion holding a pheasant.
Owner: Piotr Chilpala.

Photo #14:
CP Jacks The Duke, National Hunting Dog Association Pointing Retriever AND
Amateur Pointing National Champion points a pheasant
for owner Piotr Chilpala.

Photo #15:
Julie Knutson working on water retrieves with CP Denver of Black Forest.

Photo #16:
GMPR Gunclub's Allstar JH MH, owner Greg Morgan

Photo #17:
Kassidy Knutson with eight-week-old puppy

Photo #18:
GMPR Cajun of Black Forest MH on point. Owner: Kevin Hollern.

Photo #19:
Paul Knutson planting a quail for training

Photo #20:
Ten Grand Master Pointing Retrievers assembled in one place,
all trained by Paul & Julie Knutson. Literal left to right on all 10 dogs:

GMPR Gunclub's Allstar JH MH
GMPR Star's Casanova
GMPR Killarney Kate III
GMPR Gumbo's Smokin' Harley JH
GMPR Barnone's Snake River Otter JH
GMPR HRCh Blackdog's Bonkerjohn Kate MH
GMPR Gumbo of Black Forest MH
GMPR Grits of Black Forest SH
GMPR Cajun of Black Forest MH
GMPR High Sierra Mae

Photo #21, 22, 23:
GMPR Star's Casanova with Paul Knutson, and showing off his dramatic water entry

Photo #24:
GMPR Barnone's Snake River Otter JH skims the water on the way in for a retrieve

Photo #25:
Kassidy Knutson helping out with training

Photo #26:
Jim Bonham and GMPR HRCh Blackdog's Bonkerjohn Kate MH head back
to the house after a successful afternoon of pheasant hunting

bird. If the only cover is at the water's edge, then don't expect your young dog to swim across the pond to cover, hunt the bird at the edge, and swim back across the pond. The dog will probably come back by land. Instead, throw into the water's edge from the same side you and your dog are standing, and let your dog learn to hunt water cover, even if there is not much of a swim. Islands or cover out in the water are most ideal to teach this concept. Use your head to prevent bank running or other bad habits. Find a better place to train water if your local water is not sufficient. No one said this would be easy. Use the geometry to prevent bank running. Have the mark thrown across a piece of water so that bank running really is not possible, so the easiest thing for the dog is to swim back across the water to you.

At the Water/Land Interface

Few people believe this until they see it for themselves. For many dogs, when a bird is thrown the first time right at the interface between land and water, the dog cannot find the bird! They will hunt the bank or swim around in the water, but they will not look right at the edge of the two. For dogs who will be running their first Junior Hunter/Started Dog event, or duck hunting for the first time, we make sure they always see a bird thrown right at the edge. More often than not, they have to have a rock thrown to help them locate the bird. Once they understand a bird may be found there, they learn to hunt at the edge as well. To work on this one it is ideal to have a fairly narrow channel with you and your dog on one side and your thrower on the other side. The channel or pond should be such that your dog will not run around the bank to return to you as well. Ask your thrower to toss the bird right at the edge. Start with your dog right on the edge of the other side and work until you can be some reasonable distance from the bank, and your dog will run to the edge, swim across, hunt the edge of the other side, find the bird, and swim back across to you.

The "Up and Out" Retrieve

Here's another one that humbles the proud owners of avid young water retrievers. Throw a bird such that the dog has to swim across a pond, get out of the water, run up onto the land and hunt for the bird, then swim back across the pond with the bird. For some dogs this is quite easy. For others it appears as improbable as flying. When you have spent much time throwing in the water for your dog, and then one day throw out of the water, don't be surprised if your dog hunts only in the water and never considers leaving it. That is the dog brain, not a dumb animal. Just make sure and teach your dog that sometimes he has to swim and then hunt on the land. Also make sure you have the mark set up such that he most easily returns to you by coming back across the water, and not running around.

When your dog can do an 'up and out' as easily as he or she can do a 'middle of the pond' retrieve, you can raise the stakes. Find a place to train where your dog may have to go into and out of the water two or more times. Islands, points, and multiple channels all allow this kind of training. For competitive dogs, this will be a must. For the hunter, it may make retrieves easier if a duck falls across a long distance of land and water. This more advanced work will require that your obedience is truly solid, as described in later chapters. As always, the obedience and adherence to commands is the key to success on water work. Your dog must believe in you, trust you and respect you.

Sticks and Decoys

Have you ever seen a dog out hunting that could not get out of the decoys to pick up the dead duck? Pretty embarrassing for the dog's owner. It is even worse after a hefty entry fee in a competitive event. And it is not necessary. When you are working water marks with your dog, put your decoys down in the pond so that your dog must swim though them. You can begin with a white bumper in the middle of the pond so it can't be missed. Set decoys to the side of where your dog will be going. Use a variety of scenarios to teach your dog that it is not supposed to pick up the fake birds, just the real ones. It doesn't take long. You should even throw something in the middle of the decoys so he can learn to differentiate. Try to avoid teaching your dog to go pick up your decoys if you can. It may be convenient, but it might also confuse your dog. If he can't find the real bird, the decoy will surely work in its place, right?

Similarly, a dead duck in the water has a profile of a small, dark thing. That's also how sticks, tree trunks and even garbage look in the water. Acquaint your dog with marks thrown into sticks or other pond or lake particulars, so your dog learns to hunt for the bird and not every single thing that looks like it. It is a skill that needs developed, like every-thing else. Obviously, it's a bad habit to throw sticks for your dog, unless you want your dog to retrieve a stick while the duck you shot floats down the river.

More Advanced Training in the Water

When teaching, marks must be set up such that the dog will not run the bank. That is your job as trainer. Anytime you figure your dog will not run the bank, consequently you'll put a mark close to shore and your dog will decide to hurry back to you and run the bank. Do not assume your dog is the rare exception and will always do the honest thing, because he or she is a dog and will do a variety of things. Think ahead on every mark you set up, and on every concept you are trying to either teach or practice. Prepare for the unexpected and for the dog having a bad day. A mark set up on the assumption the dog is going to do everything right will backfire, especially on the day before something important, or when someone you want to impress is watching.

Now for one of the most important concepts in water training. At some point in hunting or competition, a dog will decide to not go in the water the way you want him to, or may even refuse to get in. People are often incredulous as they watch their water-loving dog run 300 yards around the bank to get a bird instead of swimming 25 yards straight at it. For most this is not a problem, but just a hunting dog that wants to avoid getting unnecessarily wet. If you plan on running advanced   competitive events, there are training methods to teach a dog it must get in the water. If you plan on going this route, don't do it by reading a book. Get the best help you can from an experienced trainer.

With the skills of the water force and swim by, a dog can be taught to head straight for the water, even if it is at an unnatural angle to the dog. The dog can be taught to go straight past tempting islands and points, or go over the islands and points and get straight back into the water. Similarly, the dog can be taught to come directly back the same route. Once this has been established on a dog, the dog can run water blinds and run multiple water marks of significant technical challenge. Watching a well-trained dog run technical water marks or blinds looks so easy. If you go home and try it with old Yeller, it never works out anything close to the same. You can teach your young dog to enjoy the water and run relatively simple water marks. To continue to advance, you will need far more sophisticated training. Plan to get help at that stage. It is usually not necessary for the waterfowl hunter, provided the dog has enough desire to get the birds across the pond.

The Duck and Goose Blind

The actual hunting is the easy part of this endeavor. Usually, the greatest concern with hunting waterfowl with a trained dog is the safety of the dog and the ability of the dog to see the birds shot. There are cold-weather concerns with a dog hunting in the cold. Water hazards should always be considered. Positioning the dog so that it can watch the birds fall without interfering with the incoming birds is often a big challenge. Those blinds built with a dog compartment are very useful. A box adjoining the blind where the gunners sit, into which a dog can be snapped by a short cord, is pretty ideal, particularly for the dog new to blind hunting, since sitting and watching is not usually the dog's first choice behavior. Even seasoned dogs will give breaking a try in the excitement of the moment. Wherever you may have your dog positioned, snap him by a cord of 24 to 36 inches to something in the blind, so you control when the dog leaves. If the dog can see the birds go down, the job is easy. When you are ready, release your dog and let him go get the birds. The water marks you have run in training should make this "duck soup" for your dog. If your dog cannot actually watch the birds drop, you will either need to change the setup of your blind so he can see, or plan on teaching your dog to run 'blind' retrieves, or throwing a rock in the vicinity of the downed bird and send him to hunt it up on his own. A few times hunting even when the dog doesn't see the bird fall usually excites a dog enough that it learns to hunt where you have shown it the duck should be.

This brings up a training issue we have encountered occasionally. How do you teach a dog to retrieve a wounded duck that is diving beneath the water's surface? There are techniques in which a shackled duck is used to teach a dog to persevere until the duck tires enough it can be caught. We have never found that really necessary, primarily because it is no fun to torture some unsuspecting duck that way. A dog trained to retrieve well and hunt out the bird in the area the dog expects it to be, will do just that. He will stay in the area of the fall and hunt for the duck. A time or two of learning about diving ducks and waiting them out will teach the dog about that phenomenon, and he will enjoy the experience each time it happens. Good sportsmanship requires that a wounded animal be collected, and it is important to train a dog to retrieve to that end.

Cold-Weather Thoughts

Most dogs love doing anything outdoors, hot or cold. It is not uncommon for an enthusiastic dog to be too excited about the business at hand in the cold and snow and wind up with frostbite before he is aware anything is wrong. You cannot always use the dog to gauge if things are going all right or not. There are some common sense guidelines in doing cold-weather hunting.

• Make sure your dog has the coat and the feet for what you are planning to do. Dogs kept indoors do not have a coat that will insulate well enough to withstand icy water or much exposure to cold wind or moisture. Even with one of the neoprene coats available, the dog's legs, stomach, and head are not protected and they will get very cold. Feet that are used to cut-pile carpet or a well-sodded backyard will get cut to ribbons on ice, frozen branches, and hard snow. Boots can work, but they have to be comfortable and stay on, and not enchant the dog so that is spends all its time thinking about its shoes instead of the job at hand.

• Dogs to be used for hunting should start the day well prepared, just as you would. They should be well hydrated and have a light breakfast. They should have water and food available throughout the day. A bite of your ham sandwich does not count here. The energy/nutrition makeup of a good quality performance food has the best balance of what the dog needs, so carry some dry food with you in a plastic bag. A handful of kibbles every hour or two will keep the dog's body chemistry fit for action or cold.

• Shivering can mean either the dog is cold or that the dog is anticipating some action. It can be a little of both. Make sure you know your dog well enough to know why the dog is shivering. Shivering is a way to generate body heat in a dog, so a little shivering may not mean anything is wrong. Non-stop shivering means the dog is cold, so put yourself in your dog's shoes. If you were sitting in a blind shivering for an hour, odds are you would not be enjoying yourself, and may wind up compromising your immune system. That means you get sick later if there is a germ within reach.

• Keep dogs warm first and foremost by keeping them dry. Dampness is a good conduit for removing heat from the body. Dry a dog by removing the water from the coat's top layer, and avoid if possible rubbing the dog so hard you kill the air insulation layer next to the skin. Minimize his time in the water. If you have trained your dog to take a straight line in the water, then move so your dog takes the shortest reasonable water route to the bird. A 50-yard swim in icy water can even teach a dog to hate retrieving in the water, where a shorter, quick retrieve still lets him have fun without freezing his private parts off!

• Be very wary of water with ice on it. We know many sad people who have lost good dogs because they broke through the ice on a retrieve, and surfaced in a spot where the ice was solid – and drowned. It would be better to restrain the dog and lose just the duck than to lose both. Perhaps best of all is to avoid those conditions and locations that are so dangerous to the exuberant retriever.

Chapter 8

Advanced Obedience

Simplify...

Relatively formal obedience training begins around the age of six months. Before this time a dog's brain is not well adapted to learning quick responses. There are books that will give you all kind of serious obedience commands to use on young pups. We have seen a number of people with 12-week-old pups that will sit on a whistle and even stop on the way to a retrieve. Our internal cringing aside, we wholeheartedly disagree with that approach. The problem with turning the baby dog into a little soldier is that the robust attitude is squashed, or at least strongly challenged. It is the robust attitude that carries the dog for a lifetime and gives him the attitude that allows you, at the appropriate time, to be very demanding and challenging in your training. For the little pup that gleefully runs after a puppy bumper, only to be stopped on his way, the joy of the chase is taken. Soon, he will have no passion to go because some controlling human will stop him anyway. Now there will be some reader out there with a dog that was drilled on obedience from eight weeks that is now a field champion. For every dog like that, there are hundreds that had their spirit taken from them, or had their passion and attitude for serious work very compromised. One great retriever trainer told a crowd of people at a seminar, "My dogs cannot run more than a single mark at the age of a year, but at the age of two they can win a field trial." Do the right thing at the right time for your dog, and you will be limited only by your dog's natural ability. Attitude is everything.

When your dog is physically and mentally mature enough to begin formal obedience, you need to be prepared mentally yourself. It is at this point that an owner either creates his ultimate success or his ultimate failure in training. You can own the most talented dog there is and without respect, control, and adherence to certain behavioral guidelines, you will have a dog that hunts on its own with no awareness of your needs. You will have a dog that never quite pays attention when you most need it to, or a dog that embarrasses you at a hunting competition. It is this part of your dog's training, and perhaps yours, in which you will choose the long-term outcome of your work. No one ever likes to hear so much significance put on some aspect of what he is doing, but that does not make it any less factual.

If your dog will not do as you ask within a three-foot radius, what do you think its response to you will be at 50 yards, or 450 yards? As most dog owners know, the further the distance, the less the dog tends to 'hear' you, or respond. If you want any hope of controlling your dog in the field at 100 yards, you need to make certain your dog will do as you ask at your side. The whole obedience training process is premised on this simple concept. Create a conditioned response to your commands at your side. When your dog understands completely and consistently, then you begin to translate that same level of response to increasing distances. If things slip, bring the dog back in and do the basics again.

Obedience is serious work. It is relatively absolute. The dog must learn to respond to your command the first time--not because you are a marine drill sergeant and the dog a lowly recruit, but because that is how things are most clearly understood by the canine brain. Now comes the hard part about being a dog trainer. In learning and carrying out these exercises, the dog needs to feel challenged and pushed, but it also needs to feel some sense of accomplishment and some sense that this is a good thing to be doing. You cannot take the great attitude you have spent the last four months developing and then crush it with the heavy hammer of misunderstood obedience training. You are going to have to read your dog. If you have to pull him from under the bed when it is time for work, you will have to back off and simplify. Like you and anything you are learning, you are not going to learn much if you are dreading it. Be demanding, but still give your dog something to look forward to.

One of the keys to doing the formal training like obedience, force fetch and more advanced training is to start 'happy' and end 'happy'. This works awfully well with dogs. It might not with you since you know what we are doing in between is going to be demanding, but it really puts a dog in the right state of mind. Each day, as you prepare to go out and do your obedience exercises, put your training bumper in your pocket. The bumper should not be the focal point for the dog, so do not wave it around temptingly. You will need the appropriately sized choke chain, preferably the stronger links and not the thin, fine chains. You will also need a good six-foot leash and a 25-foot-long rope with a snap to use as a leash. We just start with the 25-foot cord because it gives us the luxury of using any distance we want, not limiting the work to the six-foot radius. We strongly recommend wearing gloves while doing these exercises, particularly if you have a hard-charging, enthusiastic dog. The rope should be something like the 5/16" or 3/8" nylon boat rope available in all the discount stores. You can cut it to any length and add the kind of snap you prefer on the end. Melt the ends with a candle to seal any knots and prevent unraveling. You do not want a rope so unwieldy that the dog is snagged or stopped while dragging the rope.

If your future work will involve the use of the electric collar, then put a dummy collar on your dog now and for all work you do with the dog. You should not use the live electric collar at this stage at all. There is a whole philosophy out there right now, and a well-known one, by which electric collar stimulation is used on young dogs. We wholeheartedly disagree with this concept. The electric collar can be valuable, though many that do not understand why it was developed consider it a tool of torture. If used as a convenience, then you'll never learn how to actually teach a dog anything, but you'll certainly 'jar' him into it. That will be discussed later--suffice it to say you want to create a very positive association with the sight and application of the collar so put it on every time your dog is going to do obedience or retrieve, just like the leash. Take it off when you are finished.

If at all possible, don't do much of your work in the backyard, unless you have a sizable backyard with enough space that you can be separated from the house, other dogs and other family members. They will be too much of a distraction. When you are teaching your dog something new, as with children, do it so that it is the only thing the dog has on his mind. Later when your dog understands what's going on, you will want to do these exercises in the presence of distractions because your dog must work with you despite those distractions. Find an isolated field or park where you can work without interruption.

Put on the leash, the dummy collar if appropriate, and have your bumper in pocket. Get your dog out, and without rules and commands,

Dummy collar, long leash, choke chain

use an upbeat positive tone of voice and enthusiastically toss a 'happy bumper' your dog runs immediately after. The dog is not at your side being sent on a retrieve, but out with you running after it almost before you toss it. This is fun. Talk to him and be extremely upbeat and happy. When he comes running back, do not make him sit. Just take the bumper and get him excited and toss it out again, preferably as far as you can throw it. Do this three or four times so that your dog is excited and happy, really enjoying what is gong on. At the same time, your dog shouldn't blast back into you and knock you down. He still has to have manners. Do not let this become an obnoxious dog exercise. He can be happy and excited without becoming a monster. If the dog does not bring the bumper back to you, then hold on to the end of the long rope you should use and bring him back to you. Do not make this a training issue, but make it a happy thing to get your dog in the right state of mind. Be creative, but keep the goal in mind: an enthusiastic, willing dog, ready for formal training.

After three or four 'happy bumpers' put the bumper away and begin your work. As stated earlier, keep things simple. Work on one or two things at a time. Don't advance to another command until you have mastered the previous one. Each new command or exercise should build upon and use what you have already done. Make sure your basement is sound and strong before you begin building the first floor. Be patient. Be demanding, and always be fair. Your dog should already know "Heel" and "Sit". "Here" should be pretty well understood, but probably not a conditioned response.

Heel

Your dog should already know that heel means to walk at your side. Your dog should also understand he is expected to sit when you stop. Your dog should be physically developed enough that correction on a leash and choke chain cannot hurt tissues, ligaments, muscles, or bone. Your dog should be strong and in good condition. Your dog should also be mentally capable of focusing and paying attention, and above all, comprehending what you are teaching. You must be able to read your dog well enough to know if he is getting confused or are just being obstinate. You must develop the ability to discern the difference between a dog trying to avoid work and genuinely being overwhelmed by it. If dog training were such a simple thing, books like this would not be necessary. There is much to doing this right.

Your goal is to truly create a conditioned response in your dog. First you teach. Your dog must clearly understand that "heel" means to be in position at your left (or right) side. Once your dog has learned to walk with you and stop with you, challenge his understanding of the position. Do not go or walk as he expects. Go over obstacles that are reasonable. Go through weeds or bushes. Insist that your dog be at your side.

Walk forward, then walk backwards. Require that your dog works to stay at your side. This is most easily accomplished by placing the choke chain right behind the skull at the top of the neck. This position gives

Heel at your side, shoulder to shoulder

you the greatest physical control of the dog. Think of it this way: the fulcrum, or balance point, of a dog is its withers. The neck and head are one side of the balance arm; the back and hindquarters are the other half. The 'pivot point' is the shoulder or withers. If you control one side of the 'arm', then you absolutely control the other half. Balance a ruler on your finger and test this. If you push one side of the ruler up, the other side goes down. If you move one side of the ruler to the left, the other side moves to the right. Use this concept to most easily enforce your dog's position. With the choke chain positioned at the end of the 'balance arm', you can control your dog. If the dog needs to be moved forward to stay with you, don't use tension on the leash, but use short, quick jerks to make the dog work to stay with you. When you stop, give a quick, reasonable jerk up on the leash to drop your dog's bottom to the ground. With some dogs it takes very little pressure on the choke chain, with others a bit more. Your dog will let you know how much it will take. Do not let your dog's head drop to the ground to sniff or otherwise avoid the work at hand. With the chain correctly positioned, you

Dog avoiding the heeling work

can prevent your dog from doing much of anything but respond to you. However, do not put tension on the choke chain, as you will restrict your dog's breathing.

There are some key points to keep in mind throughout these exercises. Do not nag your dog by dragging him along. That is as irritating to the dog as it would be to you if someone lugged you around at the end of a rope. Use quick, crisp movements to make your dog keep up. Your dog should make the effort, not you. When he tries, there is no pressure from the choke chain. When he doesn't, there are quick bursts of pressure, easy to relieve by keeping up with you. This should be a reasonably energetic activity, such that your dog feels your enthusiasm and energy and has the same attitude toward it. Secondly, the timing of command and enforcement is all-important. Poor timing is one of the biggest 'attitude smashers' there is in dog training. If you jerk on your innocent dog first and then give the command, your dog cannot win. He doesn't even have a chance of avoiding the pressure since you never let him know what you wanted first. This is probably the single biggest error the trainer new to dog obedience makes. You must think about what you are doing before you do it, and all the time you are doing it. Put yourself in your dog's shoes. If we jerked your neck and then started walking, you would give up and just wait to get jerked around, or you would decide to resist the pointless, irritating activity. Be sure you give your dog every opportunity to succeed here, and to feel he can learn, improve and accomplish what you are working on together.

The goal for the command "Heel" is to have your dog at your side, regardless of what you are doing. If you are walking, your dog is walking shoulder-to-shoulder beside you. If you are running, your dog is shoulder-to-shoulder. If you stop, change direction, and continue, so does your dog. Be reasonable at this point. We are not training robots, we are training dogs. Do not make unnatural, pointless movements. At the same time, your dog should respond to your movements and make a good effort to maintain position at your side. If your dog is six feet out in front of you and you give the "Heel" command, your dog should come to your side and sit down. This is taught initially very close up. When a dog is sitting in front of you, you should be face to face. If your dog is going to heel to your left side, do not let him go behind you. Step back with your left foot as you give the heel command. With quick jerks on the choke chain, if necessary, move your dog to your left and rotate inwards toward

1. Start with dog sitting in front of you
2. Step back with your left leg to encourage dog to move
3. Step forward to bring dog up to your side parallel with you

4. Dog back into default "Heel" position

you and sit straight beside you. After a few of these exercises you should no longer have to help your dog by stepping back, but have your dog naturally walk around and heel in beside you. Do not allow your dog to turn this into an avoidance game. Often a dog will come in toward you only to keep going behind you another six feet or more. That is why you do not allow your dog to disappear behind you--you cannot control what is happening. Teach the dog from the beginning to just come directly in, turn around and sit down. When running marks and bringing birds back to you, this will keep you from having to worry about where the dog is going with the bird or even having to give any command at all. The dog will bring it back to you, sit down and wait for you to take it.

Your dog should heel and sit in the presence of distractions once he clearly understands your expectations. This means if the neighbor kids are playing an enticing game of catch and you are working your dog, your dog must heel and sit without making this a new battleground. If a robin flies up in front of you, no matter how much you enjoy birdyness in your dog, your dog must heel and sit. He cannot learn that the commands apply unless something really, really interesting comes along. The commands apply always, period. You will want the dog to believe that you mean what you say when you are hunting with him. If you cannot control your dog in the park, you will not control him when the pheasants are flying.

The command will become second nature to the dog if he is required to honor the command as the immediate response to hearing it. This is a training method used by people training for life-and-death situations. The military trains the personnel on the front lines to respond to certain stimuli without thinking a whole bunch about it. If a young soldier thinks about how frightened he is and why he is there and what he can do about it, instead of dropping to the ground at the sound of gunfire, he may not make it. Rescue personnel and emergency response teams do not mull things over, they respond. Their response to specific stimuli is second nature to them; they are conditioned to respond. It is not a demeaning or disrespectful method of teaching people; it is important and useful. And so it is with dogs. If a dog is first taught a command--heel, sit or here--and then taught to respond to the command without mulling it over first, you have a well-trained dog.

The way you create a conditioned response in a dog is relatively simple. Teach first. Then using timing and pressure appropriately and fairly in a consistent and long-term manner. You teach a dog to heel, sit, and come to you with a simple, clear command for each. You use timing such that after the dog hears the command, its next action is to execute that command. We are not talking computer speed here, but if you say to "sit", then the dog needs to drop its bottom. If it takes five seconds to accomplish, the dog is telling you it does not want to do this, or is otherwise resisting you. This may be because you have nagged or created a poor attitude toward work, or because the dog just doesn't want to do it. You can fix either cause by assessing which it is and addressing that. If your dog doesn't like to sit, assuming there are no physical problems that bring about pain for the dog, then ignore your dog's opinion and enforce the response. There is no human we have met yet who enjoys paying taxes, but we all do. Your dog can sit down whether he or she likes it or not.

The final aspect to creating a conditioned response is pressure. In creating a conditioned response in your dog, you are literally getting into his head and creating the synapses or thought patterns in the brain. You can teach your dog to execute a command, and you can make sure the dog carries it out immediately. There is one further key to this concept. A dog can understand what you want. A dog can willingly do as you ask because you have made a habit of making him do it correctly. That is probably as far as most people go when training dogs. The result is a dog that does things pretty well as long as everything is comfortable and familiar. That is the nature of habits. If you take that dog and put him in a stressful or unfamiliar environment, you lose the response in him. Why? Because he is doing something out of habit, not out of a response that is so ingrained that even stress cannot affect it too much. Once your dog knows what you want and knows you will be consistent in what you ask, you add the final element of pressure with the timing of the command. You will not read many books or articles written about this because it can be so easily misinterpreted or taken out of context. We will go on to "Sit" and "Here" to clearly demonstrate the concept of pressure.

Sit

"Sit" means to sit. It does not mean to sit down and get up immediately unless you also give the magic "Stay" command. "Sit" means to drop the bottom and leave it there until released or directed to do something else. Giving the "Stay" makes you feel in control, but have "Sit" actually mean sit and you will be in control. "Stay" works well for staying on a rug in the kitchen or remaining in some location in which you want the dog to be. Sitting should also be a place in your training at which you can require your dog to work to do things correctly for you. A sit should be straight, square with the direction you are facing and at your side, or in front of you squarely, or any other place you give the command. Use this simple exercise to get a very mutually respectful outlook between you and your dog. Respect at this level, so easily achievable, will translate to respect in the field, at a distance, and with the things you plan on teaching down the line. Use that to your advantage, instead of thinking this is not so critical an activity, and allowing sloppiness or lack of thoroughness in your teaching efforts. Conversely, sloppiness here will also translate to the field and be magnified.

When your dog understands what you expect, you can begin to put pressure on your dog for doing something he understands. The plastic whiffle bat or heeling stick is used to accomplish this. As mentioned in previous sections, do not wield the stick as a threatening, "Look what I've got if you aren't a good dog..." The stick should for all practical purposes not exist unless you employ it, and disappear immediately after. You do not want the stick to be the issue. You want the timing and pressure of the command to be the issue--such a critical key concept. Carry the whiffle bat or heeling stick like a shouldered rifle, on the opposite side of your dog. By this time your dog should heel and sit reasonably well with you. Your dog should already understand pressure from the choke chain in the form of quick jerks to reinforce the correct position. The dog should not see or be concerned about the stick.

Have the dog sit a time or two as you stop. Then as you are heeling, stop as you give the "Sit" command and the instant after your dog hears the command, the bat should be used to pop the bottom as pressure to sit. Give the "Sit" command again to make things very clear. This will unnerve some dogs and have little or no affect on others. Find the level of 'pop on the bottom' that makes your dog wish to avoid the pop and sit down more rapidly. Do not allow him to get out of position or flare away from the pressure--that is an avoidance of work. It may be fear, but they must develop the ability to cope with a little pressure and still function (just as we do). Do not overdo this, either--use the

Stick pressure for Sit

appropriate level of pressure to get the good response from your dog and not more nor any less. After use, the bat or stick should return immediately to the shouldered 'does not exist' position.

You don't want to teach your dog to avoid the bat or be worried that you have it. You want to teach your dog to sit as quickly as possible to avoid the pressure of the bat or stick. Otherwise your dog will perform with great response if you have the bat, and poorly without. That is sign of a poor trainer, not a poor dog. Use the bat pressure throughout your training session, but not constantly. If it is constant no matter what your dog does, again your dog cannot win and you will lose the enthusiastic, quick response. Use it enough that your dog begins to try to beat the pressure and not avoid it, and does not lose heart in the whole activity. You will want to make the pressure to sit and heel become a routine in your obedience exercises for weeks or even months. Your goal is to ingrain the quick, "I can beat it!" response in your dog. You might carry the bat and never use it one day, or there might be a day you may have to use it more than you like. You will have to balance your dog's good attitude with the progress in creating the conditioned response. Don't hurry this, but don't take it so slowly you are busier nagging your dog than teaching him to avoid the pressure by responding quickly.

When your dog will sit quickly at your side, have him come toward you and sit in front of you. Use the bat pressure to enforce the quick sit in front of you.   You may have to use the bat to prevent your dog from flaring to one side or another. If your dog anticipates heeling to your left side and starts moving to the left, put the bat down to the left and tap the dog on the ribs or shoulder to move him back to the right. Mix up your work and pressure. If you do things the same way with the same pattern each time, you will be teaching your dog to respond to the pattern and habit, not response to the command alone. This means, do not walk out of your front door and down the block, with three "sits" and four "heels" to the corner every time. If you always step off with your left leg on the command heel, you may be teaching your dog to cue off your leg movement and not the command heel. If you always slow down before giving the sit command and stopping, your dog may cue off your speed and not your command. All of this can interfere with your use of pressure to enforce a command. You will have to stay on your toes to make sure you are not teaching your dog things you do not wish to.

Here

In this exercise, you teach the command that brings your dog to you. We use the command "Here", but you can use any clear command you choose.   The word "Here" will be used throughout, however. Precisely as in the other exercises, it is the response to the command that you are going to create. The timing and enforcement of commands is exactly the same. In this way, you maintain the consistency that teaches your dog that the rules apply 100% of the time. Once your dog is intimately familiar and responsive to this command, you can begin to use it in association with the multiple "toot-toot", or come-in whistle. Once your dog associates the come-in whistle with coming in to you, you can begin to use the whistle alone to bring your dog towards you. Established well in the yard, the come-in whistle is the only way you will communicate with your dog in the field at a distance, in the wind, or when conditions are difficult.

On the leash, tell your dog to sit. Walk in front of your dog and face him or her. Notice again, there is no use of the command "stay". In these exercises it actually can serve to dilute the "sit" command, or any other command, for that matter. The fewer commands you need, the simpler and easier your training can be.

Tell your dog to sit as you walk in front of him. Correct him immediately if he begins to get up and go with you. Stand at a relaxed leash length away. Hold that position for a moment. Do not rush this. If at any time your dog gets up to come to you without being told, correct with the command your dog is not obeying, and that is "Sit", and make him sit again. Do not complicate things with, "NO, I said sit, now you sit." Just give the command he violated and enforce it. Stay, clear, unemotional and simple.

Have dog sitting calmly in front of you

Once you can make your dog wait for you as long as you want, call your dog to you with one simple command. Use the name only if you need to get his attention, but at this point that should not be necessary. "Here" should be given calmly and clearly. Do not bark the command, or any of the commands, because you will then have to always bark a command to get the response you want. Use the tone of voice you would always like to use, and be consistent. Immediately after giving the command, use the leash and choke collar to bring your dog quickly to you. Do not pull or lug, just bring him to you crisply. You should know how to do this now. Make your dog sit directly in front of you. Therefore, the command sequence should go like this: "Here"--quick jerk to you--"Here"--"Sit"--quick sit. As always, bracket the "here" command: command, enforcement, and command. Be aware of cueing the dog with your movement. If each time just as you are ready to give the command, you shift your feet and raise the rope, you will teach the dog to go when you shift your feet and raise your hands. They must respond to the command, not your cues.

Bring the dog crisply in to you

Begin within this easily correctable four- or five-foot distance. Use enforcement proportional to the degree of resistance, if there is any. Do not allow your dog to come to you before you give the command--this is an avoidance of the work. Jumping too early is not a good thing if you allow it to go on. Enthusiasm is good, but it must be controlled. They must respect your commands, and not judge for themselves when they should react. Do not forget this.

Once your dog will come quickly in front of you and sit immediately, begin to vary the small things. Stand to the side of him and call him. Stand with a reasonable obstacle between you and call him. Regardless of the circumstances, your dog must come quickly to you and sit. Do not allow him to evaluate how he should respond. He must just respond NOW. Remember, you are now beginning to create an important conditioned response: "Here" means come here now. Period.

Dog should come willingly to "here" command

When your dog is sitting in front of you, use the command "heel" to get him into the heel position. This should be very easy at this stage.

Your dog should now heel, sit and come to you crisply and consistently. Your dog should come to you immediately, regardless of relative position or any obstacles. Though your dog should want to anticipate your "Here" command, insist that he or she wait as long as necessary until the command is given. Walk out in front of your dog occasionally and do not call him. Instead let him wait a short time, then walk back and continue heeling. He should never develop an anticipation response and second-guess you. That will show up to haunt you at anything you wish to do at a distance. Once your dog knows the "Here" command, you can begin to alternate the 'toot-toot' of the come-in whistle. Eventually,

Dog should go to default "Heel" position without help

work to replace the verbal command with the multiple, crisp whistle, so that you can communicate with your dog at a distance.

To use pressure to create the extremely important conditioned response to "Here" you will again use the choke chain and long cord. Starting close in where you have good leverage, you will use a strong jerk on the cord the instant after you have given the "Here" command. Use the pressure, even if the dog is coming towards you. Again, you want him to react as quickly as possible the instant he hears the response, and you do this by creating pressure he will want to avoid by responding even more quickly. Usually a dog's initial response to this is to anticipate your command and get up and begin coming to you before you give the command. This is rewarding to see, but it is not something you can allow. A dog cannot 'guess' what you are going to ask. He must wait to see what you want.

Heeling and Sitting Off Leash

This should be the easy part now. Your dog will heel, sit, and come, forwards and backwards, through, around and over things. Your dog is learning that there are no other options than compliance, and that every command you give absolutely will be carried out and carried out in short order. With this base, we begin to have some fun.

1.   You will use the choke collar and the four- or six-foot cord attached to it. This way your dog is off leash, but can become 'on leash' instantly. Put the leash on and 'happy' your dog. Begin by holding the cord just like the leash and do the heeling and sitting routine. In the middle of things, drop the cord and continue. If you carry a bat for sit enforcement, remember to carry it on your shoulder, out of sight of your dog. It should not exist when you are not using it and should not exist again the instant after you have used it.

Heel and sit in your mind, exactly as if your dog were on the six-foot lead, in your total control. Require the exact same level of response. At any point if your dog slows in response, correct exactly as if the dog were on lead. Bracket the correction with the command, "Heel"--jerk the dog into place with the short cord--"Heel". Again, correction proportional to degree of resistance, though by this time, any resistance should be viewed very negatively because your dog definitely knows better.

Continue to occasionally reinforce the "heel" and "sit", even if your dog is doing the commands well. This, used in reasonable moderation, serves to more firmly establish the conditioned response in your dog. It helps to make "sit" an unquestioned command, and make it become a subconscious response. The same will go for "heel" and "here". Consistency and repetition will make it become second nature for your dog, though this does not happen in a few days. It is a result of your consistency and commitment to the effort.

This key aspect of reinforcing a known command is what sets successful trainers apart from those who are not. They go to the extra effort to entrench a thought process in the dog, and this process is to carry out any command given. This "entrenchment" is purely a result of the relationship of respect that has been established between dog and handler. This respect arises from consistency of action, the requirement of adherence to commands, and the repetition through which every dog learns.

2. If at any point your dog regresses in the exercises with the short cord, immediately put the long cord back on and simplify things. Re-establish the response level in your dog. If you have to do this, that is normal, but it does mean you didn't make the headway you thought you had to begin with. Do the leash work for a month if necessary, but if it is dragging on, you need to question how effective your enforcement and correction techniques have been. They may have been overly harsh, or more likely, not strict enough. Every dog is different, so do what it takes for your dog. It is more humane to get the point across clearly and quickly than by slowly trying to nag it into them. Nagging creates resentment, and that creates a huge packet of problems. Do not nag, do not abuse. Just communicate the point clearly.

3. Once you have reached the point at which there is no difference between the six-foot cord and the short 12-inch cord, continue the exercises with the short cord on. It will be available for correction and enforcement, but not used otherwise. Do everything you do with your dog with the short cord hanging off the collar. The cord will mean nothing to your dog. This is now equivalent to off-leash work. We leave the short cord on for months, sometimes years, depending on how much correction a dog is determined to get. You might consider making it a somewhat permanent fixture when you and your dog are doing things

together. This will allow you to enforce commands at any time easily. You will know at what point in the future it should come off, if ever.

Getting Your Dog to Come to You at a Distance

This is the single most requested aspect of dog obedience. How do you get your dog to come to you all the time? Can you imagine a seeing-eye dog deciding not to return to his person? Or a hunting dog picking up a goose and high-tailing it for the hills? That would be very unacceptable. Therefore, it is important that you approach this training segment as if it were a life-or-death issue, because it is. If your dog starting chasing a _____ (rabbit, squirrel, pheasant, stick, ball, you fill in the blank) across a road with traffic, could you call him off 100% of the time? You should be able to. That is the standard you need to have in your mind as you go into this.

It is absolutely critical that you passed all the performance checks that came before this. Your dog must believe in you and your commands. Your dog must heel, sit off leash under all circumstances, forwards, backwards, in circles, on yucky stuff, near loud noises, around tempting distractions. If you are shaky here, go back. Your dog should also understand clearly the command you used for coming.

1.   For this element, you need the longer cords. Ideally, you should begin with one about 25 feet in length, and graduate to a 50-foot cord. This is the really funny part to watch, especially the first few times people try it. Be prepared to look pretty silly. Do what it takes to get this point across to your dog, however.

Attach the 25-foot cord to your dog's choke chain. Knots come undone at inappropriate times, so use a snap attachment if at all possible. 'Happy' your dog again with the long cord dragging. Begin your heeling and sitting exercises with the cord in your hand and the remainder dragging behind you. Do not trip. This will get your dog in the right 'state of mind', and that is one of immediate response to you. After enough heeling and sitting, backwards, forwards, etc., begin the initial "here" exercise you now know so well. Do it just as if you had the six-foot cord on. Tell your dog "Sit", walk in front by about six feet, wait an appropriate time, give the command "Here" and require the immediate response.

Do not allow your dog to use the rope as any distraction. In your mind and his, it should be no different than the short cord or the leash, so treat it as such. Maintain the same standards--quick response in coming and sitting. Begin to increase the distance between the two of you. Do not do it all at once. Go only five or ten feet in one day. Do that until it is just the same as if your dog were six feet in front of you.

Gradually extend the distance the full length of the rope. Shorten the distance, if necessary, if you begin to lose the response you need. You should be in a position to enforce with an abrupt jerk on the long rope if necessary. Still, do not let your dog come before being called. You should use gloves during this exercise, for obvious reasons.

2.   Once you have mastered the 25- and 50-foot "Here", you are ready to take a new step. At this point you will have to use your judgment. Perhaps the 25-foot cord is all you will need. The 50-foot cord introduces a greater distance for you to require good response from your dog. This may or may not be necessary, but we like to use the 50-foot. Now you begin to step outside the standard training regimen. Allow your dog to drag the long cord. By this time, he should tend to ignore it. 'Happy' your dog, maybe heel and sit a little, then take your dog for a walk in the park or the field with the cord on. Keep the distance between you and your dog less than the cord length. Be prepared to step on it if you need. When your dog is generally walking or sniffing, call him. You might use his name to get his attention: "Spot, here." As you do this, be in a position to enforce the command. Step on the cord if your dog keeps going. Bracket again: "Here"--abrupt jerk on the cord--"Here". Make your dog come directly to you and sit.

Do this exercise in as many environments and conditions as you possibly can. Introduce as many distractions as you can. Be as inventive as possible to entice your dog not to comply, while being prepared to demand complete compliance. Through repetition and consistency, your dog will learn not to second-guess your commands, even under unique circumstances.

Wrapping Up Each Training Session

Do obedience work for no more than about ten minutes. Though you may be intense and ready for great progress, your dog is not. A dog's brain can take only so much, and after that you are nagging and boring him. Worse, you are making him begin to dislike the work, not because you are too tough or too demanding, but because you don't know when enough is enough. Do not reach a point of diminishing returns, but stop when the dog is still absorbing and retaining the ideas. Have a goal with each session in your mind, before you begin. For example, plan on having the heeling and sitting go very well, including over obstacles. Then get some very good responses on "Here" without your enforcement. When you get that, quit.

Some days you will get just what you would like to get. Another day, your dog will act like you got the wrong animal out. Take what is there. If it is a bad day for your dog, then accept less but end on a successful note of some kind. If the "here" exercises are a struggle, then end with two or three good responses to "here" at a close distance of a couple of feet and quit. When you are finished with the last command or exercise, pull the bumper from your pocket, give a genuine and throaty "Goooood dog" and throw the happy bumper. You want to relieve all pressure from the dog's mind and to have him once again run whole-heartedly after the bumper, without rules. Throw several of these with great enthusiasm and fun. Then put your dog up. You will find after starting 'happy' and ending 'happy' each session, your dog will come to really enjoy these training sessions, even though you are demanding in between. You are giving him something to look forward to, he trusts you and knows it is coming. This way he is even more willing to work hard for you.

Obedience is a way of life, not a training session. Obedience does not imply servitude or any lack of respect. It does imply that your dog understands its behavioral guidelines and incorporates them into its daily activities. That can be hunting, competing, or hanging out with the kids. You are subject to these kind of 'behavioral guidelines.' Why shouldn't anyone's dog be subject to the same thing? If you came to our house and jumped on one of our children, or chased our other dogs, or ran through the field busting all the birds before we were ready, we would not invite you over again. Our long-time question has always been, then why should an animal developed to work with mankind not be subject to behaving within its abilities just like the more advanced humans are?

There is a school of thought that it is cruel to teach a dog its job is to comply. That theory holds that dogs should hunt or coexist with us out of love and desire to please. It has been shown time and time again with children, that those children raised in a loving environment who were also taught to respect themselves, their family members, and the community around them have fewer problems in their adult lives. Children who have to get up each morning, go to school, behave in school, do their homework and clean their rooms tend to better in college than those who never had to do things that they did not really want to do. Most of us have had our greatest moments after we worked very hard at something, endured unpleasant times but coped, learned and became more because of it. Our greatest sense of value and happiness comes from contributing and from disciplining ourselves to become more, to be better. There are few living creatures that do not want a sense of accomplishment and a sense of value. We earn it though effort, discipline, and struggle, and finally, achievement. In truly understanding and caring for an animal, as that is the greatest gift for your children, it is also the greatest gift for your dog.

Chapter 9
Whoa Training

By the time you begin working on formal obedience, your dog should be very familiar with the concept of standing still on all four feet to the command "Whoa", or whatever simple command you choose to use. For the last three or four months you should have been working on whoa for at least a couple of moments almost every day. There should be no association with bumpers, birds, retrieving or anything, except just stand there until you release the dog.

Just as you teach your dog to heel and sit long before you expect to control him in the field, you should whoa your dog long before you expect him to be steady on point. Very young dogs, even dogs that are only a year or so old cannot or perhaps should not be expected to be steady on point. That is like asking a teenage boy not to stare at a bikini-clad beauty queen. Ask what you want, but the maturity can give you only so much control. Your job is not to make the very young dog be steady. Your job is to build into the young dog the tools you will use to enforce the steadiness when the time is appropriate and the dog can handle that level of control.

There is an evolution in the whoa process. First the dog is taught to stand still with the whoa command. This can be done in a variety of ways. We prefer to start it on the GRT board as described in the earlier chapter. The board serves to define clearly in the dog's mind that it must stay in one place on the board. The board initially makes a definable area for the dog. On the board is okay, off the board is not. Once the dog understands the board and its significance, you can carry the board with you when you go to run marks, take a walk, or go somewhere. Get out of your vehicle, put the board down and whoa your dog for a minute or two. Teach the dog that whenever you are 'whoaing' it, it stands still regardless of what else is going on. The only thing you want to avoid is rewarding the whoa with a retrieve or making some association with going to get something and standing still. Begin simply by teaching your dog it has to stand still.

When your dog will stand still reliably on the board, walk out in front of the dog. Scuff around in the cover and kick, as if there was… a bird or something in there. You are getting your dog accustomed to watching you flush a bird, or at least going through the motions. Teach your dog it must remain in place no matter what you do. If the dog comes off the board to check what you are doing, calmly place the dog back on the board standing, reinforce with the whoa command, and see if you can return to your 'flushing' activities. This may take a day or two or a couple of weeks. Continue working with patience to make your dog remain in place as you go about various things in front of the dog. You will also wish to avoid coming up from behind the dog as you walk out to kick through the cover because this may create an almost competitive aspect to getting to the cover, and your dog may want to 'race' you to it.

By the time you have effectively taught your dog to stand still and wait for you to finish your gyrations out front, you must challenge your dog. This is most easily started on the GRT board. You do not always have to whoa on the board, but in the beginning it makes things clearer to the dog. The board makes the initial challenge easier to understand and correct as well. The whoa should always be done with the leash on, and also the dummy collar if your other work involves that. Place your dog on the board and whoa it. Walk out front. Be patient and deliberate. Give the whoa command and pull on the leash gently as if you are trying

Challenge your dog to remain on the board

159

to pull the dog off the board. The dog should attempt to resist your efforts to move it off the board. View resistance as a very positive thing. Now pull with enough force to actually pull your dog off the board. When he comes off the board, correct him as if he had intentionally walked off the board. Firmly give the whoa command and place the dog back on the board. This will make your dog even more resistant the next time you try to pull him off.

If the dog does not resist your pull, either you have been too mild in teaching him to stand on the board, or you have not whoa'd for a long enough period of time to make it a comfortable, understood thing for the dog to do. Go back on whoa for several more days before challenging the dog again. Keep in mind that this takes months to do. If your dog does understand whoa and still does not resist your challenge, you may have to make your correction for coming off the board more severe, so that your dog will certainly want to avoid being corrected. You can have a more severe correction by picking the dog up by the collar and its tail and setting it abruptly back on the board. You do not want this to become too much of a punishment, since standing needs to be a positive thing in the long run. Patience and consistency are your biggest allies in this endeavor, rarely increasing force.

Accustom your dog to being primped while whoaing. Run your hand along their back and under their tail. Push against their hind legs in a forward direction with the whoa command to further develop the resistance in the dog to forward movement. Walk out in front of them; kick around in the cover. Walk back, primp a little, and walk out front again. Make your dog get used to many different things going on, all while he remains motionless. As with obedience, if you do this exactly the same way every time, you will teach your dog to whoa only under certain behaviors of yours. If things change, he will not understand he is still expected to stand still.

When your dog is whoa'd well enough that you can really challenge him with the leash or your movements and he remains steady, it is time to up the ante on his ability to remain motionless. There is still no place nor reason to introduce birds to the equation yet. You want your dog so conditioned to stand still that when it is time for birds to be a factor, your dog may not even consider not honoring your instruction to stand still. It is much easier to work in the field with a dog trained with that perspective than it is to try and get a dog to stand still while it wants nothing more than to go chase a bird. Here are several things to do with your dog in the whoa process:

• As your dog is walking along with you, give the whoa command. Your dog may understand and stop in a standing position, or may not understand and continue walking or even sit down. Enforce the stand as usual. A few times of this and your dog will learn to stop and remain standing when it hears the whoa command. It is not advisable to do this in the middle of obedience drills, because your dog is responding to pressure to sit or move, not stand still. Do not confuse issues if you don't have to. If you plan on teaching your dog to honor the point of another dog, you will have to enforce the whoa even though your dog is not the one pointing. Begin the process now by having him stop and stand because you instructed him to.

• Whoa your dog and then, when you are out in front of him, toss a bumper along the ground in front of him. Give the whoa command simultaneously. Correct if the dog even moves a foot. This is the beginning of teaching a dog to withstand enticement it does not want to resist. Start by doing it only once a whoa session, but up the number until you can toss the bumper anywhere and the dog will remain in place with the whoa command. Do not give any signals, cues, or commands that might lead the dog to believe you actually want him to retrieve what you have

Entice the dog to move with a tossed bumper

thrown. As always, if you start to loose ground and your dog is not nearly steady enough, go back and simplify. Do not push this any faster than what works with your dog. Patience is your best ally here, not force or frustration.

• Use the wind direction to your advantage. A hunting dog will always be checking what is on the wind. If you face your 'whoaing' dog into the wind, it will not have to make any effort to check the wind. If you place the dog crossways to the wind or with the wind coming from behind the dog, it will naturally try to turn its head or body to be in a position to get more out of the breeze. In all training with a field dog, think about the terrain and environment, and be aware of the impact of the small things important to a dog that may be no thought to you.

It is important to challenge your dog and its staunchness during whoa'ing. If you present challenges like pulling the dog gently off the board, or tossing something around in front of him, he will learn to withstand a desire to move. You are going to want the dog to withstand his desire to move when he is faced with the scent of sight of a live bird in the field. Acquaint him with that level of self-control where it is manageable and you can teach the dog to restrain himself.

Whoa Breaking

As with the force fetch and other training techniques, there are a variety of ways people finish the whoa breaking of a pointing dog. The pointing breed people have successfully whoa broken dogs for a very long time and do it well. It is our contention that not all of those methods are advisable for the retriever, not because they don't work, but because they don't always fit in with the philosophy used throughout the rest of the training program of the retriever. The methods in which dogs are being restrained or harnessed have never demonstrated their usefulness to us. The barrel is a good way to reinforce whoa, however. We have found that the 55-gallon industrial barrels we use for doghouses work well.

Place the dog up on the barrel

Keep the dog on the barrel

*Dog should relax and allow primping
fairly shortly*

Be wary of metal drums, as they can be quite uncomfortable to dog's feet in very hot or cold weather. The drum should not be too slippery, either. The barrel should be held steady so that it is possible for the dog to remain standing on top of the barrel without having to be a circus acrobat as well.

At first you will probably have to lift your dog onto the barrel. This is often another humorous thing to watch at the beginning. Dogs are not entirely comfortable standing atop a rounded object. They will try to leap off, sit down, or very often, lean on you. None are allowable, of course. You must give the whoa command and make your dog do what it always does with that command: stand still.

Don't place yourself so closely that the dog can lean on you, and restrain your dog with collar and tail-hold so that it can't leap off. Enforce the command that should be well understood by now--"do not move your feet". It may take a moment or two, or even a day or two, until your dog is mentally willing to stand up there on that barrel. Like it or not, however, the dog can and must learn to stand still.

The beauty of the barrel is that the dog no longer has the luxury of inching its feet a little or readjusting its position. It has to remain motionless. The dog falling off the barrel or jumping off should be viewed as a refusal to honor the command to stand still, and the dog should be corrected by abrupt placement, by tail and collar, back on the barrel. This teaches complete lack of movement better than anything we have tried.

We had one funny little dog named Rosy that used to have us in stitches when we whoaed her on the barrel. You could put her up on the barrel, (and she is a staunch pointing dog in the field), step away, and literally count the seconds until she fell over off the barrel on her side-- never moving a foot! She was like a domino that merely tipped over, completely rigid. We have no explanation for why a dog can be whoaed on the ground, staunch in the field, and incapable or at least unwilling to stand upright on the barrel. It was always comic relief when we'd give it another try, however.

The dog stays willingly on the barrel without help

The dog must clearly understand the concept of remaining in place on all four feet. It must do so even if bumpers are tossed or someone is kicking cover all around in front of him. The dog must also stop and stand when given the whoa command while it is walking or trotting. We are now in a position to challenge him further. Often we start with the barrel when we introduce the 'bird factor' to the whoa. This is so the dog really knows it is not supposed to move. The dog is on the leash and collar, placed on the barrel and given the whoa command. This should be very 'old hat' by now. The dog, in its mind, should be relaxed and prepared to stand there for however long you plan on doing silly things around it. Now you set a live bird down about six or eight feet in front of it. Ideally this should be a quail that is not going to run off or fly away, or a pigeon that can only walk around. You do not want to start with some big horrendously tempting or frightening bird. Instead you want a bird that is readily visible, smells good and will stick around, even if you

Put the whoa to the test with a live bird

must clip its wings or prevent it from flying off.

Don't say anything unless you have to. If your dog stays in place, then be quiet and don't interfere. If your dog begins to move, is thinking about moving or actually does move, use the whoa command and put him back in place immediately. Treat the consideration of movement just as you would actual movement--get into your dog's head if you can. Do not be so slow and unprepared that you actually allow your dog to go catch the bird. You will undo weeks or more of your training. That is why the dog is wearing the leash and you have practiced this many times prior. The bird should be moving around and making things so very tempting for the dog. Your dog is to remain in place and not move one bit. Correct any movement with the whoa and an abrupt replacement by the collar and tail. If the bird moves behind you or towards the dog too closely, bump it back in place with your foot and maintain your dog's staunch position. In the beginning, do this only for a moment or two. As your dog learns the drill, you can extend the time. Never allow your dog to get the bird. When you are finished, have someone pick up the bird and put it away, then release your dog and leave the area. Never teach your dog that if it is patient enough it can still go and get the bird. It never gets the bird, not until it is flushed and shot and only then is the dog sent on a retrieve. Much later, the mature hunting dog will learn to pick up live cripples or just go after a bird you want it to pick up, but that is the job of the force fetch, not the enthusiasm level of the young dog.

Dogs are released from the whoa for three reasons: because you are finished whoaing and they can walk freely with you, to continue hunting, or to retrieve a shot bird. They are not released to have fun chasing a live bird around. Unless that is what you want in the field, do not teach them that now.

Whoa breaking with the live bird serves several purposes. It shows the dog what behavior you want in the presence of a live bird--stillness. It also familiarizes your dog with the presence of a live bird. That way, when you begin your upland work, your dog will not be too excited or over-stimulated by the smell and presence of a live bird. As mentioned many times in other training sequences, do your up-front work in the yard thoroughly, and things go easily and smoothly in the field.

Use of the Collar in Whoa Breaking

No work should be done with an electric collar until the dog is fully collar conditioned. That chapter should be read and so thoroughly understood that it could be recited before considering its use here. The collar is not mandatory for whoa breaking, but it is an additional tool that can be used in the field if desired. Some dogs may require a little more pressure to hold their point than others may and the collar can be of value with the hard-charging aggressive dogs. The use of the collar in whoa breaking is slightly different than in obedience and control work. The basic concept for the dog is the same. First the dog must understand the command, in this case "whoa." The dog must have had pressure to honor the command that it clearly understood; again, in this case the abrupt lift by the collar and tail as the dog was placed back in the proper position. The dog must know how to do everything first, before the collar pressure is introduced. Your dog should be familiar with the live bird in front of it and with being pulled off the board and repositioned and corrected. These drills should not be just reasonably familiar to the dog, but in fact ingrained. Otherwise the use of the collar can backfire on you.

Whoa your dog. At this point you should know which would be the best way to tempt your dog, if anything will. You may wish to place the board in the yard and walk your dog over it. Give the whoa command just as the dog reaches the board. Your dog will know to stop and remain on the board. If he doesn't, you have an avenue to introduce the collar pressure. You may wish to use the live bird flapping around in front of the dog or you may actually have to pull the dog off the board and then correct him for not remaining on the board. To use collar pressure on whoa breaking requires that your dog leave the initial position in which you placed him, or where he knows he is supposed to be. You will introduce pressure on the dog to return to that initial spot. You are ingraining on the dog's mind that once he 'sets up' he cannot leave until he is directed to. Leaving brings about bad things, remaining in place brings about good things. It is that simple logic you must keep in the front of your mind.

Collar pressure in whoa breaking should not be overwhelming. The dog that requires a high level of stimulation in collar conditioning will not require that same level here. The pressure is not to generate a quick conditioned response as it is in collar conditioning. It is to convince the dog that remaining in place is the only thing to do. If you use high levels of stimulation on the collar-conditioned dog, he will revert to the responses you taught him to give in the obedience work, and it likely your dog will just sit down when you use it. That is the last thing you want a good pointer to do. Instead, use a level of stimulation that is high enough to genuinely irritate the dog, but not so high that it reverts to obedience responses. Too low a stimulation will teach the dog to completely ignore your collar pressure in whoaing the dog, which is probably the worst thing you could do. We have found that settings between 1 and 3 work with most dogs, using the 2 primarily.

Using the live bird temptation, the sequence of events for your dog's mind need to go like this: Whoa the dog. Have someone toss the live bird out in front of your dog. For the sake of illustration let's say we have a big chukar that is flapping its wings and jumping up and down. Your dog takes two steps off the board. You of course have hold of the leash so the dog cannot break and get the bird. You give the whoa command clearly to your dog and then hold the button on continuous (not momentary). As you hold the button down, you make the dog re-establish its initial positioning by placing him back in position. You immediately let go of the button when the dog is back in place. If the dog tries to sit, do not let him. If the dog tries to resist and go get the bird, you may have to up the level of stimulation or make sure your timing is correct, since you are not 'convincing' the dog he needs to remain in place. If your dog screeches and panics you have the collar set too high. Drop it to a more appropriate setting. The goal is to make your dog understand he has no choice but to remain in place, no matter how much he wants to go get the bird. Collar condition your dog to whoaing with collar pressure in the yard. Do it with birds, do it with the walking whoa, do it if you have to force your dog to fail so you can correct him. That does not seem imminently fair, but it is the only way to let your dog know there are consequences for not remaining in place. If your dog is worth two cents, he will want to go get a wild bird in the field. If you develop the tools to control that situation in the yard, you won't have a dog breaking the point and chasing wild birds when you aren't right there to stop him. Collar pressure on whoa should always be a 'nag' to resume the position, not a jolt. Nag the dog back into its original position and remove the pressure immediately. This is the same way you will reinforce whoa in the field while actually hunting birds. Condition yourself to handle whoa this way, so if your dog begins to creep or break on a bird, you are prepared to use the low setting nag to get him back into the whoa position. As with all collar work, your timing is critical. Don't allow the dog to walk forward. Remember you need the transmitter, reach for it, grab the dog, yell whoa and then remember to hold the button down, drop the button when you pick up the dog and make the whole thing a confusing mess! Be prepared, and hold the button down as you return the dog to its position. You might try some dry runs before actually having to correct your dog.

Whoa breaking is not teaching a dog to point. It is a tool to use when a dog points a bird but does not want to remain at point. Whether it is a pointing retriever or an English pointer, the really good dogs are aggressive and bold about wild birds. Few naturally hold a five-minute point because it's so fun. Fun for those dogs is getting the bird. It is training that creates the dog that will hold a point for an extended period of time. Of course there are some pointing dogs that hold points for longer times without all the whoa breaking, but more often than not they are the ones that aren't going to break ice to retrieve the bird they pointed for ten minutes.

Honoring

Pointing retrievers can be taught to honor the point of another dog like any other pointer. With retrievers it does not always come very naturally to stand back and let another dog have all the fun. Some find it unthinkable, literally. With time and opportunity it can be taught to most pointing retrievers. A dog must be whoa broken to be taught to honor. You must be able to give the whoa command when the dog is going along and have him stop and honor the command, even if he isn't pointing anything. The pointer trainers use silhouettes to teach dogs to honor. A cutout of a dog pointing is placed in the field or pops up when the dog walks near. When the dog sees the 'pointing dog' it is given the whoa command and made to remain in place. Done repetitively, this teaches the dog to whoa upon the sight of a pointing dog. It is a good idea and it works. If you have no other pointing dogs with which you can train, it may be your only way to teach your dog to honor.

Eventually you will have to have your dog honor the point of another dog, if you plan on ever hunting with other people and their dogs.

Once your dog is whoa broken then it will take time and repetition to teach him to apply it on the honor in the field. When you do your upland work as described in Chapter 13, you will need to know where the bird is and make sure the other dog will wind it first. When the other dog (most hopefully trained as well as yours) points the bird, you whoa your dog and enforce the whoa through the entire process, including flushing, shooting, and the retrieval by the other dog. It will take time, consistency and a lot of training to ingrain the natural honor in your dog, but it is very achievable and a whole lot of fun in actual hunting.

In summary, whoa breaking is not teaching a dog to point. You could whoa break a Doberman pinscher, but it will not make the dog point a bird. It is the tool you use to develop and reinforce the staunch point. Whoa breaking is not a quick training technique you work on for a few weekends before hunting season. It is something you should ideally work on all year before hunting season. It is not a forceful process, but a process of attrition: consistency and repetition. You do it until it becomes a conditioned response in your dog, and you will rarely have to say a word to your dog in the field. Do not teach your dog during the process that it is rewarded by a retrieve--that is a separate exercise. Get creative and enjoy this process as well, and you will be impressed by your own dog when you go hunting. The extra effort will be pay off tenfold.

Chapter 10
Whistle Training

The use of the whistle allows you to control your dog at distances beyond those your voice can carry, in windy weather, and in water as well. It is important to understand, however, that the whistle training session assumes you have done much work with your dog before this point. An untrained dog should not be started with whistle training; instead, the whistle should add to the dog's repertoire of commands.

Before beginning this program, your dog should have all the basic obedience down completely. This means your dog should heel and sit, on or off leash. Your dog should come immediately when called, and you should have a command specifically for coming to you. Your dog should do all of these things in the presence of distractions as well as without. This is going to be important because we are going to use the good obedience behavior to teach the whistle control. Take the time to make sure this is solid before proceeding.

Tools Required for Exercises

You will be performing both basic obedience and field exercises in this program. To accomplish this you will need:

• Choke chain and a piece of nylon rope a foot or two in length to attach to your dog's choke chain. This rope should have a snap attachment for attaching to the choke chain. The rope should be very light, but strong.

• The same rope mentioned above, but in lengths of approximately 25 and 50 feet. This rope should have a snap attachment for attaching to the choke chain.

• At least two good field whistles. These can be found in your pet supply stores, sporting goods catalogs, and dog training supply websites. A commonly used brand is the Roy Gonia clear whistle. If you are going to be in conditions in which it will be difficult for sound to carry, like fog, wind, running water, etc., make sure you have a whistle designed for this application. Louder is not necessarily better, but penetrating is the goal. Don't blow your whistle with someone standing in front of you. A whistle intended to carry a long way can actually hurt human ears close up.

• The plastic whiffle bat or heeling stick.

The Goals of this Exercise

The objective of this training program is to be able to use the whistle to control your dog at a distance. In your mind, this distance should range from six inches to several hundred yards. By control, we mean that your dog will stop on the whistle, and with another whistle command, come back toward you. Notice the use of the phrase 'toward you'. The 'come-in' whistle can be used to bring your dog all the way to you, or just to bring your dog in your direction until directed to do otherwise. Your dog's response to the whistle, at any distance, should be exactly the same as it would be to your verbal commands at your side or very close to you. Do not let distance dilute the crisp response from your dog. "Sit" means sit. Now. "Here" means come this way. Now.

It is important that you have already established the strong relationship of respect with your dog before you begin this aspect of training. The more firmly that your dog believes in you and your insistence on compliance, the easier this whole exercise will be. As a matter of fact, the key to the success of whistle training is the same key to the success of anything you do with your dog. You need to have created the conditioned response in your dog to follow your orders. Once you have the fundamentals of obedience, and so the complete respect of your dog, you will merely teach the dog another command for the same actions he or she already knows. In our training program, the whistle introduction is virtually unnoticed by the dogs, because they are tending to the business of doing their job. They are conditioned to carry out the commands, so whether they are told to sit or whistled to sit, they are expected to sit.

Make sure your dog is very sound in the obedience basics as you prepare to teach the use of the whistle. You will find this is a simple aspect to introduce to your dog. You can teach your dog to do many things on the whistle, using the teaching technique you will learn now.

Beginning Exercises

To make the concept of reacting to the whistle even easier, you are going to take your basic obedience tools and add some small variations to them. You do not need your whistles around your neck yet. They can sit patiently on your table-top until you do a few more days worth of work. Of course, wearing whistles does make you look and feel like a dog trainer, so if you always wear them, go right ahead. Go back to the six-foot leash and choke collar. Do the standard heeling and sitting routines: vary speed, direction, introduce obstacles, go backwards, etc., etc. Review the "Here" routines by having your dog sit and wait for different intervals, never coming until directed to do so. Have him come to you over obstacles, at unusual angles, etc. Now we will add a few variations. Do only one at a time, and do not move until you have installed the new things as solidly as the basic exercises.

1.   With the six-foot leash, 'happy' your dog first. Remember this is to put your dog in a positive and willing state of mind. 'Happy' for a very short span of time, 20-40 seconds, just long enough to get your dog in a good spirit, then begin work. On leash, begin the heeling and sitting exercises. Your dog should stop when you stop, and when you command to sit. Now add a variation to that by giving your dog the command to sit while you continue to walk. Be prepared to enforce the command. If your dog does not sit immediately, correct. Carrying the plastic bat or heeling stick will allow for quick corrections.

The bat should be carried on your shoulder, in your free hand, like a rifle. It should not be apparent to your dog, except for the brief second it is employed on his bottom. It should immediately go back to the rifle position on your shoulder. That bat must never be waved around. It is intimidating and your dog will be thinking more about avoiding the bat than doing the work. Use it only for the popping noise it makes and the effect it has on your dog. It should be very quick. The bat or stick is not used to hurt your dog, but it is effective because of the sound and feel it has. Use it on yourself to demonstrate this effect. Use this to correct any slow response on a sit. This is critical for the result you want of having a dog sit on a whistle at a long distance, particularly with distractions or the enthusiasm of the chase he or she is on at the time.

Begin by walking slowly the first few times you require your dog to sit, while you continue to move. This makes teaching the concept of your dog stopping independently easier for your dog. As this is mastered, you can increase your speed. If your dog does not sit or hesitates, quickly repeat the command, step back to your dog, use the bat to force the sit, give the "Sit" command again and continue moving forward. Do more traditional sits in which you stop also, then perform the 'moving sit' again. Intersperse the two until your dog will sit every time you give the command, regardless of your motion.

You are teaching your dog to honor the sit command under unusual circumstances. This is the first step in the process of whistle training. Continue to perform obedience exercises and create interesting versions of "sit" yourself. The idea is to have the dog carry out the sit command when other things are going on. Another good place to introduce this concept is in the "Here" exercise.

2.   On the six-foot lead, tell your dog to "Sit" and walk in front, holding the lead at almost full extension. Give the command "Here". Require that your dog come quickly toward you. Back up after giving the command and keep going backwards, requiring that your dog continue toward you. Stop and allow your dog to come right to you and give the command "Sit". Get your dog used to your going backwards in this way. Do it a number of times until he is clear what you are doing.

Once your dog will continue to come towards you as you walk or run backwards, and sit immediately upon reaching you, it is time to introduce the sit on a 'come-in'. With the six-foot leash, tell your dog to sit, walk in front of the dog and face him, as you have been doing. Just as before, give the "Here" command and begin to move rapidly backwards. Your dog should be trotting after you. Give the command "Sit", and be prepared to enforce it immediately. If your dog sits, continue backward and stop a good ten or 15 feet away. If your dog hesitates, correct immediately by going calmly but quickly back toward him, pulling up on the leash and giving the bracketed command "Sit"--pull up abruptly on leash--"Sit". Teach your dog to sit in the middle of transit toward you. Work on this exercise until you can put on the longer rope, then go the full rope length away, still holding on to the rope, call the dog, give a "Sit" command somewhere in the middle and have your dog sit immediately. Be patient and consistent. If you work on this almost every training session, through repetition you will condition your dog to sit under any reasonable circumstance.

It is a little frustrating to be going into whistle training and not even getting to use the whistle yet. You will find this is going to work out well for you, however, provided you take each step in order. You are evolving another conditioned response in your dog's mind, literally creating the synapse path in the brain that will be used in the whistle training of your dog. Often, people are impatient in formal training programs, because the process does not move at a pace they enjoy. The pace you may personally enjoy is irrelevant to the effective education of the canine brain. The purpose of this portion of the training is to teach your dog, through repetition and requirement of quick response, to sit on command while moving or while just wanting to move. This is key to stopping a dog on a dead run after something he wants very much. It can also save his life if you need to stop him from going somewhere that may be dangerous, like a busy street.

Don't teach your dog to stop on a whistle while on his way to a marked retrieve. This has to be one of the biggest mistakes people make using whistles. It is fine to have control over your dog, but it's another thing to send your dog on a retrieve---something you have taught him to do with great enthusiasm and heart--only to stop him for no reason besides you just felt like it. That can ultimately be very disheartening to a good dog. We once had a young man new to dog training join us for puppy basics. He had a real nice young pup with a great attitude about retrieving and everything else. Though he trained with us occasionally, he also read all the books there were out there on training his pup. He really liked the ones that told him about using the whistle on his baby dog, and teaching them to stop to the whistle. To prove how well this was working one day, he threw a bumper for his dog, sent her and then blew the whistle when she was en route. She slowly stopped, turned around and sat down, head hanging, obviously disappointed. He was just beaming. Then he gave her a "Back" and sent her on towards it. She got up and loped out to it and brought it back. His joy was huge. When he came out a month or so later, we were running marks with the dogs. He sent his dog on a mark, and she trotted out towards it. The first and shorter mark she got. On the second one, a little longer, she made it about two thirds of the way and then began to smell around, basically having quit the retrieve altogether. He was dumb-founded. He had no idea why his dog was behaving so poorly. His dog wasn't misbehaving, she was doing what she had been taught to do. The joy of the enthusiastic retrieve had been literally ripped from this young dog, just so he could feel like he was controlling the dog. Never lose sight of the ultimate objective. Dogs are handled on marked retrieves only when there is some danger to the dog or the dog is completely off track. Those occurrences are rare. If it's necessary to stop the dog, it doesn't do any damage to the dog's attitude.

Progress Test

Put the long cord on your dog, but don't hold onto it. Let your dog drag it with him. 'Happy' your dog. Head out on a walk to the park or field. Have your dog heel at your side. Give the "Sit" command as you continue to walk. Does your dog sit? Keep walking until you are a good 20 feet beyond the length of the rope you have been using. Stop and call your dog. Let your dog go 15 or 20 feet and give the "Sit" command. Does your dog sit? Call him again, let him walk six more feet and give the "Sit" command again. Does he sit? If not, use the long cord and go back to the exercises. Your dog should sit as many times as you command on his way to you. The sit is not a one-time shot. If your dog does pass this test, release him to walk freely around you on your walk. Keep the dragging cord very near you. As your dog is inspecting the flora and fauna, give a clear command to "Sit". This is a very key response. Does your dog sit, turn around and look at you, or completely ignore you? This tells you how solidly you have the "Sit" in your dog's mind. If your dog does anything but sit, reinforce immediately: "Sit", make him sit, "Sit". You are not ready to proceed until your dog does all of these things repeatedly.

Do not go on until you have a dog that sits at a distance, when told, and when he doesn't really want to sit. Use the long rope to your advantage here. Take all your walks with the long rope on. When your dog is actively doing something within rope range, give the command "Sit" while simultaneously stepping on the rope. Do not let him come back to you. Make him sit. Carry the bat with you unobtrusively so the dog knows the 'pop' is coming if he doesn't sit. Here is one of the few places carrying the bat prominently and visibly to the dog is appropriate. If you tell your dog to sit while stepping on the rope and his tendency is to run back to you, raise the bat as you are moving toward your dog, giving the command "Sit". Your dog should have distinct memory of the bat and its enforcement properties, and he'll want to sit before you get there. If not, take the dog back to the spot at which you wanted him to sit and enforce the sit and continue at this type of exercise. If this is too advanced for your dog yet, take a few steps back to the long rope exercises and work on the conditioned response on the rope for a while before trying this again.

Introduction and Use of the Whistle

Finally you get to put the whistle on. Some whistle usage advice first: get two whistles and hang them around your neck. Whistles break, freeze, fill with spit, get a bug in them or otherwise malfunction at the most critical moments. Always have a ready reserve. There are whistle lanyards available everywhere, try and get one that doesn't hurt your neck while hanging there for hours at a time. Another important aspect of whistle usage is your ability to whistle. When people first use a whistle, they often make the mistake of blowing through it as if they were blowing out a big candle. This is hard, and the sound does not carry very well this way. Good whistle usage actually involves pressure. When using a whistle, it is held between the upper and lower teeth, with the tongue held over the opening. You put some air pressure in your mouth and just release the tongue from the opening to get a quick spurt of sound. This brings another key aspect of whistle usage to bear. Different kinds of hunting dog people use different whistle signals. Regardless of which signal you want to use, the whistle sounds themselves should be crisp and short. At close distances the crisp, short sound should be low volume. At distances, the crispness remains, but the volume goes up as necessary. Volume of sound should approximate the intensity of the command. You would not scream a "Sit" at ten feet unless you were preventing your dog from being harmed. You would yell a sit at 100 yards. Use the whistle similarly. Use the intensity of sound where appropriate.

Another extremely critical thing to remember when using a whistle is this: Sound is carried through the air. Whistling downwind carries better than whistling upwind. Adjust for the conditions under which the sound will carry. In case you are an electric collar user, or want to become one, remember this: the electrical signal from the transmitter to the collar travels faster than the sound waves from the whistle. Therefore, if you blow a sit whistle and hit the button on the transmitter at the same time, the dog will be corrected before he understands that for which he is being corrected, a dangerous situation. Also, when a dog is breathing heavily or running through water or heavy cover, he might not hear your whistle over the noise of breathing, splashing water or brushing grass. Take these things into account as you work your dog. Wind blowing through tall grass can mask whistle sounds as well. The bottom line is keeping your wits about you when you using a tool at long distance. There are many more factors than you might be aware of. At the same time, do not let outside influences be an excuse for poor dog obedience.

You are going to introduce your dog to the whistle. You can use any kind of whistle sequence or command you like, obviously. Traditionally, a single, crisp blast means "Sit" and a short series of blasts means "Here". You can whistle the directions for quartering or any other thing you like, but at least begin with the basics. We use a single "Toot" for sit, and a "toot-toot" for here. A long series of blasts is unnecessary; besides, you have trained your dog to respond immediately, so you do not have to give more than a quick command. Whatever you use, remain consistent. Use low volume close in and greater volume with greater distance.

As always, start back with the basics your dog should know so well. Use the six-foot leash and choke collar, and go back to the heel, sit and here exercises. Review with the traditional commands of heel, sit, and here. Begin only with the exchange of one command. Don't start on both the sit and here at the same time. Teach one thing at a time always. Start with the sit. You have now reached the easiest part of this whole program. First, bracket the new command with the known command. When you stop, tell your dog "Sit"--blow the single, low volume whistle--"Sit". Continue this for the whole training session. Depending upon how rapidly your dog learns and absorbs new information, you can begin to drop the last "Sit". Use the verbal and whistle sit commands everywhere you would normally. During heeling and sitting, use them together. During the here drill, use them both for the sit. This may take one or two days, or a week. Read your dog's responses and judge when you can begin to drop the verbal sit and just use the whistle alone.

Remember this: Treat the whistle command exactly like the verbal. Reinforce the lack of response with the bat or heeling stick. Response must be quick and crisp. Once your dog understands the single blow means sit, bracket the correction exactly as before: "Toot"--pop with the bat--"Toot". Just slide the conditioned response you created in your dog to sit right into the same thing for the whistle. Your dog should sit immediately. Do not use the loud blow close in because it is overkill and it tends to make your dog callous to the obnoxious noise. Make the whistle calm and only as loud as necessary, which is not much. Just as if you had taught your dog to respond only to commands that were screamed at him by yelling out all the verbal commands, with loud whistles you will teach your dog to respond to the whistle only if it is loud enough. You create a situation in which he can decide what is loud enough, and then you have completely lost. Do your basic obedience exercises until you can use the whistle in place of the sit, with the same immediate response.

Now use the whistle for the come-in. You will replace the verbal command "Here" with the toot-toot whistle. Exactly as you did with the sit, using the basic obedience exercises, begin to bracket the new toot-toot command: "Here"--toot-toot--"Here". Begin this with the six-foot leash and close in. Again, keep the whistle crisp, calm and not too loud. After your dog has heard the verbal and whistle commands together enough to associate them, begin by dropping the last "Here", and continue the basic "Here" exercises. Before completely dropping the verbal command, go to the long rope and repeat the long rope "Here" drills. Use both verbal and whistle here until the conditioned response is installed for both, then go entirely to the whistle.

Once this has become second nature to your dog, go back to the extensive exercises outlined earlier, in which you are walking with your dog at heel, give the sit whistle and continue moving. Whistle your dog to you and make him sit on the way in, then whistle in again. As with all other fundamentals, the more you practice these drills that become somewhat tedious with time, the more you will install the conditioned response, and the more response you will get in the field later. Go on the long walk with your dog dragging the rope, and whistle when your dog is extremely interested in something else. When he sits, let him wait, then whistle him to you. Make him sit several times coming in. Be careful not to overdo the sitting, because your dog can lose his momentum and enthusiasm you initially created in having him come running to you when called. You will have to maintain your dog's enthusiasm while teaching control and conditioned response. It is always challenging to be a good trainer.

It might seem very simple, but by this time you have done a lot of training with your dog. The key is the conditioned response, the unquestioning compliance with your command. You have created this not through fear, intimidation, or by negotiation with your dog. Some dogs learn very quickly and are very willing to comply. Other dogs learn through far greater repetition than others and are not so inclined to get with the program. Both can be trained this way, but each takes a different amount of time and patience. Assess your dog realistically, no matter how much you may love him, and deal with what you have. Take the time to work out the small, unexciting details, and your dog may surprise you when the fun stuff comes around. Definitely do what has been described here, but feel encouraged to come up with your own inventive ways to create and reinforce the conditioned response in your dog. Just make sure that you follow the same philosophy used in all the fundamentals: be fair to the dog, make sure he understands what you are asking, give clear, simple commands, require crisp, immediate response, and reward the efforts of your dog. Remember to never give a command you are not prepared to enforce.

Progress Test

Put the short cord on your dog, but do not hold on to it. Let your dog drag it as you head into the park or field. Do a few obedience exercises first to get your dog in the right mindset. Release him to run in your close vicinity. Blow the sit whistle. What is his response? Whistle him to you. Does he come immediately? Blow the sit whistle as your dog is on the way to investigate something. Does he sit? If not, go back to the long cord and work the drills more. As a final test, walk your dog at your side. With whistle in mouth, enthusiastically toss a training bumper as far as you possibly can. Make sure your dog has seen it. At the same time, blow the sit whistle and make your dog sit at your side. You should already have worked on heeling while throwing the bumper and requiring that your dog maintain a heel position or sit position. Your dog should honor the sit, even if you continue moving. This will give you an idea of how well you have installed the whistle command. Enforce immediately if your dog does not respond. This is what the long rope is for. Remember to avoid stopping your dog on the way to a marked retrieve. There are almost no applications in real life in which you stop a dog heading correctly for a bird. That is the biggest spirit-crusher there is. Dogs are stopped on blind retrieves because they are not sure where the bird is and expect direction when they are off track. When a dog is doing something correctly, do not make the mistake of stopping him as if he was doing something wrong. Though you understand the difference, dogs rarely do.

Whistle-trained dogs are a pleasure. They can be controlled at distances and under unusual circumstances. Whistle training is very possible when the obedience basics are solid and the whistle is introduced afterwards, and used in a variety of circumstances in which the commands can be enforced. Be patient, be consistent, and work every day if you can. Training sessions should last no more than ten or 15 minutes, but on walks and in ordinary circumstances, the training can just be a part of the activity. Do not dampen your dog's enthusiasm by overdoing any drills, but don't let sloppiness arise during any drill. Require crisp, immediate responses, and reward good effort from your dog with verbal praise. Physical praise is too distracting during a training session. Use a reassuring touch or pat only during training. Keep it simple. Have fun with it.

If you start your pup on a program that creates enthusiasm for work and willingness to comply with you, only your dog's natural abilities and intelligence and your ability and commitment limit you. Your dog should heel over any obstacle, in any direction, forwards and backwards, with any temptations or distractions close by. Your dog should learn to sit on command, verbal or whistle, regardless of your proximity, or distractions. Your dog should learn to come when called verbally or by the whistle, regardless of distance, distraction, or obstacle. Once this is firmly entrenched in your dog, the force fetch will be easy to begin.

Chapter 11
Force Fetch

Force fetching a dog means simply this: you teach a dog that you expect him to pick up whatever you direct him to, and that he is to hold it until you take it from him. It is an essential piece of the foundation you build on your dog. Just as with obedience, if you cannot successfully ask your dog to pick up something at his feet without great enticement and pleading, you have no hope of asking your dog to pick up something it either does not want or does not see, at a distance. The force fetch can give you the conditioned response to pick up whatever you ask the dog to pick up, without the dog deciding how it feels about carrying out that task. It is also the response on which advanced training is built. You will be hard put to send a dog out 50 yards on a blind retrieve if you cannot send a dog reliably three feet from you. It also teaches your dog to carry a bumper and ultimately a bird by the body, and not by the rope, wings, or foot. It teaches the dog to retrieve without mouthing or playing with it along the way.

By this time, you should have established a strong control factor with your dog. This means your dog should understand that "Heel" means to walk at your side and to sit immediately when you stop. He should also understand whatever command you use directing him to come to you. Force fetching is the process by which a dog is trained to pick up an object on command. It is possible to hunt with a dog who is not force fetched, but any training or corrections done on a dog not properly forced may and usually does result in the dog's refusal to retrieve. This can be entirely avoided by having a dog that does not question the command to retrieve.

Force fetching is usually started at six to eight months, after the adult teeth are in completely. There is often pain and discomfort during the transition from baby teeth to adult, and this discomfort should not be allowed to create negative associations with retrieving. Up to this point, your dog should have been enthusiastically encouraged to deliver to hand, but you have had no real means to correct any refusal to carry and deliver.

After the completion of force fetch, your dog will be far more inclined to deliver to hand, and you will definitely have the means to correct him for dropping birds. A more significant reason exists for force fetching a dog. The force fetch teaches your dog to retrieve under pressure, and to learn to accept and deal with that pressure. This makes the force fetch the foundation for most modern training programs that require a dog to run blinds and handle.

Tools Required for Exercises

You will need the following equipment to carry out the force fetch:

• Choke Chain that fits the dog's neck loosely, but not so loose that it can easily be pulled over the head.
• 20-foot cord or lead, preferably nylon so that it will not wear or break with use.
• A 'dummy' electric collar, if you plan on using that down the line, or a wide nylon or leather collar that can fit firmly around your dog's neck, just behind the ears.
• Plastic knobby training bumpers, not the 3-inch diameter, but the narrower version.
• An empty shotgun shell or other something very similar. You will see the application shortly.

You may have read or even seen the force fetch done on a table. There are plenty of dogs that have been successfully force fetched confined up on a table. We choose not to for several reasons. The real purpose of the table is convenience for the force fetcher. This process requires bending over a great deal of the time and it can be quite difficult on a trainer's back. For some this is the only way it can be done. In terms of the dogs, however, it is far less stressful to incorporate movement and natural contact with the ground into what they are doing. Dogs are not naturally 'static' and they learn more readily when they can move around a little, heeling and sitting during these exercises. Secondly, as you begin to transition the concept of reaching for a bumper towards and finally on the ground, it is easier on the dog if he is actually on the ground. For those going on to advanced work with handling, it is a simple thing to reinforce any refusals to fetch with an ear pinch and the familiar groundwork. For dogs that have been taught on the table, it is not such familiar territory.

The contraptions used on the table are also not so quickly available to reinforce any refusals. For these reasons, we work to keep things as simple and natural on the dog as possible.

"Hold"

Before beginning the force fetch, it is important that you have a strong obedience foundation on your dog. This is because when you begin to subject your dog to pressure he or she has never experienced, often the dog that is weak in obedience will stop carrying out the obedience commands completely. If a dog doesn't believe it really has to sit when directed, then when you make it uncomfortable it will stop reacting to the command at all. You will have a dog that not only doesn't want to hold a bumper, but will not even sit down. You will see how strong a foundation you built when you begin the force fetch.

The force fetch begins with the idea of 'holding' on to the bumper until told to release, or "Drop". It would be difficult to teach a dog to pick up something if you have not first taught him not to spit it out as soon as he picks it up. Begin by placing the bumper in your dog's mouth as he or she sits by your side. You may have to pry his mouth open to put the bumper in. Do not expect your dog to reach for it or even willingly accept the bumper. Use the lead attached to the choke collar, or the dummy collar, to prevent your dog from moving away from your side. Keep the dog in a sitting position, say "Hold" when you get the bumper

Place bumper in dog's mouth

in the dog's mouth, and encourage the hold response with calm but positive praise.

At first, you may have to literally hold the bumper in the dog's mouth in order to get the 'hold' response that you can praise. Some dogs will put up a real battle at this point. Do not let that dissuade you. Be patient and excruciatingly persistent in your requirement to hold. Counter the resistance with insistence on holding, even if you must actually hold the dog's head and mouth and bumper in place. Be cautious about holding the bumper and closing off the dog's breathing passages. Hold firmly but on the bone of the nose and not the sinus passages. Once your dog sees that he cannot win, the resistance will lessen. Praise any real effort and your dog will begin to hold without major struggle. Often,

Holding dog's mouth closed over bumper

when a dog is being made to hold the bumper and begins to stridently resist, you can use secondary pressure to get his mind off of being made to hold. When a dog begins to really resist the hold, give a strong "Sit" command. Make him sit, even if you must you use your foot to pop his bottom. The command and pressure to sit may redirect the dog's focus and calm him down. The dog must now sit and hold, a new concept of doing two things under pressure at one time. Give your dog a few days or more to adjust to this new idea of performing under more stress than that to which he is accustomed.

A dog will often begin to lower its head to avoid the activity at hand. Use the chain or collar to keep the dog's head up. You will need to do this while maintaining the sit position and the bumper in the dog's mouth. It can be a little challenging the first few times you attempt it. Set one simple goal each time and work towards that each day. This is harder on the new handler than it is the dog. Keep your sense of humor and focus on the objective.

Once your dog successfully holds the bumper for a period of time, a moment or so, remove the bumper with the command "Drop". If, for any reason your dog attempts to hold on to the bumper, calmly give the "Drop" command again, and rotate the bumper gently counterclockwise in your dog's mouth. This helps to open the jaw slightly, allowing you to remove the bumper. Never yank or pull the bumper out of the dog's mouth. This can create a "biting down" response in your dog. This is the last thing you want in a retriever. Your goal is to teach the dog to open his mouth and release at your command to drop. Throughout all these exercises remain calm but determined. Any show of emotion signals your dog he or she has 'gotten to you', and they can sometimes use that to avoid further work.

After your dog has begun to get the idea, you can correct the dog when the bumper is dropped or dangling by cuffing the dog under the muzzle with your open hand, and placing the bumper back in your dog's mouth, while giving the command "Hold".

It is an important training principle that a command be taught before pressure is used to enforce the command. Do not apply pressure for refusals to hold until you feel you have adequately taught the dog clearly what "hold"

Reinforcing Hold with Open Hand Chin Cuff

187

means. As your dog becomes more successful, have him hold the bumper for longer periods of time. If the bumper is chewed, rolled, dangled or otherwise 'played' with during the hold, treat that as a refusal and give the command to "hold" again, with a correction of a chin cuff. Your dog will quickly learn to hold the bumper firmly, but gently. Once you feel your dog understands "Hold", test it by tapping on the bumper while giving the hold command. The dog should maintain its hold on the bumper. If he drops it, then reinforce the hold by placing the bumper back in his mouth and stiffly give a chin cuff with the hold command. Tap the bumper again to show the dog that he must hold when you direct him to, even if there is challenge offered to the hold.

You should now be able to walk away and return to your dog, with him sitting calmly, holding the bumper all the while. A jerk up on the choke chain can be helpful when used with the "Hold" command, to prevent the

dog that likes to drop its head to avoid the activity or even to slowly drop the bumper. One of the easiest mistakes to make in this process is on the actual "Drop" command. If each time your hand reaches in the direction of the bumper, your dog actually winds up releasing the bumper, the dog will soon begin dropping the bumper when your hand appears any-where near. To prevent this, move your hand around the dog's face, down on his chest--give him a pat, move your hand back up, tap the bumper. Teach your dog to drop only when the drop com-mand is given, and not to drop to some other physical cue you may inadvertently give.

Tap on the bumper to challenge the holding response

The final step in the Hold training is to have the dog walk, heel, and sit, all while holding the bumper. As reliable as your dog may have been on the 'hold' while sitting, it is almost a sure thing your dog will spit the bumper out as you try to get him to move with it. Be prepared for this, and correct immediately when the bumper is first spit out. Place the bumper back in your dog's mouth and continue to try to move, using the command "Hold" as a reminder. This can be a very challenging section of

Have the dog hold bumper while you touch the dog

your training process. With some dogs it goes so smoothly, and with others it becomes a field of conflict. It is your job to keep the activity a positive one--starting happy, ending happy and making some bit of progress in the middle. If you find yourself becoming frustrated or questioning whether this is really worth pursuing, understand you are part of a large population who has gone through the same thing. Once you have force fetched enough dogs, you come to realize you almost always get through this with success. A little humor might do you well if you find yourself feeling as if you are not making progress. Often, when you have come to the conclusion your dog will never walk and sit while holding the bumper, you will have the best training session ever. This is usually not because the dog has read your mind and wishes to prove you wrong once again. It is more often because you have relaxed enough that your dog relaxes also, and progress can continue. If it gets a little too frustrating, lay off for several days. Starting up again with a different attitude can make a huge difference.

Begin heeling while holding the bumper by actually holding the bumper in the dog's mouth and you begin to walk. This often shows the dog want you want more clearly. Correct any drops as you would if the dog were sitting, but continue to require that the dog move forward. Praise effort on the part of your dog. It usually takes a day or several to have the dog suddenly grasp the idea that you expect him to move and hold.

Help your dog by holding the bumper as you begin to walk forward

As happy as you may be when your dog begins to enthusiastically carry the bumper throughout the obedience exercises, do not forget the important nature of the drop command. Do not happily rip the bumper from the dog's mouth to throw a happy bumper. Still reach down carefully, even holding on to the rope for a moment, before giving the drop command. Have your dog wait, albeit excitedly, for the drop command.

Hold the rope without having the dog release, release to the drop command

The goal at this point is to have your dog go through all of your basic obedience drills of heeling, sitting, coming to you, etc., and holding the bumper continuously without dropping. Do not move on until your dog can reliably carry this out. A very trainable dog will complete the 'hold' training in a few days. Some may take longer, but with patience, consistency, calmness and persistence, you will get through this stage. Your dog should hold the bumper with routine obedience pressure, pops on the bottom with the stick, or jerks on the chain. Do not proceed until you have this soundly.

Do all obedience exercises with dog willingly holding bumper

The Ear Pinch

The ear pinch is the key and the heart of the force fetch. Through this process, your dog will pick up an object on command in response to pressure. The concept and use of pressure is all-important here. The discomfort of the ear pinch will be relieved by the act of fetching. That is all you are teaching at this point. It is simple, but critical. The dog will learn that it can remove the discomfort of the ear pinch by carrying out the fetch command and reaching for the bumper. The ear pinch is ideal because pinch pressure is used on a flap of skin alone, so that there is no way the dog can be harmed, aside from a skin scrape. The grip that will be shown below allows you to have a good hold of the dog's ear and a hold on the dog's head. As said before, if you control the dog's head, you control the dog. This method of maintaining a good hold on the dog's head as well as the ear allows you to prevent the dog from moving away from you or avoiding the work. Dogs will often turn the ear pinch into a battle of remaining in place and the whole aspect of what you are trying to teach is lost in the effort of trying to get your dog to just be obedient.

Begin by holding your left hand (if your dog is at your left side) under the leather collar strap or dummy collar strap located at the back of

Hand grip through the collar

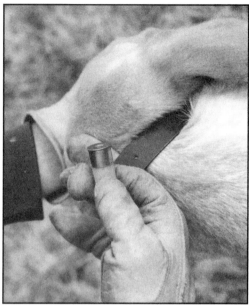

Brass shotgun shell

the dog's ears and skull. You will see why collar position is important momentarily. Beneath the collar, your left hand should reach for your dog's right ear, with the thumb not beneath the strap. If you have the hand and nail strength, you can use your thumb and index finger. Most of us use the brass base of a shotgun shell as the hard object pressed against the sensitive part of the ear, near the ear opening, but not in the ear itself.

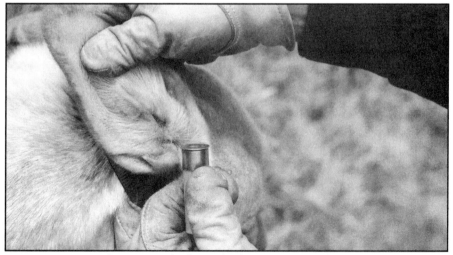

Open the ear and place the brass part at base of ear,
fingers holding the shell in place against ear

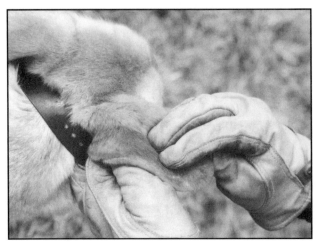

Fold the ear back over the shell

A pinch at the tip of the ear yields far less discomfort avoidance than that close to the base of the ear. The fingers hold the brass base of the shell against the inner part of the earflap and the thumb is against the ear making contact through the ear with the brass base. This positioning of your hand serves several purposes. With it your right hand is free to hold and manage the bumper. As mentioned earlier, when you control the head, you control one side of the 'balance arm'. When you control one side, you then control both sides. You can keep your dog in position with this hold.

Once your hand is positioned to pinch the base of the ear either with the nail of your thumb or index finger, or with the brass base of the shotgun shell against your thumb and index finger, you can begin. Your hold on this position needs

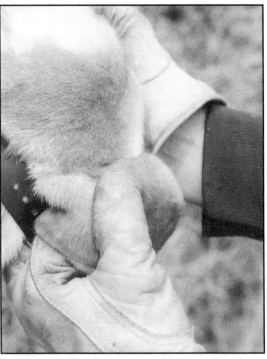

Place the thumb on the outside of the ear in contact with the brass shell

to be one you can maintain throughout the exercise. Now, you will give the "Fetch" command and gently pinch the ear between your thumb and index finger or shotgun shell, while you place the bumper into the dog's mouth with your right hand.

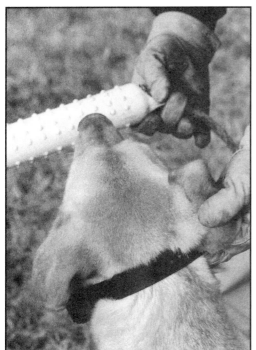
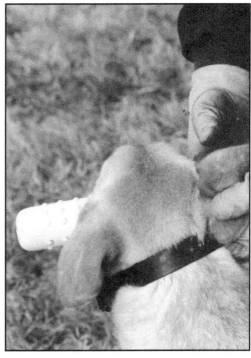

Hold bumper right in front of dog's mouth, say "Fetch", pinch and place bumper in mouth

The idea is for the dog to understand that getting the bumper in his mouth relieves the pressure. Continue to repeat the sequence until the dog begins to get the idea. Offer plenty of praise as the dog holds the bumper between command sequences. Dogs really show different aspects of themselves at this juncture. Some dogs will get the idea, dislike the ear pressure and begin grabbing for the bumper anytime it is held even remotely close to them. Others will become stoic and not react no matter how hard you pinch. Their jaws will be clamped shut with the strength of an ox. This is where reading about the force fetch really fails. The concept is simple and can be written so clearly. Carrying it out successfully is not always so simple.

If you have a dog that immediately begins grasping at any bumper you hold, do not allow him to do that. Dogs like that are avoiding every kind of pressure and that is not acceptable. They must wait for the fetch command; remember, you are in control here, not the dog. If you have a 'grabber', then use the sit command as you bring the bumper close to him. If he begins to reach, use the sit command and make him remain sitting and not grabbing. When you have regained control and he is waiting for the command, wait a moment and then give the fetch command. You should reasonably expect your dog to sit as told, and fetch when told, and to do each separately and as you direct.

If you have a clammy dog that becomes a statue when you apply ear pressure, you may have to be quite patient, and a little inventive. Don't think that if some discomfort isn't working, more will be better. Sometimes you may not be causing him discomfort enough to make him decide to eliminate it by reaching. Other times the dog will not care how much discomfort you inflict, it will just freeze on you. You must find out which you have and react accordingly. If you are pinching as much as you can and the dog's reaction never changes, then change the game some. Try pulling forward on the ear as you pinch, or changing the location on the ear where you are pinching. Do not just grind mercilessly on the dog hoping you will 'break' its clammy nature. It sometimes helps your dog's attitude to mix heeling drills with the bumper in his mouth with the fetch command sequences. Do something a little different and then come back to the ear pinch. Often, the next day the ear is a little sensitized to the previous session, and the pinch suddenly works well. Don't give up and don't stick with just one way of going about this--alternate what you do, keep your dog's attitude up, and keep at it. Remember, you are more intelligent than your dog. You can work this out.

If, during the ear pinch, your dog drops the bumper, remind him to "hold". On the first day of ear pinch, you can usually get the dog to open his mouth and begin to reach for the bumper. For the first few sessions, you want to hold the bumper just in front of your dog's mouth, so he hasn't far to reach. Keep each training session under ten minutes or so, especially in hot weather. Try to make a little progress every day, and end the session on a positive note. This is most easily accomplished by reducing the level of difficulty of the task required near the end of the session. This leaves your dog with some feeling of accomplishment after a difficult and demanding session. Start each session with a happy bumper and end it the same way. Sometimes a dog will stop retrieving during the force fetch. If this happens, curtail the happy bumper until he regains his interest. Do not let that worry you that you have killed your dog's interest in retrieving. He will resume his earlier attitude toward retrieving when he regains his sense of accomplishment after completing the force fetch.

Every day your dog should be required to reach farther towards the ground for the bumper. This should begin right next to his mouth, and progress slowly toward the ground, if only an inch or so at a time. Remember to incorporate forward movement each time your dog reaches for the bumper. As the dog reaches and takes the bumper, even if you help by placing it in his mouth, walk a few steps forward and have the dog sit down again. All fetching and retrieving involves going forward, and it should start that way now. As soon as the dog gets the idea of reaching for the bumper, stop placing the bumper in the dog's mouth. If you continue to place the bumper in his mouth, you will teach the dog to open its mouth to the pressure and that you will take care of the rest. Teach your dog the pressure ends when he reaches for and takes the bumper. The bumper should travel eventually to just off the ground. Finally, you will put the bumper on the ground. This 'on the ground' step changes the whole game, and is usually meant with an unexpected resistance. The good progress you made to this point and you and your dog's feeling of accomplishment can completely vaporize at this step. For some dogs, it is as if they never heard the word "Fetch" before.

KEY POINT: The biggest mistake made by people force fetching dogs is in timing and pressure. Even seasoned force fetchers easily make small mistakes in this process, only to wonder why the dog is not respond-ing the way they know it should. You must put yourself in the 'shoes' of the dog. Think about what you are communicating. The dog is seated and you give the "Fetch" command. The dog must first hear the com-mand. If the dog is reaching for the bumper, there is no reason to use pinch pressure. If the dog is not reaching, the dog must first hear the command and then feel the pinch pressure. The instant the dog responds by reaching, the pressure must stop.

So many times we have had people come by with their 'force fetched' dog, only to have the dog not pick up a bumper lying on the ground in front of him. Of course, the owner is completely bewildered by this behavior. To watch the owner correct the refusal usually tells the story. He will grab the ear and pinch the dog's ear, all the while dragging the dog's mouth down to the bumper. The dog is just pinched and dragged all the way to the bumper. There is no place in this scenario for the dog to relieve the pressure by responding. The dog is just being made to do it. So, the dog has been taught to endure this pressure of ear pinch and collar tug and when its mouth reaches the bumper, open it up and take the bumper. This isn't a force-fetched dog, it's a nagged dog that endures discomfort but doesn't really have any idea why. Teach the dog to respond to the fetch command and that when it does, things are good. When it does not, if feels pinch pressure until it does respond, and then the pressure is gone.

You may have heard of dogs that bite or snap during force fetch. This usually doesn't happen because the force fetch is so brutal, but because the dog is either being subject to pressure from which it cannot escape or because the dog has never learned to function under some duress. Occasionally you may just have a dog that likes to react by biting, and you will have to deal with that aggression quickly. It's poor timing on your part if the dog can't escape the pressure. By this time in your training, you should have already acquainted your dog with the concept of functioning under some pressure in the obedience training on heel, here and sit. We like to use the analogy of the smart kid going to MIT who never had to study in public school. He has never learned to bear down and continue to work when things are tough or demanding, and may fail completely, go home and never become what he was capable of. Another kid, not nearly as smart, with experience in dealing with challenge and difficulty, may work hard and do very well at the tough school. It isn't the intelligence of the kid nor the toughness of the school that is the reason for success or failure, but the ability of the individual to cope and continue to function. It's important that you bring a dog conditioned to working with and dealing with fair and appropriate pressure to the force fetch stage. Your force fetch will go much easier--for both of you.

If you do have a dog that wants to bite at your arm to alleviate the pressure, you can prevent that from happening. If your dog is a snapper, then when you grip the collar with your right hand, bring the left ear over and maintain it in your grip along with the shell and the other ear. Unless the dog has very tiny ears, this is not difficult. Then, if the dog begins to bring his mouth in your direction, your grip on the outside ear can keep it from coming at you. You will control both sides of the dog's head, and can prevent any rotation in your direction. Continue with this grip until your dog stops trying to escape pressure by biting, but is instead escaping it by reaching for the bumper.

Once your dog will reliably fetch the bumper you are holding even when it is touching the ground, you are ready to take the next step: letting go of the bumper. You will find that this completely changes the picture for your dog. The dog that would consistently reach down to the ground for the bumper you were holding will not reach down for that same bumper once it is no longer attached to your hand. To help the dog through this stage, you can either step on one end of the bumper, elevating the other end and making it easier to reach, or you can lay the bumper on

Bumper should be fetched off ground with you holding it.

Place bumper on foot to ease transition.

your foot, elevating it in that manner. This seems to ease the dog into the transition of picking the bumper off the ground. As long as the bumper was 'attached' to you, the dog was comfortable with reaching for it. Once you begin to 'detach' the bumper, this changes the game for the dog. With the bumper on your foot, the ear pinch pressure is applied identically at this point, to the way you did the first day. Your left hand should be beneath the collar, with the dog's ear in your right hand in the pinch-ready mode. Give the command "Fetch" and use the pinch until the dog moves to pick up the

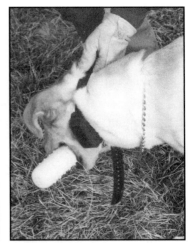

Collar gripped in left hand, ear and shell holding right ear, pinch pressure until dog reaches for bumper

bumper. Stop the pinch when the dog reaches for the bumper. Always have your hand under the collar and with ear in hand, no matter how good or poor your dog's response is. Never let him learn he can avoid the pinch by your lack of readiness only by reaching for the bumper.

Once the dog is picking the bumper off the ground, walking forward and sitting, give the command to drop and take the bumper. Have your dog heel forward, drop the bumper in front of him, and give the fetch/ear pinch command again. Some dogs may merely put their mouths around the bumper without actually picking the bumper up. In that case, you must heel forward and then repeat the sequence when they inevitably leave the bumper behind. Turn back toward the bumper, give the "Fetch" command again and be prepared to use the ear pinch to enforce the fetch. As the dog's response improves over time, you will only begin to reach for the earflap and he will dive for the bumper. This is the response you are looking for: the dog has learned to control the pressure by completing the task quickly.

It is helpful when teaching the fetch off the ground to use your left hand to hold the collar and control the dog's movements, and to use your right hand to hold the shell and actually pinch the ear. With this hold, you can direct your dog to the bumper easily. It is extremely important to be aware of your timing and use of pressure during this process. Keep foremost in your mind that the goal is to have your dog relieve the pressure by fetching. When your dog reaches for the bumper, you stop the pinch. It is a common mistake to just grind the dog all the way to the bumper, pinching until the bumper is in his mouth. Again, when you do this, the dog cannot win. No matter what he does, he gets his ear pinched. You kill any good response in him and he just waits for you to pinch him to it. Give the fetch command first, apply pinch pressure if the dog does not reach for the bumper, and stop the pressure when the dog does reach for it. You are teaching a dog to avoid pressure, not endure it. A common response in a dog at this stage is to reach for the bumper, even put his mouth over it, but never pick it up. If your dog begins this, give him one chance to make sure it is not confusion of some sort. If it is not and the dog is just refusing to pick it up, then treat it as a refusal and use the ear pinch again. Place the bumper on the ground in front of the dog, with collar in hand and shell in the other. Give the fetch command. As your dog reaches down but does not take the bumper, pull him back up. With no bumper in his mouth, you now use ear pinch pressure back down to the bumper and pick the head up again. Teach the dog he must pick up the bumper because you are going to pull his head back up and if he doesn't have the bumper, he will get the pressure until he does. Be calm and deliberate and require that your dog pick the bumper up. Praise the good effort. End on a positive note.

Walking Fetch

As soon as your dog is fetching the bumper off the ground reliably, move right into the 'walking fetch'. Begin by using one white bumper. As with all drills, this should be an area with very short grass and complete visibility. Start by heeling the dog on lead. Stop and toss the bumper down about three feet in front of you. Give the fetch command and begin moving forward. Your dog should quickly reach for the bumper. Continue walking a few steps forward and stop again. If your dog doesn't pick the bumper up, give him one chance and then correct any clear refusals. You should get to the point at which you can toss the bumper down and have to correct your dog for not remaining seated until you give the fetch command. Make your dog wait until you give the fetch command. Make sure your dog is not cueing off your leg movement. Give the fetch command and don't take a step. If your dog doesn't move to pick up the bumper, correct the refusal with an ear pinch.

Walking fetch

You must realize that you have taught him to go when you moved, and not off the fetch command. Make certain you are teaching your dog to respond to the fetch command alone. Your goal in this exercise is to be able to toss the bumper down, give the fetch command and have your dog dive for it and continue walking and holding the bumper with you. Stop, take the bumper and do it several more times.

Now you can mix the game up a little. Scatter white bumpers around your training area. Separate from one another. Have your dog on the lead and begin by heeling. When you approach a bumper, give the "Fetch" command and apply the ear pinch. Do this right from the heeling position while moving--don't put the dog in a sit position before giving the command. After your dog has picked up the bumper, continue to move forward with the dog in the heel position. Remove the bumper with the "drop" command, either while still moving forward or after stopping, then give a "sit" command. Discard the bumper behind you and proceed ahead, repeating the whole sequence when you approach the next bumper.

Once your dog is lunging for the bumper on each "fetch" command sequence, you may begin giving the command without applying the ear pinch. If you get a refusal to fetch, you must immediately repeat the "fetch" command with an ear pinch. You may also walk right past a bumper without giving a fetch command, and keep the dog at a heel with the "heel" command, not allowing him to pick up the bumper. Your dog must learn to fetch as directed only.

It will usually take 15-25 training days, one session per day and no more, to get your dog through the walking fetch. This sounds very nice on paper, but force fetch is never easy, and can induce all kinds of unusual responses. Your dog may try to escape the ear pressure by moving away from you, or even more likely, responding aggressively and trying to bite you. In the process, force fetch can look more like a wrestling match than controlled dog training. It is important to remain unemotional and objective during force fetch.

Aggression toward the trainer should never be tolerated, and may even be a sign the dog is unsuitable for further training. Do not allow the dog's aggression to enable him to escape training pressure, because in doing so, you will have reinforced the aggressive response in your dog. Stop it immediately by whatever force is necessary.

Some dogs are quite stoic in response to ear pressure. If your nails are not strong enough, or hands not strong enough to squeeze the shot-gun shell between your fingers and your dog's ears, you may not get any response to the ear pinch. Various devices may help overcome your dog's high pain threshold. A single metal-tipped collar prong attached to the dummy collar may create a better ear pinch surface than your finger. You may have to get creative in coming up with an ear pinch device.

Some dogs exhibit a stubborn response to force fetch pressure. Day after day, you can pinch these dogs and they never get snappy about picking up the bumper, and they may refuse every other "fetch" com-mand. Both stoic and stubborn dogs often improve their response when plenty of heeling is incorporated into the command sequence. That is, don't just have the dog sit in one place. Move forward between each com-mand sequence.

If you make no progress after 15-20 days of force fetch, try put-ting the whole project on the shelf for a week or two. When you return to force fetch, your dog's response may change completely. We have seen this layoff work for many dogs who otherwise seemed to hit a wall during force fetch.

Conclusion

The ease with which your dog masters the force fetch often fore-tells his reaction to yard work that follows in the whole handling program. The dog that learns to master the pressure easily will probably learn to handle more easily than the dog that makes you work for every inch of progress. There are also cases in which dogs were almost impossible to get through the force fetch, only to excel later at advanced work. Force fetch is the foundation on which all advanced work is premised. With a thor-ough, patient and persistent approach to force fetch, your dog should emerge with a healthy attitude toward pressure that will serve you well in the training that lies ahead.

For those dogs that will be taught to handle, that program con-tinues, based on a strong force fetch foundation. Unlike some approach-es we have read in which a dog is taught to handle by merely teaching him to cast in certain directions, we choose to teach the dog first that its job is to go when asked, and when that is clearly understood, stop when asked as well. Too often people teach a dog to turn left to pick up a bumper or turn right to find one, or even go backwards a certain number of feet, and believe that will serve to get their dog across a river or a large field to pick up a bird he didn't see. Sometimes it will. More often it won't. Modern training methods make things a little clearer to the dog, not by brutalizing the dog into going, but by simplifying and teaching concepts one at a time to the dog. Doing that correctly takes more than a chapter, however, and our next book is already started, to address the program to teach your dog to run blinds and handle with as much exuberance as they run marked retrieves.

Chapter 12
The Collar

Know how to train without the collar

Discussions revolving around use of the electric collar are equivalent to discussions about what happens as a result of this year's election. People feel pretty strongly in every direction. There are a number of schools of thought regarding the use of the electric collar. No training of a dog should be for the sake of any tool, including the electric collar. It should be nothing more than one of several tools you use to create the enthusiastic, confident, conditioned response in your dog. Can a dog be trained without an electric collar? Yes. Can you stop a dog chasing a wild bird across a distant field without one? Probably not. If you understand how and when a collar can be used humanely, you can make an informed choice regarding whether or not you wish to add it to the tools you have for use with working and hunting your dog.

A good trainer knows how to train a dog without an electric collar. It is as a calculator is to a mathematician. The mathematician must first understand how to carry out higher-order equations and derivations from first principles, and then the calculator comes in and makes the job easier that he understands fundamentally. It also allows him to do more than he could without it. It doesn't necessarily increase his knowledge, but it does increase the scope of what he can do. You must first understand how a dog thinks and how to teach, reinforce, and create the responses you need from the dog. When you understand that fundamentally, then you have the addition of a tool that makes what you already do a little easier and increases the distance at which you can function.

An electric collar is another form of pressure. Throughout obedience training, you have used crisp jerks on the choke chain and pops from a heeling stick to put pressure on the dog. First you taught the dog what you expected, then you enforced the response and finally you corrected the dog for not giving the correct response. Each time you jerked on the choke chain or popped the dog's bottom, the dog understood what you wanted and why you were putting any pressure on him. You also taught him he could avoid the pressure by carrying out the command. You should not have used pressure to punish or demoralize your dog. You used it as a means to get your dog to quickly do as you asked. Your dog learned that pressure was not something from which it cowered and ran, but something it could conquer and eliminate. That is the same way an electric collar is used.

When your dog has a strong obedience foundation and has been subject to pressure in obedience and force fetch, you will more clearly understand where it is appropriate to apply pressure and what to expect from your dog. It is not enough that your dog knows how to heel and sit and fetch. Your dog needs to know how to function with pressure, what the pressure is there for, and how to get rid of it. You need to know when to use pressure and when not to use it. You don't go out one isolated day and decide that day you will jerk your dog around and pop him on the behind a whole bunch to condition him to pressure. You make obedience a routine and way of life, and utilize the appropriate use of pressure to create a good conditioned response in your dog. Provided you have conditioned your dog to the use of fair and appropriately timed pressure, you can condition your dog to the electric collar so you will have the ability to enforce commands at a distance.

The first time a person has his hands on an electric collar, he often feels like he has a Light Saber or Jedi Sword in his grasp. People have no idea of the damage they can do, and they are a little frightened of their new 'power'. At least the smart ones are. Instead of talking about how you feel about it, let's talk about how your dog will feel about it. As mentioned earlier, if you planned on using an electric collar, you should have been placing a dummy collar on your dog since it was five or six months of age. You want the dog to see the dummy collar come out and be quite excited about getting to work. This does not happen in two weeks. Make it a part of the dog's life, from the time the dog is big enough to wear the collar easily. A dog should wear a dummy collar for months before you ever use a live collar on the dog.

Contrary to some schools of thought, we do not collar-condition a dog until it is well through the basics, including obedience, force fetch and extensive retrieving and marking. All of the obedience work, retrieving work, whoaing work, force fetching, and daily walks should have been done with the dummy collar on. When a dog is strong in the fundamentals and mentally mature enough to grasp another form of pressure, he can be introduced in the same place he was initially introduced to performing with pressure. In all honesty, it is our contention that you should be fully schooled in 'dog-think' and dog training before you begin to use a tool that can be more easily misused than any other--with unpleasant and unnecessary results. No matter how smart you are, you need to learn dog thinking first.

Collar Conditioning

The term 'collar conditioning' means that you are going to condition your dog to carry out known commands and responses with some pressure coming from the electric collar, along with the choke chain and heeling stick, and finally in place of the jerk and the pop. Don't even consider introducing the live collar until you have conditioned your dog to carry out commands with the pressure from the chain and heeling stick. So many times we have heard people make the sizable purchase of an electric collar, with plans to use it on their dog the next time he wouldn't come back in the field. So there is a dog that has been essentially taught that the field was its playground, and it could run and frolic at will. One day, they strap this contraption on its neck and then, when it begins to do what it has always done, Wham! A bolt of lightning from the sky hits the dog. And these folks expect this dog to understand the complicated thought process: "Oh, I was running around and not listening, so now they have a way to make sure I listen whether I want to or not by inflicting this weird new pain on me. I better hightail it back right now!" Probably not. Instead, the dog is going to think the ground hurt him, or the bush he was sniffing, and he will be sure to avoid that from now on. He may even panic and bolt, or decide it isn't even worth going out into the field any longer. A bolt of lightning is not the way to introduce or use this tool with a dog.

You want to make sure your dog has been well acquainted with collar pressure in the obedience exercises in the yard with "Here" long before you actually use the command "here" in the field with the collar pressure. With collar conditioning done well and thoroughly, you will find you won't have to use it much in the field, and that should be the goal. Introduce the collar wisely, and you will need it fewer times than you might expect.

To begin, think about what you are going to do each training session before you do it. Set a goal for yourself for each time, as you have been doing throughout your entire training process. Keep things very simple, for you and for your dog. You will collar condition your dog with the ever-familiar obedience exercises. These should be second nature to your dog, including the pressure you use in them. To make things easier on yourself, go out for a couple of days and redo your obedience with emphasis in your mind on pressure and timing. Put heeling stick pressure on your dog randomly for sit. Put choke chain pressure on your dog alternately for here. Get your timing clear in your mind. "Sit", pressure from stick, "Sit". Command first, quick pressure, command. Praise your dog for his attempts to eliminate the pressure by responding quickly. Start happy, end happy. Get the timing sequence so clear in your mind that you do it as second nature. Just as you would not dream of using a heeling stick on your dog without having made clear what you wanted first, (command – pressure – command), you will not want the collar pressure to ever reach the dog before you communicate what you want. Never has your timing been more important. Never have mistakes been easier to make.

The first time you plan on introducing your dog to the collar pressure, again have a simple plan in your mind. Most collars have varying levels of 'stimulation'. A "1" is usually a very mild stimulation. A "5" is a high level of stimulation. If you start on a very low level and work your way up, a way you may hear suggested occasionally, you can actually teach your dog to endure the pressure and become immune to it. You don't want to do this. You don't want to nag your dog into complying. Conversely, you don't want to dial it up as high as it goes and flabbergast your dog with too much pressure. Every dog is unique in how he responds to pressure and you, as the trainer of your dog, should have a good feel for what level of stimulation your dog may require. When in doubt, be conservative. Consider putting the collar on your palm and feeling the stimulation yourself. Begin with the lowest setting and increase. You may be surprised to find it is not as awful as you initially believed.

Plan on introducing the collar pressure on one thing only. The sit command is the easiest. You will not use the collar every time, but sporadically throughout the exercise. Start with the happy bumpers as usual. Hold the transmitter in your right hand and the leash in your left. Don't wield the transmitter any more than you would wield the heeling stick. It should be a non-factor--don't make it one. Begin your heeling and sitting. Carry out the heeling and sitting without event the first time. Do a couple of sits without pressure. Then, give the sit command and hit the momentary button set on a mid-range setting of 2, 3, or 4. Follow immediately with the sit command again. (Sit--electric collar nick--sit) Just as the jerk on the chain or the pop on the bottom was quick and to the point, so should be the collar stimulation. Don't wait for something to happen. Your dog needs to sit. Make sure he does by using the leash and choke collar in conjunction with the collar. Dogs will do one of several things the first few times. One may be nothing, and you will wonder if the collar is working. The other is to emit a squeak of surprise and either sit or jump up as if the ground had bitten them. Make them sit down. Your goal is to create the conditioned response of sitting to eliminate the pressure. If your dog does not respond at all to the pressure, then your collar is too loose, not working, or set too low. If the dog is surprised but sits--that is good. If the dog overreacts, either the collar is set too high, or the dog is just overreacting. Do not allow the dog to use that to get out of sitting.

If you are nervous and insecure about what you are doing, you can be assured your dog will be as well. You must think of this in the exact light as doing obedience exercises with the heeling stick. If you pop your dog on the bottom with the heeling stick and he flares or moves away, what would you do? You would quickly make him sit. Do this the same way. Keep the objective clearly in your mind. You are conditioning the dog to sit with some collar pressure. Continue with your exercises. Proceed with conviction and you will get past this unfamiliarity, and your dog will begin to share that attitude as well. Heel and sit a few more times and then use the collar pressure again. Introduce the collar pressure only with the sit to start, and end with some positive response in your dog, preferably one in which he can't quite get seated quickly enough. That is the response you are looking for. Do not overdo this by putting too much pressure on the dog, because again you have the situation in which the dog cannot win--he will get pressure no matter what he does.

You should notice a remarkable response to the sit command after a day or two of collar conditioning on it. When your dog understands the pressure and continues to function and work to beat the pressure, you can add the "here" command to your collar conditioning. Give the sit a few days of work so your dog actually becomes comfortable with the sessions.

Here

Your dog should understand the new form of pressure for "Sit" and respond well to it. You do not stop the intermittent pressure on "Sit", but you add another element--the pressure for coming to you or yielding. Your dog must thoroughly understand the "Here" exercises. The jerk on the choke chain should be very familiar and something your dog has learned to escape by coming quickly to you when the command is given. With transmitter in one hand held unobtrusively and leash in the other, proceed with your routine obedience exercises. With your dog on the long cord and sitting in front of you, give the "Here" command with choke chain pressure first. The next time you do it, replace the choke chain jerk with a nick from the collar, "Here"--nick--"here". Hold the cord in your hand in case the dog does anything other than come directly toward you. Usually one of two things happens. Almost always it is that your dog really beats it to you. Or, you may get a stoic response in which your dog just sits there. What would you do if you were doing "here" exercises with the long cord and choke chain and your dog did not respond? That is the same thing you do now--give the command again, put pressure on your dog again and make him yield and come to you. This is not done by holding the button down, but by using the collar pressure nick on "Here" and the choke chain pressure at the same time. Your goal is to teach your dog to escape the pressure by carrying out the command quickly. You will not teach him to escape pressure by allowing him to quit on you entirely. If you have done all your groundwork, the dog will understand that it 'wins' by yielding. As soon as your dog does come towards you, stop the pressure.

You will not find numerous articles on collar conditioning, and when you do, they are usually brief and to the point. This is because it is more realistic to give someone the concept in sound collar conditioning, but almost impossible to describe all the things that might actually occur in the process. Any use of the collar is best learned by watching an expert and being watched as you begin to use it. This is the case not because the collar is so frightening or so horrific. It is because a dog will often do unexpected things to avoid any new form of pressure. If you are looking for reasons not to use the collar you can probably find them. Of course, if you are looking for reasons to avoid the choke chain, long cord or heeling stick you could as easily find those. The key to successfully collar conditioning your dog is to have a single goal each session. Keep things simple and very clear to the dog. Teach your dog to respond. If you find yourself responding to your dog instead of driving the training session, stop, regroup in your mind and start again.

After four or five collar conditioning sessions, your dog should be acquainted with pressure to sit and to come towards you. Your job is not to 'acquaint' your dog with the pressure, however; it is to 'condition' him to the pressure. Think of it with your long-term goal in mind; you ultimately want a dog that will not misunderstand the collar pressure you use when he is chasing a bird and does not want to stop and return to you. If your dog is wholeheartedly chasing a flying pheasant across a section of land and you give the "Here" whistle, the first time it happens your dog may decide it cannot stop the chase. The "Here" whistle followed by the familiar collar pressure will clearly remind your dog that it has to return to you. If you have only acquainted your dog with pressure in this form, it may not 'remember' too well and just screech and continue the chase, too excited to think things out. If, in your yardwork with the dog, you have thoroughly conditioned the dog to respond to the whistle and work hard to avoid the collar pressure, then you can easily remind your dog it must return and that is the only thing it can do.

Acquainting is an introduction. Conditioning takes time and repetition. Plan on taking a week or two to condition your dog. Keep your dog's state of mind in your thoughts as you work. The dog has to feel like it can win. You do not create that by easing up and rarely nicking the dog. You do it by using appropriate timing in your command and pressure application, and by giving the dog opportunity to escape with good, quick responses. You praise the good efforts and communicate your happiness with your dog's work. You vary the use of pressure by alternately using it and perhaps waiting to see what response you get without it. A poorer response means go back and teach some more.

You are teaching, not correcting. Keep that at the top of your thoughts in this process.

If your dog becomes confused or defeated, then you have done something wrong. Make sure you are doing retrieving work to keep your dog's desire to work with you positive and strong. Provided you have done your obedience exercises thoroughly prior to this, and conditioned your dog to pressure in the forms of choke chains and heeling sticks, then this should be a continuation of that work. When using the heeling stick to enforce a quick sit, you don't bop the dog every time it sits. You employ the stick at intervals so that the dog develops a response of sitting quickly without any great fear of the stick. It is the same with the collar. You do, however, need to use the heeling stick with enough consistency that the response it creates becomes second nature to the dog, and the same is true with the collar nick. If for any reason you feel you are not controlling the situation and simplifying is not getting you where you need to be, then get some good help with this. Don't just quit with "I knew I shouldn't use the collar." You are now avoiding the pressure of learning something that is not simple for you to learn. You don't want your dog to quit on you if things get tough and neither should you. If you can get yourself into the hands of someone who has done this countless times, you will feel much better about the whole exercise and you will never regret the results of good collar conditioning--especially on the occasions in which you really need it.

De-bolting

This is a term you will hear trainers use in reference to collar training. When dogs are being collar conditioned, often they will decide at some point that they do not want to engage in the games with you any longer. This is a standard response in a thinking animal. Even if the dog doesn't decide to try to leave the exercises during training, it may decide to escape or 'bolt' from your collar pressure while you are using it in the field. It is better to address this natural response before it becomes a dangerous situation in the field.

De-bolting is the process through which your dog learns that no matter how much he would like to run away from you and the pressure, the only thing he can do to relieve his anxiety and your pressure is to yield to you. You must be aware of this natural response in a dog, and be prepared for it. You will always want to carry out collar conditioning and de-bolting with the long cord on so you can keep hold of the dog. If at any point your dog decides to just leave to avoid you and the pressure, you must be prepared in your mind for what you are going to do. Look at it this way: if your dog decides he's had enough and is going to run to the kennel and you allow him to do just that, you have just taught him if he really doesn't like this, he can quit and go home. Then you will not be able to use collar pressure in the field when you really may need it, because your dog has learned to run away from it. On the other hand, if your dog decides he doesn't want to play anymore and attempts to run back to the kennel, or bolt, and you wish to end that response, teach the response you want. Put pressure on the dog with the "Here" command to come to you, and continue to apply the intermittent pressure with the command "Here" until the dog yields and begins to return directly to you. Always stop the pressure the instant the dog yields. When the dog begins to return instead of run away, you have taught him that the only way to escape the pressure is to yield to you. Praise the dog. If you embark on a number of sessions like this and when you are in the field and need to control your dog, your dog will know that it must respond to you, and running away or ignoring you is not an option.

Introducing the Collar in the Field

Familiarize your collar-conditioned dog to collar usage in the field, before you actually go on your annual hunting trip. That way, both you and your dog are comfortable with any corrections you may have to give to the exuberant new hunter. Initially your dog will understand it in the yardwork. You need to also make sure he understands any corrections given in a real hunting situation. This is easily accomplished by doing some conditioning exercises on a walk in the field. We have strongly advised that the dummy collar be placed on the dog while you go on outings, so he assumes it is part of the walking regalia. If the collar has always been part of your dog's gear, then he doesn't assume the collar pressure actually comes from the collar. Usually, they don't think that whole thing out at all, though we often assume they do since we are busy analyzing and justifying everything. If you never put a collar on a dog until you are actually using it, you show the dog that the collar is on, you have to behave. No collar on, I can't correct you. That wouldn't be too smart.

Take your dog out on his customary outing, rigged up now with the live collar instead of the dummy collar. Allow your dog freedom to explore and wander. At a logical point, call him to you. Now, in the exact manner you used the collar in the obedience exercises, you can use the collar 'in the field'. If your dog doesn't immediately respond to you, give the command again, use collar pressure in the form of a momentary nick, and give the command again. Teach your dog that the same response is required walking through the field as is in obedience exercises. Use the "Here" whistle just as you used it in obedience, and require the dog respond as quickly to the whistle. Your objective is not to overwhelm your dog with collar pressure in the field, but to make sure he understands it and is comfortable with it. Allow your dog to enjoy the outing, and still use the occasional chance to put a little pressure on "Here", and occasionally on "Sit". Don't figure that because you have taught your dog to sit on the whistle in obedience exercises that you can now require that your dog sit on the whistle out in the field at a distance from you. That is a common misconception. There are some dogs that will sit on command at a distance, but the customary response in a collar-conditioned dog to any pressure at a distance is to hightail it back to you as quickly as possible. If you continue to holler "Sit!" or blow the "Sit" whistle and the dog is returning to you, you are confusing your dog. You have taught the dog to sit when he is in proximity to you, and you have taught your dog to return to you from distances. Dogs do not automatically extrapolate to distances what you have taught them close in, though you do that pretty well. At this stage in training, expect your dog to return directly to you when called, and to sit when told at a close range. More advanced training will deal with long-distance control, not collar conditioning. You can use collar pressure for "Sit" to enforce steadiness on marks and honoring. This is not the stage at which handling is started.

Throughout all your work with your dog, you have put forms of 'pressure' on him to sit, to come to you, and to heel at your side. You have put some ear pinch pressure on him to fetch as well, but that was short-lived and not a routine form of pressure. Once your dog fetches on command, you do not continue to pinch the ear--it is neither fair nor necessary. Use this logic to dictate your future use of the electric collar. Pressure can be used on a dog when the reason for the pressure is absolutely and clearly understood by the dog. Because you give an 'over' hand signal to a dog and the dog does not go over, does not mean you can nick the dog for not taking the cast. You do not know what the dog is thinking, and you will have no idea what the pressure from the collar will mean to the dog. In fact, it will be wholly confusing to a dog because taking an over cast is a concept, and it is accustomed to pressure for specific actions, primarily "Here" and "Sit".

Regardless of how simple certain things are to you mentally, it is not the same with your dog. You must learn to understand the differences between your thought processes and your dog's, particularly if you are going to use remote means of applying pressure. If you were to watch advanced dogs running the most technical set of marks and blinds, you will find good handlers use the collar only when it is absolutely necessary, and then only on the commands on which the dog has been collar conditioned. This will be "Sit" and "Here", and for dogs through the advanced force work, "Back". In that way, it is clear that the dog understands any pressure it receives, and knows how to eliminate the pressure.

The electric collar is not a panacea for problems with your dog's behavior. Misused, it can cause more problems than it ever solves. It does not teach anything to your dog, it only reinforces what your dog already knows. Used correctly, it ensures that your dog will respond to you in the field, even when enthusiasm tells the dog it would rather not listen to you. The collar will allow you to teach your dog not to chase rabbits or game you do not want the dog to chase. It will allow you to stop your dog from pursuing a bird that you do not want your dog to pursue. It allows you to teach your dog it must respond to you at a distance, and may enable you to stop a dog from crossing a busy street or encountering some other impending danger to the dog. We can tell you many stories of how a collar-conditioned dog could have been but was not injured or lost, because it knew its job was to listen and respond to its owner. We could also tell you stories of people doing stupid and harmful things with the collar, because they were not nearly as informed about its usage as they thought they were. People who are harmful to dogs are harmful to dogs; the collar just makes it a little easier. People who are understanding and respectful of dogs are just that as well, and treat dogs in that manner with or without the collar. The collar merely extends the range and potential of what can be done with the dog.

Chapter 13
The Field

Throughout this book, we have implored you to pay attention to the small details. The emphasis on solid obedience and good attitude has been reiterated many times. You have worked very hard on establishing a program in which your dog believes in you, and understands that good things happen when he works with you. Now you will see why these things are so very important. It is time to put all the pieces together--and into action.

Dogs cannot be taught to be good hunters anymore than you could be taught to be a great romantic. You learn it by doing it. You have acquired the skills to develop the great hunter, however. There are many trainers who wholeheartedly believe all you need to do to train hunting dogs is take them hunting. That is certainly the easiest way to train but not the surest way to shaping a dog that is a joy to hunt. So many times we have had people tell us what a great hunting dog they have that in fact learned to hunt in the field. Eventually it comes to light that the dog is great but; it finds the bird but doesn't always bring it back, or it brings it back to whomever it chooses that day, or it can't be called off the chase of a fleeing bird, or it finds all the birds inside and outside shotgun range, it breaks on flushed birds and Crazy Uncle Elmo peppered it with a few BB's ...etc., etc. It is usually best to put the solid foundation on the dog, and then enjoy the next decade of hunting without having to contend with any irritating or unsafe behaviors on the part of the dog.

Your fundamentally schooled dog will not know where wild birds hide. It will not know how to pace itself throughout a day so it can hunt later as well as it does early on. It may get so excited when the wings flutter that it forgets all the rules. There are many things it will not know the first season, and even into the second. What you have done with the fundamentals, however, is prepare your dog to work with you in the field. You have the tools now to teach your dog in what range he should quarter. You have the tools to call him back when he really isn't so ready to come back. You have the tools to insist your dog pick up any bird dropped. Expect it to take two years for you to develop the master upland hunter. No matter how good a dog you have and how wonderful your training has been, it will be experience and maturity that finishes off that final superstar hunting dog.

There is a strong desire to 'over-regulate' a well-trained dog. Because you have a great deal of control over your dog does not mean you must always use that control. As a good trainer, you have to respect and honor your dog now more than ever. Because you know where a bird is doesn't mean you should direct your dog to it just because you can. Let the dog learn how to look for birds and how to find them. If your dog sees a bird go down and you send him on a retrieve, allow him to hunt the area without interfering. If a dog hunts for several minutes, as long as he is making a good effort and not getting lost or getting too hot, leave him alone. It is time to let your dog develop its own skills and learn to be confident that he or she can do the work for you. If a dog is avidly searching for bird scent, leave him to his job. Believe in your dog. Believe what you see. This is what it was bred to do.

Upland Hunting

It is advisable to set up controlled upland hunting before taking on wild birds in a new place, just as you do with retrieving. You taught your dog to mark by controlling where the birds fell and how easy or difficult it would be for your dog to locate them. While you are still training your pointing retriever, the upland work is most easily accomplished when you know where the birds are and can manage a little of what happens. If you've spent months whoa breaking and training your dog only to subject the dog to nothing but birds that either run or flush when the dog is remotely in the area, you can undo much of what you trained. In time a good dog will learn what birds do, and what you expect him to do in different situations. Show him what the expectation is now, and in the real hunt you can easily make adjustments 'on the fly.'

The scenario is very simple, and is played over again each upland training day as the dog progresses. It is very important that live birds be used in this training. Remember that these are retrievers. They are bred to retrieve dead birds. A live bird can be easily differentiated from a dead bird by scent, and your dog will know the difference. We have found nothing that works in the field except the real thing and that is a live, planted bird.   It does not seem terribly important what bird is planted, but that it be live, with the ability to fly. Pigeons can be used, and they are certainly the cheapest birds. Quail are some of the least expensive game birds you can buy from a game bird business. Chukar and pheasant are more expensive, take more room and more feed, and pheasant can be quite unpleasant to one another in small confines. If you plan on training your pointing retriever sufficiently, you will need to plan on using live birds as much as time, availability, budget, and common sense allow. Obviously, the more birds, the better your dog will be trained on upland hunting. The birds must have the ability to fly; otherwise, you may inadvertently teach your dog to catch birds.

Before the dog is brought out, two or three live birds are planted in the field. There are two good ways to do this; one is to 'dizzy' the bird by holding the bird's body and rapidly spinning the head and neck until the bird, unharmed, has lost its equilibrium. You can tuck the head under the wing and place the bird securely in some cover that the bird will not want to leave. This most closely approximates what you will encounter in real hunting situation. The other is to use bird launchers, in which the bird is placed in a wire cage or holding arms. It is either launched via remote control or by foot pedal. This way, you know the bird has not left where you put it, and you can 'flush' the bird exactly when you want, giving you leeway to control your dog during the entire operation and not have to react to unplanned events. Launchers have never been our first choice because an intelligent dog quickly learns to smell the launcher. Then you have a dog looking for launchers and then anticipating the flush, which is hardly the intent. A launcher allows you to plant and 'flush' two birds at one time. However, unless you are addressing a specific problem with a dog, they may generate as many problems as they solve. Be thoughtful about where you place the birds. They should be quite independent of one another, so that the dog will not be in a position to wind more than one bird at a time. Consider the direction of the wind, the nature and degree of cover, and the terrain. You may wish to mark the location of the planted birds with a small orange ribbon so that you do not loose track of where the birds lie. Don't mark the birds in such a way that the dog learns to locate the ribbon to find the bird. Some dogs are amazingly wily about figuring out your markers while others seem oblivious. Space the birds at adequate distances so your dog doesn't learn that hunting is a bonanza that occurs within the first four minutes. Similarly, don't space the birds so far apart that your dog may become too tired or overheated before the training session is completed.

Always watch your dog for overheating. Because you are not too hot or tired does not mean your dog is not. Most dogs are extremely excited and run five times the distance you do. This can lead to several conditions, all looking like an overheated dog. Overheating is indicated by strong panting, dark tongue, and when becoming advanced, by a very wobbly back end. If this occurs, stop immediately and do whatever it takes to cool your dog. Immerse him in water; give him some water to drink, but not the huge amount he may want. You may wish to discuss with your vet the best means to deal with overheating if your dog has that problem, and many dogs do.

To introduce and train your dog to upland hunting, you will need a choke chain and 25-foot cord. The cord should be the same one used in obedience training: lightweight, fairly frictionless and attached securely to the choke chain. Place a dummy collar or live collar on the dog if you are a user. Your dog should understand and respond to the "Here" whistle so that you may use that to bring him back in a direction toward you. This makes establishing quartering quite simple. Ideally there should be two gunners, at least, accompanying you and your dog. You should, if possible, designate yourself as the dog handler. If not, do the best you can, but you cannot shoot and steady your dog at the same time. Get help with this. Employ gunners, if at all possible, who can shoot well, for obvious reasons.

We like to whoa the dog before each upland session. It serves a couple of purposes. The dog isn't taken out of the truck to immediately run wild. That isn't a desirable pattern to create. The dog is whoaed for a couple of moments to begin the hunting session with control and to re-establish the concept of responding to the whoa command. We don't have solid data to demonstrate that this must be done, but it does seem to make a difference in the behavior of most dogs as they hunt and eventually point in the field. After whoaing, the dog is released and the hunting can begin.

You should already have the plan in your mind about what you are going to do and what you want from your dog. At first your dog may want to walk with you, if you have not already taught the 'boldness on birds' in the earlier chapter. Don't let that worry you. A few birds shot, and a good dog will have the idea. The boldness work you should have done months ago should work for you now to get the dog excited about getting out and looking for more birds. Give him whatever phrase or terms you plan to use to direct him to begin hunting on his own. Use enthusiasm in your voice--this is fun. We use "Hunt 'em up!" and "Birds in here!" to let dogs know what is going on. "Hunt 'em up!" tells them they are hunting birds, and releases them from heeling and walking with you. Once they associate the commands with knowing a bird is imminent, it generates great excitement in the dogs.

Space the gunners as far apart as you want your dog to quarter. Each gunner can, in turn, call the dog toward him, with the "Hup" phrase used to get his attention on retrieves, the 'come this way' multiple whistle, or whatever it may take to get the dog going back in his direction. When the dog reaches the limit in one direction, the gunner on the other side needs to bring him back toward him in the same manner. Continue this quartering action while you are moving forward as a front, toward the first bird you have planted. This doesn't have to be a straight line; you can curve your direction. You will need to be careful not to "push" your dog by walking more rapidly than the dog is. Pushing your dog teaches him to walk with you instead of using his nose and hunting for birds. You must be patient in the early stages and let your dog learn to take the initiative himself, and not rely on you for all direction. This is always a little tough on the Type A's out there who want to make this a great dog right now.

Initially your gunners will encourage and show the dog that it is supposed to run back and forth between them. The objective is that the dog learns to quarter between gunners without being encouraged or directed. Show the dog that it is to traverse that distance by calling it or encouraging back and forth, but stop the whistles or cues as soon as the dog shows it understands what it is supposed to do. Teach your dog to quarter on its own. Be quiet when you can be.

The dog should be dragging the cord behind him. Your dog should already be accustomed to this cord, and ignore it. If it gets entangled, walk over, free the rope, and continue. If the dog doesn't respond as you wish, with the rope you have a tool to ensure the dog will respond. If the dog continues too far to the right, and ignores your directions back to the left, pick up the cord and stop it from going further. Change its direction with the rope. You need to do this without quelling your dog's enthusiasm for the hunt, so use good judgment. At the same time, don't let the dog run wild and get out of your control. This is why the earlier obedience foundation is so important. If you have taught your dog to do nothing but listen to you and work with you, he will do this now as well, and you won't have to deal with the issues of lack of control.

Most dogs begin to learn about quartering quickly. Don't worry if your dog still sticks close to you. Then you walk him out and quarter yourself, always enticing him to hunt. Be patient. Some dogs are aggressive enough they would just as soon go out in front of you. Others have to learn the rewards of moving ahead, and they will do that after they find a few birds and get to retrieve them for you. Do whatever it takes to get your dog excited, and acquaint him with what his ultimate purpose is-- finding live birds.

As you begin to near the first planted bird, be aware of the wind direction. You want to be downwind of the bird, and close enough to your dog to be able to get your hands on the rope. Your job is to watch the behavior of your dog. In the beginning you should get nearer your dog, and be prepared to possibly require steadiness in the point. You will be able to tell in most cases when your dog has detected the scent. Don't stop him from proceeding toward the bird. As the dog gets up to the bird, watch your dog. When your dog points (not hesitates or searches, but points) your job as trainer is to not interfere. If your dog holds the point, say nothing. Anything you say at this time would be interference to your dog's attention and focus. If your dog begins to creep or show movement toward the bird, you now use your ever-familiar "Whoa" command. It is at this point that you will reap the rewards of how much 'foundation building' you have done over the past months. If you whoaed your dog a few times when you remembered, you will have a dog that has a vague memory of you wanting him to remain in place. That vague memory will be most likely washed over by a tidal wave of desire to get the bird. If you conditioned your dog to remain in place, then your pointing dog will most likely remain in place. This will be familiar territory for both of you: You giving a calm "whoa" and even primping your dog, and your dog standing still for you. However, for the pointing dog, the stand is no longer a calm erect stance. It is usually a head down pointer stance. Do not interfere, just reinforce it positively.

If your dog actually does move, do just as you did in your whoa drills. Bring the dog immediately back into the position with the firm whoa command. Teach your dog that the rules apply right here as well. You should have your dog hold its first point for at least a moment. Without overdoing and causing the dog to lose interest, you should teach the dog that the point is a steady, continuous thing without specific time limits. After a moment have someone flush the bird and shoot it. You need to be in a position to make sure your dog remains steady to wing and shot. If your dog moves, invoke the whoa command and make him remain in place. The only reason to ever let a dog chase a bird is in the few circumstances that the control should be sacrificed to build up a good, enthusiastic attitude. A dog should love this, and if he doesn't, either the dog is not a hunter or you have done something wrong. Never lose sight of the importance of attitude.

One of the biggest mistakes we made in the beginning was to make the point on a live bird unpleasant for a dog. In our earlier stages of developing the training program for these dogs, as soon as the dog got excited and pointed a bird, we were all over the dog if it moved or made any attempt to get the bird. The dog was yanked back or picked up and set unceremoniously back in place. A time or two of this behavior and as soon as the dog found the bird it became nervous, even turning away and avoiding the bird. Why? Because any time it found a bird and got excited, we got in the way and were so busy messing with or correcting the dog that it associated the live bird with unpleasantness. So, we taught it that live birds were not a good thing. This falls in the stupid-trainer category. The whole key to this program is the initial stage of boldness on birds as a young pup; enough that the dog is ecstatic about finding live birds, and does not worry about what happens when it does. Then, after the dog has been fully whoaed, with birds in the yard and much temptation, the whoaing in the field does not detract from the excitement of the live bird. So important.

When the bird has been shot, keep your dog at whoa for a few seconds and then send him for the retrieve on his name. This should be ever-familiar territory as well for your dog--marking and retrieving should be sort of like eating and breathing. You may have to be prepared for whatever dramatics your dog will go through, and be in a position to make the dog remain in place, and if possible make the dog watch the bird fly and fall. This may mean literally holding onto the dog and keeping him in a position so that he can watch the bird. With some dogs this is not difficult, and with others it is a wrestling match. Think ahead, and be ready to make sure what needs to happen does happen. Once your dog understands how the game works, you will no longer have to teach him to watch or even remain still.

Important: If the pointing dog does not point the bird or bumps it while hunting, don't shoot it and reward the non-pointed bird with a retrieve. Never allow him to retrieve a bird he didn't point as he should have. Think about what you are communicating to him if you do send him on the retrieve. If he begins to point and then goes ahead and charges the bird and you shoot the bird and let him get it, he has just successfully been taught that he doesn't have to hold still to get the bird. On the other hand, if he learns that when he doesn't honor his first inclination to freeze and hold he gets nothing, he will learn more effectively that you want the steady, pointing behavior. You may sacrifice birds you do not wish to sacrifice this way, but it is better to return a few birds to nature than it is to teach your pointing dog that he really doesn't have to point.

So many times people have looked at us with an incredulous expression when we don't shoot a bird. Their attitude is that there is something inherently amiss on the planet to have a hunting dog and a flying bird--and not shoot. If you drive all the way to South Dakota to hunt pheasants, then by all means shoot the birds you can hit. If you are training your dog to go to South Dakota next season, then be a dog trainer and not a hunter. Think about what you are doing. If you are teaching your dog to be a staunch pointer, then show him that non-pointed birds go away, and pointed birds are fair game. You will be glad you did when your dog locks up on a pheasant and it takes you several minutes to get there.

Steady to Wing and Shot

When the bird flushes, your dog should remain standing and watching. This is where your basic obedience really pays off. As the bird first flushes, give the whoa command again to make sure your dog knows it is expected to remain in place. Hold onto the rope so he can't break and chase the bird. If the dog still wishes to break, give the whoa command and make him stand in place. Do not let him creep around. He needs to learn to watch the direction of the bird and mark its fall. When the bird has been shot and dropped, hold your dog for a moment, and then send him on his name to retrieve the mark. Use here whatever form of pressure you have customarily used to enforce steadiness on whoa'ing and marks. If steadiness on shot birds becomes a battleground, end the battle quickly. You can go back to your yard work and obedience, and walk with your dog and suddenly toss the bumper up and in front of you. At that instant, as described in the whistle usage chapter, enforce the whoa with rope pressure or collar pressure. Familiarize your dog with steadiness in that situation, and then reinforce it in the upland flush situation. Use the rope or other familiar obedience pressure, if necessary, to ensure your dog's swift and direct return to you with the bird. Make him behave just as he does in the drills.

In the event your dog was too excited or confused to watch the bird and mark its fall, don't be too concerned. Walk out with your dog and have him find and retrieve the bird. This is another reason you never use dead birds for pointing, because they are for retrieving. It is common to have dogs too excited by the proximity of the shotgun blast and the feathers flying to watch the bird fly and go down. Experience and your control will teach your dog how the game works. Once you have located, flushed, and shot your first bird and had your dog retrieve it, you are ready to proceed to the next bird. Get the rope in the right position so you can continue to control your dog. If necessary, give the "Hunt 'em up" command, and begin the exercise again. After the first time, your dog will begin to relish this activity. Again, there are plenty of retrievers who have little interest in this. If you go out several times and your dog never gets any more excited about it, consider whether this dog is best used as a hunting dog.

Dogs who are very confused or even disinterested in the beginning can be many things. They may be too young to begin the upland fieldwork. Not all dogs are ready at the same age. They may not have heard a shotgun blast until then, which is a mistake in the dog's training. Their retriever training up to this point should have long ago introduced the gun. The dog may have never been introduced to the excitement of live birds in the field, something that ideally should be a part of their early development. The dog may be a slow learner, or may not feel well. There can be a variety of reasons for confusion or apparent lack of interest. The lack of interest may also be just that--a complete disinterest in hunting--and we have seen that many times.

Do not reach a judgment too soon. We have trained several excellent pointers who would never have made it had we given up when the pointing was not shown in early training sessions. Continue to work with your dog several times a week if possible. If no interest is shown, stop doing the upland work for a week or a month. Then go back and try it again. If there is improvement, you had pushed too early. If there is no improvement, wait another month, and try again. Eventually, your dog will tell you whether he wants to do this, and whether he is going to point. Don't try to make your dog into something he or she is not--it never works.

Too much pressure in the yardwork appears to interfere with a dog's behavior in the field. If you are collar conditioning a dog with "Sit" and "Here" and then run out in the field for upland training, your dog may be so concerned about you that it will default to the all-safe "Sit" position when things start to happen. Don't expect your dog to switch back and forth between responses to you. Go ahead and do your collar conditioning, but get through it to completion. Then relax your dog before going into the field.

There are always questions regarding upland work that have to do with lack of fundamentals. What do you do if your dog creeps? A dog that creeps is not honoring the whoa command. Enforce the whoa breaking. Never reward lack of staunchness with the shot and retrieve. What do you do if the bird runs on the dog? If the bird is gone, release the dog from the point the way that you do in whoa training and tell the dog to continue hunting. If a dog sees a bird and initiates a chase that you do not want, tell him "whoa" or call him back to you. Enforce the command. You should have whoaed a moving dog in your whoa breaking drills. As much as we would like to have it appear that advanced upland work is technical and complicated, it is common sense and an application of the basic tools you developed in the yard.

It is experience and time that will develop a top-flight upland hunter. If you hunt wild pheasants, hunting wild pheasants will develop those skills necessary in a dog for that type of hunting. If you hunt quail or grouse in Texas, you must hunt there so your dog learns about the terrain and cover in which those birds hide, and how those birds move and evade predators. Some dogs that are not quick to pick up the technical skills of force fetch and marking have an innate ability to hunt birds better than many formally trained dogs. Nothing teaches hunting like hunting.

When upland hunting with a trained dog, you should expect your dog to quarter within whatever range you need without your cues. The dog should listen and respond to you. It should not hunt until you direct it to, and should return to you when you ask. The dog should be aware of your movement and changes in direction, and respond to what you do without being directed. It should learn to find the birds that are there and hold its point until you arrive and flush the bird. Your dog should remain steady until the bird is flushed and shot and continue to remain steady until you release the dog for the retrieve. If you only winged a bird and you want the dog to pursue it for you, then release him when you see the bird is not immediately going down. The dog should be able to mark the area in which the bird fell and diligently hunt that area until it finds the bird. The bird should then be brought back immediately to you and handed over unchewed and unscathed.

Hunt Dead

Often in hunting, there is a dead bird out there 'somewhere', and neither you nor your dog is exactly sure where. Or, you may know where it is and you want your dog to go find it. For this, you will want to acquaint your dog with the concept of hunting for a dead bird. Very often, pointing dogs new to upland hunting will run out and re-point the dead bird. This is always kind of funny, because no one knows what he or she should say then. It is just fine if your new dog points the freshly shot bird--it smells live, after all! Just tell him to fetch, and he will know to pick it up. You can generate a command for him to go hunt a dead bird, to cue them there is a dead bird out there, or you can just tell him to "hunt 'em up," and soon he will learn the difference between the live and not-so-live.

We sent one very experienced Grand Master Pointing Retriever after a duck that had been winged but not dropped--hunting, not training. The duck flew away from the pond and into the sagebrush about a quarter mile away. The dog knew it was out there somewhere, and hunted in front as we walked in the direction the bird flew. As she got downwind of the injured duck hiding in the brush, she stopped and pointed. Now this is a dog that has won field trials, has a Master Hunter title, and hunted for three years straight. She knows what ducks are, and she knows what upland birds are. Now she's out in the sagebrush, and found a duck hiding in the cover. It was an interesting thing to observe...what was she going to do? She pointed the duck for a few seconds, and then you could actually see the confusion in her face. She looked quickly over at us, then immediately resumed her point. She knew something was amiss, but by gosh, this bird was alive and in the cover, so she held her point. One quick "Fetch" and the duck was on its way back to us, flapping and protesting. Give these guys a chance. They usually know better than we do what needs to be done.

Backing

So what if you and your hunting buddy both own pointing dogs? Hunting them together can be a lot of fun. It isn't much fun, however, when the second dog comes busting in and overwhelms the first dog on point. Most dogs need to be taught to back the point of another. An aggressive dog will be too competitive to naturally sit back and watch another dog on point. Backing should be taught starting in the yard, as described under Whoa Breaking. First teach the dog the concept of stopping at the sight of another dog on point. Do this in the yard until the dog's response is automatic, with no command from you. Then in the upland training when you know where the bird is, you can set the dogs up so one finds it first, and you are in place to use "Whoa" and enforce the backing response in the second dog. It is not difficult, but it does take time and repetition. Labs can back the same way other pointing breeds can back. You will also need to teach the pointing retriever to honor the retrieve of another dog for this to work well. Just because you can get your dog to honor the point of another dog, does not mean that dog will automatically honor the retrieve. Plan on working both in your yardwork and retrieving training, so the backing dog will also let the working dog bring the bird back single-handedly.

Mistakes to Avoid

Some dogs are avid hunters from the get-go. There are ten-week-old Labs that will search tirelessly for stuff in the cover. Let them learn about birds in there and you will have to drag them away. Other dogs show little interest in anything aside from 'hanging' with you. Just like people, dogs develop at different rates. Whether physical, mental or emotional, some dogs do not seem to even understand aggressiveness or hunting for a while. Some never develop that tendency, some seem born with it, and others acquire it with time. Do not read this book or listen to someone with all the answers and make a quick judgment about your dog. If your dog is good, you will know it. If your dog is slow, you may not know what its potential is. Usually, a dog's desire to retrieve is very related to its desire to hunt, since they are both means to the same end. If you have a dog that loves to retrieve, you most likely have a dog that will love to look for live birds--once it understands and is ready. If your dog isn't big on retrieving, odds are it will be less inclined to expend energy looking for something it hasn't even seen.

Teach your young dog to be bold on birds, if it has that desire. Do not upland hunt with your unskilled young dog if you can muster the self-control. We have been asked hundreds of times how to stop a dog that was hunted as a baby from eating birds or chasing birds. Rephrased, the question is, "How do I stop my dog from doing what I taught it to do?" Why not just avoid the problem entirely, and teach right from the beginning what you want from the dog?

That said, be wary about trying to teach something to a dog before it is ready. Many times we have received the question from well-intentioned dog owners: "How do I get my dog's pointing style back? It seems to have gotten worse over time." What happened is the dog is taken out bird hunting and when it pointed, immediately the owner jumped in with whoa and steadiness pressure and every other way to interfere with the dog. Soon, the dog is more concerned with what the owner is going to do than it is focused on the trophy, and the style goes to heck or the dog quits pointing. If a young dog is pointing a bird, your job is to not interfere. If the dog creeps or moves, use "whoa". If whoa doesn't work, either your whoa breaking isn't finished or the dog is too young to put the whole package together. Figure out which one it is and react appropriately.

Make sure all the components of training are maintained. Now what does this mean? A well-trained dog understands obedience. It comes when it is called, sits when it is directed. It understands marking a fallen bird, waiting to be sent, going to the area of the fall and hunting diligently for the bird. It also understands that "Hunt 'em up" means to stay within a certain range of you and use its nose, eye and experience to tell it where birds are, and to point them out. Each of these separate activities demands a different mental emphasis on the part of your dog. If all you do is obedience, making your dog focus completely on you and your every word, your dog will not learn how to focus on its own senses and intuition to look for live birds. If you do nothing but hunt live birds, your dog will focus only on its nose and intuition, and lose the skills of watching a bird fall and diligently hunting that single area. Each of these areas of training demands something from a different aspect of the dog, and it is always best to maintain all of them to keep the whole package functioning in the field, in the blind, in the house, and in daily life. Any skill or discipline you possess will weaken with lack of use, and it is very true for these dogs.

Don't train the exact same way all the time. A lot can be told about how a person trains a dog when you see the dog actually hunt. We had one individual come out with a pointing dog, only to see the dog point every obvious clump of cover in a field. There were no birds in the obvious clumps, but apparently the dog was so accustomed to finding birds in obvious clumps, that out of habit, it went directly there. It is challenging to be smarter than an upland hunting dog, but it is necessary in training. Predictable or habitual training teaches a dog those habits, and not the skills of hunting. Just as throwing every mark a dog gets at a distance of 73 yards teaches the dog to hunt in a 73-yard radius, planting every training bird 150 yards from the car in a clump of cover or under a deadwood pile results in a dog hunting those situations exclusively. Think dog when you are training a dog, and think wild bird when training upland hunting if you can.

There are so many strange products for dog training on the market. Each time we make a trip into the 'big city' to a sporting goods store, we stand there wide-eyed like Ellie Mae and Jethro, looking at the dog training aids. Scented things, feathers to tie on things, cans of bird smelling stuff, bumpers that look like birds…it is amazing. If a dog can smell specific odors in the concentrations of 5 parts per million or less, we're figuring they know the difference between a real live pheasant and canned pheasant scent. We sure hope they do, as we don't want them pointing any discarded cans of the stuff! It's also a pretty good bet that a feather tied to a training bumper is actually different to a dog than a live chukar hiding in the brush. There are no doubt good uses for many of these products. If it takes a feather tied to a bumper to initially get your dog to retrieve, then by all means tie one on. Do not for a moment believe you can trick a dog with artificial things, however. Scent sprayed on an object hidden in the field will not do much to teach your dog to hunt wild pheasant. Who wants to learn about dating by going out with a cardboard cutout?

Finally, make sure your dog is in good condition to upland hunt or train. Dogs should carry no excess weight in any season. Dogs should have cardiovascular and muscular fitness if they are expected to run for any period of time. This is not acquired sitting in the kennel or backyard. Imagine yourself sitting idly all summer, and then suddenly being expected to run multiple 10K races. You would think that was stupid, and you would probably injure or at least humiliate yourself. Don't do that to your dog. Keep him fit and healthy and prepared for some great upland hunting adventures.

Some Dog Stories

We have had literally hundreds of pointing Labs through our training kennel. All of the dogs you see pictured throughout this book have been with us. Some of them pointed the first live bird they ever saw. Some did not. Some pointed the first wing it ever saw, while others merely attempted to eat it. GMPR Gumbo of Black Forest MH, a great dog that has produced some great dogs, pointed a wild quail on a walk when he was 12 weeks old. GMPR Cajun of Black Forest MH, another producer of Grand Master Pointing Retrievers, didn't point live birds until he was about nine months old. We won't know if it was something we did or did not do, or just the nature of the dog. We have had dogs that became spectacular pointers be so aggressive initially on live birds that we were concerned they would ever become staunch pointers. We've had great dogs point meadowlarks, and great dogs ignore them. The bottom line has become that if a little dog points birds, it should be a good pointer if we get the solid foundation on it and it is then offered ample opportunity to learn to hunt. If a little dog doesn't point birds, we don't jump to conclusions until they show that behavior for the first year or more. Stories abound about non-pointing Labs that started to point at the age of three or six or nine years, or some magical age. Perhaps had these 'potential' pointers been whoa broken, the phenomenon would have been discovered earlier. We have seen pointing Labs that have never heard the word "whoa" become great pointers.

Still, all of these unique animals were trained with a solid foundation and then allowed to acquire their own skills of marking, hunting, searching and finding. People who come to train upland with us are often surprised at how little 'training' is going on. They must envision coming to a professional trainer and seeing all kinds of training gizmos and commands and little 'tricks'. Instead what they see is a dog, some birds and some people with very little to say.

Chapter 14
Dogs and Attitude

Attitude is everything....

Throughout this book and around many dog trainers, you will repeatedly hear about 'attitude'. The term is very often misinterpreted. It is simple to conceive of your dog's attitude being important, but what does that really look like on a day-to-day basis? What does this mean and how do you know if you are maintaining the kind of attitude you need for effective training?

A dog should enjoy what he is doing. That does not mean every day and every training session must be easy and a great joy. It does mean that the dog should believe that this is a good thing and look forward to it, even though there will be days you both may wish were a little better. Think of the kid on the swim team or the football team. Practices are not always pure pleasure, but there is a great deal of 'pleasure' from the work, the process, and the notable improvement. However, if that kid begins to believe he can never succeed and doesn't measure up, then he won't. There must be an appropriate balance between demanding enough so that there is progress made, and yet enough success that it seems within reach.

One of the most difficult things to do well while training a dog, is to put your personality aside and do the best thing for the dog. People who are a bit dry and boring train that way, and so training is dry and boring for the dog. It is almost impossible to have an enthusiastic, robust attitude toward fieldwork when you are being taught and coached by someone who has no spirit whatsoever. The best thing you can do is to put yourself in your dog's shoes. That is not as easy as it sounds, but give it a mental go sometime when you are planning out a training session.

Dogs don't think so geometrically or logically as we do. Time and time again we have heard the protestations of handlers when they were upset with their dogs, "But he knew that bird was out there, he just wouldn't go where I told him to go!" Or, "When I give him a left cast, he knows he is supposed to go left!" The question is how do we know what they are thinking? How do we know what they know? We are guessing, and some of us are a little better at that than others. What we know is what we would be thinking in their shoes. Be aware that your thoughts are not those of your dog.

Sometimes a dog is really trying to do what you ask, but is not doing it the way you would like. He may be hunting for a bird you had thrown with all his heart, but in the wrong area. Or he may be doing obedience exercises with you but you are nagging him with your repeated commands so that he loses any good response. Then it is easy to get mad or frustrated. Now put yourself in your dog's shoes. Here you are, doing the best you know how and your coach is mad. There are two options: give up, or try even harder. Either one is likely to garner an even more negative response. A few sessions like this and your dog will lose heart. Read your dog. If a dog goes out on a mark and isn't bearing down or trying, you have reason for a little frustration. If your dog goes out on a mark and is hunting where the dog truly believes the bird is, though it is not the area of the fall, you have no reason for anger. Your dog is doing its best and that is all you can ask. You cannot ask your dog to be perfect, anymore than you can be perfect. You can only ask that your dog gives the best effort. If you punish or correct the dog's best effort, you communicate to the dog that it is a bad dog. There is no greater blow to a dog.

Conversely, if your dog runs out on a mark and frolics through the field with no intent or seriousness about the work of retrieving, you can't sit idly by assuming your dog is giving you his best effort. There is a significant and recognizable difference between a dog frolicking and exhibiting a casual attitude toward work, and a dog that is really bearing down but not in the right place. Don't punish or correct the dog giving you his best. If he makes an error, show him the error and try it again. If the dog misses the mark, have your gunner help him and run it again. Help your dog figure out whatever threw it off in the first place. Praise him for his effort when he is returning from a job well done. This will serve to make your dog even more willing to try and give you his best effort and enjoy doing it.

For the dog that is choosing to frolic instead of work for you, be careful about your reactions. Do not assume you know what the dog is thinking. Your dog may actually believe it is perfectly okay to folic a bit before finding its bird. If it does it is most likely because you taught it that it could do that, very often as a pup. In that case, direct your frustration where it belongs, at the dog's trainer. Figure out what you might have done to create that attitude and go back and redo that training.

When a dog has a very lackadaisical attitude toward work or retrieving, assuming it is not the very nature of the dog, you can go after the attitude in indirect means. It is not usually advisable to go after a 'problem' by going directly after the problem. It is very much human nature to do that, however. If a dog is dawdling over a bird instead of picking it up, the handler usually will walk out and begin the force fetch all over with the bird and the dog, because the dog is not picking up the bird. The result of 'in your face' corrections is usually that the dog will be even more hesitant to go out and pick up that bird since it became so unpleasant the last time it did just that. The dog is not thinking your thoughts, "Whew, last time I went out and dawdled over the bird he came out and pinched my ear so I sure won't do that again." Instead, it is more likely your dog is thinking "Whew, bad things happened last time I went out and picked up the bird, I am not even going out there this time." The use of indirect pressure can be very effective in correcting dogs with problems.

Indirect pressure means going after your dog's mental state instead of the immediate problem. The best way to clarify this is with some examples. We can use dawdling over a thrown bird as a good example. Some dogs with a lazy or lackadaisical attitude will run out to a mark and stand over it without picking it right up and returning. This can mean a variety of things, and often you cannot be sure what has caused it. Instead of going out and pinching your dog's ear because he is not picking up the bird, correct your dog for not returning to you, since in fact the dog is not returning to you. Call the dog back to you and correct your dog if he doesn't return immediately. You will notice that a dog that has been force fetched will quickly pick up the bird before coming back. You have corrected the dog for something it clearly understands with no negative associations with the bird. Whether you use the collar or the long cord, you can require that your dog return immediately. Do that a few times and the problem of dawdling over a bird will go away. You made your dog do what you were asking in a very clear manner and wound up also making your dog pick up the bird quickly as well.

Another example of indirect pressure to solve a problem is a dog that jumps on people. That has to be in the top ten of all dog problems. People have commands for not jumping and commands for what to do when they have jumped. It is an interesting concept--if you have a command for not jumping, does that imply there is one for jumping? Curiosity aside, indirect pressure if often a good way to deal with this problem. It is hard to be equipped to deal with a jumping dog at all moments. You can however be prepared to require that your dog sit at any moment. When a dog is taught that it must sit immediately when given the sit command, then use that to preclude jumping. Do not turn jump-ing into a 'knee in the chest' or 'heeling stick over the head' duel between you and your dog. Take control of the situation by using the well-under-stood concept of sitting on command. When your dog is going to jump, tell him to sit and enforce that. Then the issue is not jumping but sitting and your dog must react to you instead of you reacting to your dog.

In general when dogs are not focused in their work or not giving you the level of effort you should expect from them, you can use indirect means to address the particular items that you find troublesome. Obedience is almost always the best place to accomplish this. It was your obedience exercises that were utilized in the previous two examples, one using "here" and the other using "sit". That is another compelling reason to emphasize the basics of obedience. Those few simple taught behaviors will be used to refine essentially all of your dog's behaviors at home or at work in the field. In addressing problems in this manner, you do not sacrifice your dog's attitude and spirit toward work. And you don't have to be able to successfully read his mind to work on problems.

Do remember that though dogs should behave and work efficiently with you, they are not machines. They are living creatures. They have good days and bad days. When they are lazy and unfocused, use obedience concepts to get them a little more serious. When the dog is giving you his best effort, praise him for that since that is all you can ever ask. When you are happy with your dog, let him know it. When you are not happy with your dog, put your emotion aside and teach the dog that a lousy attitude doesn't work and that you can outwit him. He will respond like anything would, by going with what makes life easiest for him, and that is working with you.

People and Attitude

We have talked quite a bit about maintaining your dog's attitude. What about yours? How much of an impact does your attitude have on your training and hunting? Let's put it this way--almost always the dog is a direct reflection of its trainer. Probably more than almost always. As mentioned a few paragraphs earlier, if you think training your dog is boring, then it is, and your dog finds it the same way. If you think this is the highlight of your day, then it is, and your dog's as well. If you believe training your dog is a necessary evil and you'll do it, but only what is absolutely necessary and nothing beyond, then you shortcut and your dog will do the same to you when you need him most.

There is an interesting phenomenon that occurs when people are 'training method' shopping. Many training systems are developed upon this phenomenon and a great deal of money exchanges hands because of it. Let's take a gentle-hearted couple whose family has always had lap dogs and kittens for family pets. The dogs ate people food and rode in the front seat of the car and the kittens did whatever the heck they wanted. They've bought their first Labrador. Now you want to sell these people on a training method, so they'll go to your class or buy your book or video. What is the best way to get their interest? If you tell them to buy a choke chain and heeling stick, you have lost them. Without knowing anything else, they will not want to choke or hit their dog with a bat, so they move on. Now, tell them that you will teach them to teach their dog through love, kindness and positive reinforcement, and you will have their keen interest. Not because of the real nature of the training system, the results or actual nature of the animal being trained, but because you made them feel right at home and comfortable.

Conversely, take the person who has broken horses for a living and hunts to actually put food on the table and maybe thinks spanking his kids is always the best punishment, and tell him to 'love' his new hunting dog into good performance. He's gone. Tell him about using ropes and significant pressure to teach, and he'll want to read on. Again, not because the results are there in front of him, but because he is intrinsically comfortable with the tools described. That is what we all do. We look for the system or techniques that sound like something we would like to do.

What is the point of this discussion? The majority of what you do with your dog is a result of making yourself comfortable more than it is anything else. It is very easy to describe with words, concepts like 'crisp obedience' and 'quick enthusiastic responses'. It's pretty darned hard to actually create those. That takes stepping outside your familiar mental territory, and looking beyond. In reality, you cannot love your dog into true, consistent performance, and you cannot intimidate them into it. You must find the way to communicate with and teach your dog, and thereby gain your dog's respect. When you can do that, good results will be a combination of loving what your dog is doing, being frustrated upon occasion, being patient, consistent, fair, and true to the nature of your dog, not your picture of how things should be. When you realize how many limitations you may impose on your training process, you can begin to eliminate them. When you stop trying to be in complete control, but instead can think about the details of what you are doing and how they impact your dog, you can create good results. That's probably why you bought the book, isn't it?

Chapter 15

Over a Cup of Coffee

Dogs are doing what they have been taught to do...

The world of people and their dogs is an interesting one. There could be a book written, perhaps in part comedic, discussing the nature of people and their relationships to their animals. In our own business, we work with people almost as much as with the dogs, and it is as important to understand how and why people do what they do as it is to understand that about the dogs. We have also found in our own daily work with the dogs that it is of paramount importance to understand how our own foibles, emotional baggage, idiosyncrasies, and weaknesses can be incorporated into our dog training. It is uncomfortable to consider actually being the cause of a problem with your dog. It is uncomfortable to consider that your reasons for training the way you do or interacting with your dog the way you do are more self-serving than appropriate and fair to your dog. And it is human nature to avoid anything that brings about discomfort.

Have you ever noticed that the way someone drives in the rush hour is similar to the way he lives his life? Some people relax and don't fight what they cannot possibly change. Others become aggressive and almost hostile because they cannot move the way they would like to. The emotional state of an individual becomes more apparent when you watch him handle the challenge of rush hour driving. It also becomes apparent when you watch someone work with an animal he or she cannot completely control. Training a dog has to be a teamwork thing, and constant adjustments must be made during the process since there are two living creatures trying to balance their own reactions with the desires and reactions of another. The rush hour analogy is a good one because there is a goal (to get some specific place) and to reach your goal you must react to

239

the frequently unpredictable actions and reactions of others. You must read and adjust continuously. If you don't, bad things happen in both endeavors.

Some of us are very goal-oriented. Very often, people who buy books to learn how to do something want the results without the irritating involvement of someone else. So in dog training, they know what they want and they expect to get there and have the next three and a half months until opening day of teal season in which to do it. Dog needs to fit program. Then there are those of us who have a dog in lieu of a child or even a close friend. There is nothing wrong with having a dog and not one of the others; it isn't right, however, to expect the dog to fill the role of a friend or child in an emotional sense. That situation exists with alarming frequency, however. It is true that dogs are our friends, and sometimes the very best of those. It is also true we must nurture, raise, teach and care for our canines, but they are not human children. They are still dogs. When a parent watches a child play a game of soccer, there are those who watch with pride or at least appreciation that their children are out on the field. Then there are those who are playing the game through their children, and every goal is their own, every mistake, theirs. As the child goes, so goes the parent. People do that with their dogs as well. Their dog has no weakness, since they certainly have none. Standing back, it's easy to see someone's error in that. In looking at your own actions it is not so visible.

We tend to have the same kind of embarrassing emotions tied to our dogs. It is very easy to sit back and make judgments about people and their relationships to their dogs. It is even fun to read about quirky people and their dogs. It's not so easy to look at ourselves and objectively evaluate what we do and why. In general, assuming you have a dog with enough brains and talent that it actually is capable of doing the work, the overwhelming majority of problems you encounter are of your own creation. Either it is something you are teaching the dog, or something you are missing completely and should be doing. Almost without exception, dogs are doing what they have been taught to do. That is so important it will be restated: dogs are doing what they have been taught to do.

People come to us because their dog will run away if they let it off the leash. If they took it into the field they may never get it back. The look on their faces is interesting when they are told that they taught their dog to do that. Mentally they scramble back in time to see if they ever did anything to teach their dog to run off. A momentary recall assures them they did not teach their dog to run off, and also assures them we may not be as nice as someone said we were. Familiar with their mental process, we will ask them what they did with the pup when it was young. Answers are usually that the dog hung out in the backyard, but they took it camping twice. The pup loved to chase the chipmunks. It had a doggie door so it could come and go as it pleased. The neighbor kids threw Frisbees for it, but not too many times. So they assure us they never taught their dog to run off.

But they did teach the dog to do whatever it chooses to do, whenever it chooses. The young pup, much beloved by the family, could come and go at will. It had no behavioral restrictions. It never learned it has tasks to perform or guidelines in its life. So it was taught to honor its natural inclinations. One of its natural inclinations was to run and see what was out there. And it does that now, just the way it was taught.

Occasionally people teach their dogs to be mean or aggressive. Some retrievers have that aspect to them. Some people have that aspect. Because someone would like to belt everyone that makes him or her mad doesn't mean they will. If people learn that they must control themselves, the majority can control themselves. If a pup is aggressive and people find it entertaining, the dog learns aggression is a good thing. If a dog becomes aggressive to other dogs in the training group, neighborhood, or in its own yard and nothing is done about it, the dog assumes its natural status of pack leader. A dog that assumes that status usually includes you in its pack as well. That makes training awfully challenging, since the pack leader should be the trainer, not the dog. Some people can be taught to restrain themselves from being so aggressive to others by merely discussing the repercussions of their aggressive actions. In that case that would be the appropriate method to deal with the problem. Others may have to suffer the repercussions of their actions to learn not to do that again. A small number may never learn. The individual should define the method of dealing with inappropriate behavior, not the teacher. Letting dogs fight serves only to establish among the dogs which is the pack leader. It in no way teaches them not to fight.

A natural question we receive repeatedly is "How are we supposed to know when we are 'teaching' our dog something we do not mean to teach him?" It sounds simple, but when you begin to evaluate your actions, it isn't so simple after all. Think of it this way: What is the actual problem? For the people whose dog runs away when they let it loose, what is the problem? They perceive it to be that the dog runs away. The real problem is that the dog doesn't listen to them, understand, or respect their wishes. There will be many more problems than just running away. The dog will not do much of anything they ask, unless the dog sees an immediate reward. Do not 'treat the symptom', but cure the disease. Try to state the whole problem in one sentence. List all the symptoms: the dog doesn't come when it's called, the dog drags everyone on the leash, the dog chews up birds or bumpers, the dog jumps on Grandma...etc. When you have your list of symptoms, set it down and walk away. In a day or two pick up your list and imagine you are looking at a list of problems that your least favorite brother-in-law's dog exhibited. In one sentence, how would you best describe the real problem? That often makes it a little easier to evaluate. If your rotten brother-in-law's dog is a spoiled, obnoxious animal, chances are any dog described the same way is the same thing.

Many of us have dogs we wish were a little better mannered, a little more responsive. We can actually look at our animals and know they could be better behaved. Very often the issue is not that an individual cannot understand the methods and philosophy behind training a dog. It is that that person is not comfortable carrying out dog training to the degree necessary to have a really nicely trained dog. How many of us have either said or heard said, "If it is something I would not do to myself, I will not do it to my dog." This is a defense for not having a kennel or a crate, or considering using a training collar or even a choke chain on a dog. That certainly sounds humane, makes us feel like really good guys, and gets us out of all kinds of work and responsibility. Few of us voluntarily offer one-third of our paychecks to the federal government. We do it to avoid the alternative of jail. Few of us spring out of bed on Monday mornings because we can't wait to get to work soon enough; but we do rise and get to the right place at the right time because the alternative is more unpleasant. Even a smaller number of us order the broiled chicken and broccoli for dinner because it's our favorite thing to eat. We do all of these unpleasant things because they are in our long-term best interests. We do that because we care about our families and ourselves more than we care about our immediate discomfort. It is no different with our dogs.

Teaching an animal to spend time in a kennel or sit on a whistle quickly is not mean or abusive. It is doing what is best for that animal. Having the ability to call your dog off a chase that may endanger its life is worth training it to that level. Because the training is not imminently gratifying and pleasurable is irrelevant, as is your desire to pay taxes. Don't put your spouse in a kennel because your spouse is a human and that is not appropriate. Your dog can go in a kennel because it is a dog and they can thrive in kennels and kennels almost always beat the alternative.

Breeding Dogs

This is a big subject. This is a book dealing with training, not breeding dogs. We are asked repeatedly by people if they should breed their dogs. We offer some food for thought based on working with all different kinds of dogs for a long time. First, there are too many dogs. There are too many retrievers, too many of most things. Does the world need your pups? Not at all. If you want to breed because it would be fun for the kids to see or because it would be fun for you, take a quick trip to the Humane Society first. Look at all the adorable retrievers in there. Purebred, registered, good, smart and unwanted. Do not produce animals for your own gratification. If you have ten people clamoring for a pup because your dog is unbelievably talented, athletic, and healthy, then give it some heavy thought. It costs more to have pups than you will make if you are extremely responsible. The only way to know if your dog has talent and ability is to spend time training and then doing something with your dog. Training costs money and takes time. Hunting and competing takes money and time. Those are the only ways to find out how your dog measures up. Because you just like your dog doesn't mean it meets a standard the world will want. Find that out first. Because your vet likes your dog, that's nice, and implies certain health issues are sound, but that is not enough. As outlined in the puppy section, when you are looking for a pup, get the best one you can from people who really care and have proven their dog is worth reproducing. Expect the same thing from yourself if you have the nerve to create more animals. If you plan on producing more of an overly plentiful commodity, then put yourself in a position to stand behind your 'product'. Then, actually stand behind your product.

Trainers

There are lots of dog trainers. To be called a professional trainer requires only that money exchanges hands. There is no accredited University of Retriever Training. There are also significant variations in training methods. By definition, every trainer believes wholeheartedly that his or her method is the best method. Consumers new to the market are vulnerable, as with any product or service. Ultimately, if you are considering using a trainer or looking for a trainer there are several things to keep in mind during your investigation.

Sales talk, fancy advertising, and neat hats are all nice. They are nothing more than that. One dog that did awfully well eight years ago is a good thing, but that doesn't make a successful career. For a consumer who doesn't come into the buying market informed, experienced, or knowledgeable, the only thing left on which to base decisions is performance record compared with peers. A trainer may have recently titled a dog with some grand sounding title and appear to be just what you are looking for. If, however, there is a another trainer who has achieved that title 25 times already, that may change your standard. You do not have to have a trainer that runs competitive events and works toward dog titles. Titles are a convenient way to know a trainer can train a dog and at the same time is willing to put himself or herself on the line with others to prove it. You will find the most experienced and professional trainers don't feel that their venue for dog performance is the only way to go. One of the greatest retriever trainers to date, a man who has trained more national field trial champions than any other single trainer, will sit down and discuss how to train a good pheasant hunting dog with you. That is neither beneath him nor uninteresting. The best of trainers love the dogs and the process, and do not castigate anyone for how they choose to use their training. Usually a trainer very offensive about what others are doing is very defensive about something. A trainer should be expected to care about your dog and to care about you and your education. A good trainer should genuinely enjoy the process of training, even with its frustrations and challenges. There should be a connection between dog and trainer and a strong relationship of respect without fear.

When leaving your dog with a trainer or working with a trainer, you should expect to have confidence that you and your dog are in good hands, and that you can trust what is said and what is done. A trainer must level with you positively and negatively about your dog and its progress. People don't like to hear that their dog is average or that it has some trait they didn't want the dog to have. A trainer has to be willing to take the disappointment and sometimes worse from the owner in his diligence to honesty. Neither should a trainer tell you whatever you want to hear to keep you happy. Similar to what you expect from your doctor or dentist, you want one that is charming and funny and attractive, but you need him or her to be extremely accurate about the job.

Training Methods

There are variations on the theme of field training of dogs. Some are similar; some are quite dissimilar. How do you determine the best way to train your dog? Normally the book, seminar, or video with the most compelling wording and prettiest pictures is the first choice. If you take your pup to the professional down the road and he force fetches on a table and tells you to run your dog behind a truck every day, then that becomes your method of choice. People often default into a training method more than search out the one that is best for their dog. It is obvious what method we feel is the correct one, but the point is, how do consumers converge on the method that really is best for them? The same way the consumer should converge on a trainer. Performance record compared with peers. In this case, what are the results that can be demonstrated by one method versus another?

As mentioned earlier, do not be lulled by those methods that capitalize on your desire to be a warm fuzzy nice guy. Don't be lulled by those methods that make dog training sound like it can be easy and quick. Losing weight, quitting smoking, getting in shape, raising children, or having a good marriage is not quick and easy. There are plenty of advertisements and books that tell you that on the cover, but actually doing it lets you know that it's never true. It's just another way to separate you from your money.

Man and dog (in the non-gender sense, of course) have been a natural team for a very long time. Being true to the nature of the relationship doesn't involve gimmicks or new concepts. Dogs and humans have had things worked out successfully for centuries. Treating one of man's working partners like a stuffed animal or a human being is a disservice to the dog. The method which honors the dog and its nature, temperament, and genetic intent has to be the best for the dog. Nature never intended a working dog to be an equal to you. Nature also never intended you treat an animal with spirit and purpose without respect and an outlet for those characteristics.

The Difference Between Respect and Fear

Good animal trainers understand the distinction between respect and fear. You will hear the word respect used frequently by dog trainers. People often misinterpret it. Perhaps in part because respect is not so important in today's world. Young boys on skateboards knock people aside in shopping malls as they play on a weekend. Students do not feel they have to listen to teachers lecturing. "Yes, Sir" and "Yes, Ma'am" are ridiculed and not actually used in conversation. Certainly if people don't teach their children respect, they will see no need to instill it in their dogs. Take a close look into the world of animals. Animals don't cross animals they respect. A wild dog will not attack another animal it doesn't believe it can conquer. It will attack an animal it does believe it can conquer. It doesn't have to fight every one to find out which is which. How does it know the difference? A stronger animal knows it is a stronger animal, and that it will prevail. The weaker animal senses the same thing and there is no need to demonstrate the reality of it. The lesser animal respects the strengths of the greater animal and life goes on for both. It is the nature of a dog to determine where it lies in the hierarchy of its 'pack' and then to act accordingly. Nowhere in this framework do the words 'nice,' 'loving' or even 'fair' enter. You can be the nicest, fairest, most loving owner in the world, but if your dog doesn't respect you, you have little impact on the dog outside being its provider of pleasure and food.

Knocking a dog over the head or keeping him confined in a kennel doesn't gain its respect. Respect is earned with a dog the same way it is with you. Fear is a single focused emotion. Fearing something means the animal will do everything in its power to avoid the source of fear. The only thing accomplished by the creation of fear is the avoidance mechanism. That is the premise on which invisible fences work. Cross the line with the collar on and the dog experiences pain, hence, they avoid the line. In cases like that, fear is appropriate. In training, you want your dog to believe its job is to learn what you are asking it to learn and to work with you to do something you both enjoy. It doesn't do that because it loves you, but because it respects you. Whether that is a comfortable concept or not, it is the way it is. Given a choice between listening to the person who feeds the dog or listening to the person who works with the dog, the dog will virtually always honor the person who provides them work and its rewards. That is respect.

Foibles

People transfer their own problems to their dogs. Doggie psychologists probably deal with this phenomenon constantly. It can be difficult to deal with a dog's behavioral problems when in fact you are dealing with the owner's behavioral problems. Feeding is a good example of this. The majority of dogs are overweight. Dogs rarely need to be overweight, assuming they don't have a systemic problem that precludes a good feeding regimen. Dogs are overweight because we feed them more food than they require. Why does an intelligent, informed person feed some animal they love more than it needs? Usually because they don't think the animal is overweight (we still don't know how they come to that conclusion) or because the dog 'looks so hungry' or 'deserves a reward for doing something so well.' Animals eat to stay alive in nature. If they gorge, it's because they don't know when they may eat again. Since our dogs aren't subject to the survival mode of eating, it is our responsibility to feed them what they need and nothing beyond that. Whether they want more because it feels good to them to eat is completely irrelevant to their health and well being. If a muffin makes you feel good and so you give the same pleasure to your dog, you are transferring your unhealthy relationship to food consumption to your animal.

For every rush hour driver that tries to run you off the road, there is a driver that passively hangs back and lets the crazies go by. That kind of person may also never go into the boss's office and ask for the raise promised three years earlier. There is passivity in certain people that makes successful dog training very difficult. Some folks are comfortable reacting to what goes on around them, instead of working to define or at least effect what goes on around them. We have worked with people who wait for the dog to do the right thing. The idea of actually making the dog repeatedly do the right thing until it becomes second nature doesn't register. There are trainers who capitalize on this phenomenon and will tell you that over time you can wait for your dog to discover what pleases you and let them learn through your 'pleasure' what it is they should and should not do. Passively waiting for your dog to discover what makes you happy so he figures out what behaviors you want probably works about as well with dogs as it would with children. Imagine passively sitting by and waiting for your children to discover on their own that drinking and staying out all night is not the best thing for them? Or letting them discover on their own what happens if they do no homework and flunk out of school?

Bickering between people associated with a dog can interrupt sound training. Now this is a strange sounding one, and we have never seen it brought up anywhere else. We have so many times had a dog brought in for training by its married owners. One is always determined and glad to have the dog with a trainer. The other is worried about the state of mind of the dog and its adjustment to the new life. It is obvious one is behind this exercise and the other has little choice. That doesn't bode well on the personal side as it is. Time goes by and the owners become part of the training process. When one of the couple is there and he is being taught how to work with their dog and how to overcome certain little problems, he reveals how the other person actually caused those little problems. The next time, when the 'problem causing' person is out working with their dog, she reveals how in fact it is the behavior of the other person that actually causes most of the problems with the dog. So each is informing us how the other person is the problem and the dog is proof. If the dog is more the sounding board and tool used to demonstrate the unworthiness of the other person involved, it will be difficult for the dog to progress and thrive at home. When the dog and its training is not the real issue, it will be hard to be successful. That is also a very uncomfortable one to diagnose close up.

Perhaps above all other personal 'foibles' we bring into the arena of learning how to train a dog, fear of not measuring up is the greatest. Most of us don't do things we secretly might wish to do. Have you ever known anyone who loved to sing, but would never sing in front of people? Or someone with a knack for drawing that would never take a course in art? Some people would love to join the intramural softball league or the local chamber orchestra, but don't. What if they were not good enough? Then everyone else would know. Better to avoid the whole thing completely and never really find out. It is no different in gaining skills in dog training and then putting them into practice. What if you really are not very good? Your dog will be proof of your inadequacy.

It is true some people are quite naturally gifted in working with animals. Others are not so lucky. Both can be successful and both can fail. As with almost everything in life, it is not the gifted one that is the greatest success. It is the one most determined, most committed to the effort; the one that just will not quit, even when it looks like he should. We have repeatedly witnessed dogs we knew to be below-average animals become successful, well-trained, even titled dogs. Their owners would not take failure as an option. This is not to say any dog can be trained in the field because some just don't have the raw talent to become something they are not. Some dogs have a level of talent that is hard to reach or hard to develop. A person committed to getting the most out of his dog can reach it and can develop it. A person looking for reasons not to dig and not to try harder will find them and avoid the work. In working with your dog and pushing his limits, you will find that you do the same thing with yourself.

The more you come to know your dog the more you come to know aspects of yourself you never would otherwise. You will see negative traits you will not like: impatience, frustration and shortsightedness. You will also see things you did not know about yourself that you like very much; a person capable of connecting with an animal on a unique level, a person who can learn things completely alien previously. You might find that you are better with dogs than you ever thought, and can actually help others struggling to learn about their dogs. You may find what brings about problems in your dog training efforts are also the things that bring about problems in other parts of your life. Your dog just points it out to you in a kindly way. You never really fail in your dogs' eyes; your dog just waits until you get it right.

Dogs

There is variation in dogs the same way there is variation in people. There are smart ones, not-so-smart ones, and everything in between. There are those born with great talent, some talent, and absolutely no talent whatsoever. There are those with great heart and spirit, and those lacking both severely. These are things you cannot change.

You will, at some point, have to see your dog honestly. It may not be possible to look at our own children as honestly, but it is important to muster that with your dog. It is only fair and you owe it to your animal. Some folks spend years and much of themselves trying to make their dog into a seasoned, titled field dog. Only, the raw material necessary is not there. That is not fair to the dog. It gets to live its life disappointing its owners. Other people buy a truly talented and gifted animal and then leave it set in the backyard until it finally dies, most likely of boredom and frustration. Both are heartbreaking cases, not for the owners, but for the dogs.

Some dogs have all heart and go in the world, and not a brain cell beyond those sustaining body functions. Other dogs are so darn smart it's scary, but have no interest in feathers. The majority of dogs are reasonably intelligent, like retrieving, might point if they come from those lines, and can be taught many things if you take enough time. Very few of us have the superstars most of us think we do. People understandably misinterpret a high desire level in a dog. A dog that loves to look for a bird is just that: a dog that loves to look for a bird. The great talent also needs a good nose, the ability to think about where a bird might be or should be, and the ability to take the pressure of training to develop and refine its hunting skills. If you can separate yourself emotionally from your dog, you need to look at the dog objectively. Some cannot and view the dog as an extension of themselves, like their truck or their gun. Insult the dog and you insult them. Why do we need to look at our dogs objectively? Because you have to be fair to your dog. If you ask more from it than it can give, you will always be disappointed and your dog will reflect your disappointment. If you don't ask enough of the dog, it will know you aren't much of a dog handler and take advantage of you. If you understand what your dog has to offer and create the opportunity to reach all the dog has to offer, you make the most of your dog. Every dog we know wants that as its life. You are very likely most satisfied in your life when you strive and accomplish. You are not so happy when you try and are just not good enough, or when you have absolutely nothing to work for. Place your dog where you would like to be--at the highest potential.

The Electric Collar

These days, there is more debate over how to use a collar than there is debate on whether a collar should be used. The electric collar is terribly convenient, as you have to do nothing more than buckle it on and push a button. Anything that easy to use is also easy to misuse. People have developed training programs in which everything is premised on the use of electricity. We have read compelling logic regarding pushing buttons before any signal is given, giving warning sounds before pushing buttons, pushing buttons when pups are four months old…you name it, someone has it figured out and phrased it convincingly. Any tool that is created to make things easier on the human is usually further refined to continue to make things easier on the human. There is nothing wrong with convenience. We employ it ourselves when we can without sacrificing something more important. There are those who will argue this issue with us ad nauseum, but our contention is that you should know how and be able to train a dog without a tool of convenience before you actually use that convenience. As stated earlier, a mathematician should know how to extrapolate large numbers before using a calculator or computer. Then he is not a pawn of his tools. A dog trainer should know how to force fetch or whoa break a dog without contraptions or equipment, and how to get a dog to go on command without using the collar first. Then he isn't stuck if the collar is broken or drained or missing or the table collapsed.

Correctly used, the collar is valuable. It is the only way certain things can be enforced. Our advice to collar users and potential collar users is this: educate yourself in the fundamentals of dog training. Understand the importance of teaching, correcting, and reinforcing with pressure. Digest the concepts of timing in commands and reinforcement until they are second nature to you. When you truly understand the basis of teaching and working with a dog, then the collar will not be so intimidating or confusing. You will understand the use of appropriately applied pressure, and most importantly, your dog will understand it.

Parting Words

People who buy books to learn about dog training usually buy all the books they think look like they have something to offer. In doing so, you will read many different things, different approaches, and different philosophies. No one undertakes the task of writing a book about what they do if they do not believe that their system is really the best. In the final analysis, it is not the compelling rationale or the appeal to what makes you comfortable that matters.

Think of yourself in your finest moments. What brought you to that point? Was it the culmination of great effort and struggle? Could it have been the end of years of exhaustive research resulting in new information? It is highly probable that your greatest moment has been a result of dedication, commitment and attention to the fundamentals of something. It will be no different in this endeavor.

There is only one thing that 'speaks' in the end. It is not you and it isn't the authors of this book. It is the dog work itself. A dog that is utilizing all of the talents and skills it possesses doing what its genetics drive it do, at your side, with great heart, spirit, and love of the work. That says it all. Think about what you are doing. Think about your ultimate objective. Understand what you want to do, and formulate a solid plan. Enjoy it, see progress. Science has now 'discovered' that working with an animal, mere association with an animal, results in lower stress levels and greater mental health. There's a news flash. Go do good dog work.

Epilogue

If you were to make a study of "Success" there are several things you would most likely do. You would look closely at sports teams that repeatedly win championships. You might evaluate individuals who have built great businesses, theories, or enterprises. A visit to Mother Theresa would have been on the list. Watching Michael Jordan practice basketball and Tiger Woods play golf would be on the agenda. You might go back in history and evaluate what Albert Einstein and Albert Schweitzer said and did. There are many places, people and enterprises that personify or portray success. Though there are notable differences between what Mother Theresa and Michael Jordan have done, there are few notable differences in how they went about it.

Michael Jordan, arguably the greatest to have played the game of basketball, was known to throw 2,000 free throws in a single practice-- routinely. The greatest repeating football world champions were known as much for the emphasis placed on daily drills as they were for great quarterbacks or other players. Mother Theresa spent long hours reading scripture she knew by heart. In short, these great "successes" were not so because they had some gift dropped on them from the sky. They excelled at what they did because they spent time on the basics, the fundamentals of what they were about. Not only did they spend time on the fundamentals; they emphasized the fundamentals above any other single thing they did.

Great people, great businesses, and great animals that remain great over the long haul are neither lucky nor particularly blessed with something. They work harder and pay attention to the basics. They never outgrow or become bored with the basics. This is as true in dog training as it is in wrestling, badminton, or accounting. The more you understand the fundamentals of dog training and the more you work on those, the greater your successes in the field or in the competitive arena will be. A good dog is a good dog, whether it hunts 30 days a year and plays with the kids the remainder of the time, or runs field trials 30 weeks out of the year. The fundamentals for both are the same. Success in the world of dog training is not defined as a certain title or a certain price tag on a pup.

Success is a healthy, robust dog that believes in working with you in whatever you are doing. It is the greatest thing in life. When you and your dog are a genuine team, when each shoulders his portion of the load well and loves doing it, you are a success. It is for your long-term success that this book is written. There are few things better in life than a great dog that is both friend and partner.